Everyday Ethics for Practicing Planners

Everyday Ethics for Practicing Planners

By
Carol D. Barrett, FAICP

A BOOK OF THE AMERICAN INSTITUTE OF CERTIFIED PLANNERS,
AN INSTITUTE OF THE AMERICAN PLANNING ASSOCIATION
Washington, D.C.

This book is published on behalf of the American Institute of Certified Planners, an institute of the American Planning Association.

Copyright 2001 by the American Planning Association
122 S. Michigan Ave., Suite 1600, Chicago, IL 60603

ISBN (paperback) 1-884829-61-9

Library of Congress Control Number 2001 135201
Printed in the United States of America
All rights reserved

Interior composition by Kelmscott Press, Inc.

Contents

Acknowledgments

Many people deserve recognition for their contributions to *Everyday Ethics*. Some contributed indirectly. Over the years, Jerry Kaufman, Elizabeth Howe, and Marty Wachs researched topics, wrote articles and books, and delivered papers that challenged all of us as professionals.

Others proffered hands-on assistance. Bob Joice, AICP, provided text, commentary, and helpful criticism along the way. Carolyn Torma made valuable editorial suggestions, offered ideas for expanding the introductory material, and helped with revisions to some of the commentary. Margot Garcia, AICP, Ph.D. redrafted several scenarios in an effort to improve both the format and content. Joanne Garnett, AICP, AICP Past President and APA Past President, and Bill Bowdy, AICP, AICP Past President, provided structure and continuity throughout the writing process. Their joint interest in promoting discussion and education about ethics has dramatically increased our awareness as citizens and professionals. AICP Past President Norman Krumholz, AICP, was helpful in focusing attention on the topic as well. Their long-term work is bearing fruit as the AICP Ethics Committee actively deliberates and issues new advisory rulings. Former *Planners' Casebook* Editor Mark Eldridge, AICP, used a new strategy to get the ethics message out, and I was pleased to be part of his effort. APA Counsel Bernie Dworski composed provocative arguments, stimulating further consideration as he reviewed the scenarios.

Finally, there have been believers — Rosemary Jones, formerly of the AICP staff, and David Boyd, AICP, and Steven Preston, AICP, of the AICP Multi-Media Task Force who had faith that this manuscript would be completed. My thanks for their painstaking efforts and artfully-timed prodding.

This edition of *Everyday Ethics* updates three earlier versions printed in 1983, 1986, and 1995.

Carol D. Barrett, FAICP
October 2001

Foreword

Something remarkable happened a few years ago when AICP began publishing excerpts from this document in *Planners' Casebook*. People read the material, made decisions about what they believed to be an ethical course of behavior, and took time to write thoughtful letters challenging the courses of action I recommended. To everyone who took the time to correspond: thank you. In many instances, those who took issue with my conclusions made assumptions about facts not included in the scenario. This led to a different line of reasoning. Ethical climates, which vary by region almost as much as the weather, also influence one's interpretation. Additionally, planners' perspectives on what may be ethical depend on the view they have of themselves as advocates, technicians, process planners, or hybrids. (Thanks to Jerry Kaufman and Elizabeth Howe for their thoughtful explorations of typology.) As you read the commentary you will begin to understand how I view planners and their responsibilities.

The many letters I've received demonstrate the truth of this maxim: where you stand sometimes depends on where you sit. It has never been my purpose to stake out high moral ground but merely to note that such ground exists. Working together we can move the state of the profession toward that ground.

DISCLAIMER

This publication was prepared to stimulate discussion about ethical issues. The author does not present the material as the only ethical course of conduct. Further, deliberations of the AICP Ethics Committee are in no way bound by the information presented herein. The publication has not been endorsed as the official ethical position of the organization just as no planning publication should be construed as illustrating the only way to carry out planning.

CHAPTER

1
Introduction

Planners are not expected to be the most perfect of society's members. As authority and influence accrue to a profession, public expectations rise. This public trust imposes increased responsibility on planners to offer an example of impeccable conduct.

WHY THIS PUBLICATION WAS PREPARED AND HOW TO USE IT

Most of those in the planning profession accept the concept of ethical conduct for planners as important. Most planners also believe that what they do is ethical simply because they deliberately chose a specific course of action. At the same time, in any office, one will observe a variety of different behaviors provoked by the same circumstance. For example, Sandy rigidly insists that each issue can be properly analyzed and that any course of action can be determined to be either right or wrong. Gary is more elastic in his views: life consists of variables, not constants. Mike is skeptical that a workable ethical code can be formulated for the entire planning community. Paula snickers at the lofty aspirational tone of the AICP Code. Caroline thinks that no planner, threatened with job loss, can afford the luxury of ethics. And Bernie rejects the entire concept of ethics. He says that life, planning included, is a zero-sum game. In his view, bluffing, deception, and corner cutting are acceptable to achieve planning objectives. The attorney, meanwhile, advises that it is sufficient to stay within the letter of the law.

Some benchmarks are needed to sort through this plethora of perspectives. Trying to ignore ethical problems is akin to getting rid of a boomerang by throwing it away. Ethical dilemmas just keep intruding. That's why this publication was prepared. It is designed to give planners a way to hone their ethical skills and develop a workable scheme for responding to ethical problems. A chapter in a separate publication, *Planning Made Easy*, by the author and Robert M. Joice, AICP, focused exclusively on ethics for planning commissioners. It is available from APA's Planners' Book Service.

As an ethical resource, this publication is intended to encourage discussion. It does not contain the definitive answer to every ethical question or problem. There is no such thing. The publication can help professionals clarify their ethical responses to the ever-present challenges of practicing planning. For example, you are the planning director and it is your job to make a recommendation on a conditional use permit for a manufacturing plant that emits a chemical not regulated by the Environmental Protection Agency. Project opponents present information showing that the emission is a health hazard.

- What are the facts? Is there a health hazard?
- Is this an ethical issue for the planner?
- Are there genuine moral issues at stake?

Suppose the compound is a virulent carcinogen and is emitted in large quantities. Most people would probably agree it should be stopped. The general prohibition against knowingly harming other people would necessitate this conclusion. But, suppose the emission produces only mild respiratory problems in a small percentage of the population. Further, suppose that removing the compound is so expensive that the plant could not be built at all. Additionally, imagine there is a severe unemployment problem in your community. Will there be serious disagreement among the planning staff about the appropriate recommendation?

Planners rightly believe that they have an obligation to protect the physical health of the community. But doesn't the staff also have an obligation to be concerned with the economic health of the community as well?

In this instance, there are conflicts among competing obligations, both of which appear to be valid. The conflicts that give us trouble are not those between good and bad, but between competing goods, both of which cannot be fully realized.

When faced with two competing obligations, each of which appears to be justified, one approach is to try to find a way to satisfy them both. While it often is not possible to satisfy all moral requirements in a pure form, it sometimes is possible to satisfy them in a modified form.

Most general moral rules have an "all other things being equal" qualifier implicitly attached to them. In real life, all things are often not equal. For example, the threat to the safety, health, and welfare of the public may be both uncertain and minimal. Whether or not the emissions are in fact harmful may be a matter of controversy, and there may be, as of yet, no evidence that the emissions produce fatal diseases, only significant respiratory problems in a certain small percentage of the population.

Furthermore, the obligation to the community may include an obligation to its economic well being. So, the question is what in this case is the planner's obligation to the public?

This issue involves morals, ethics, and the law. The term "morals" refers to generally accepted standards of right and wrong in a society. Ethics refers to more abstract principles that appear in a religious, societal, or professional code. Moral and ethical statements are distinguishable from laws. The fact that an action is legally permissible does not establish that it is morally and ethically acceptable. The fact that it may be legal for the plant to emit the chemical doesn't mean that it is morally permissible to do so.

People often view ethical reasoning as fuzzy and imprecise, and it certainly is true that the qualitative thinking involved in ethics is not susceptible to the same kind of precision that can be achieved in arithmetic. For example, factual disagreements may be a component of an ethical dilemma. Answers are based on what can be known and documented. In evaluating moral disagreements, appeals are made to broader and more basic moral principles that are organized into theories. The three most common moral theories are utilitarianism, the Golden Rule, and deontological principles or:

- end-based decisions
- care-based decisions
- rule-based decisions

In end-based decisions (utilitarianism), actions are right when they produce the greatest total amount of human well being. A utilitarian analysis of a moral problem consists of three steps. The utilitarian must determine:

- the audience of the action or policy in question — those who will be affected for good or ill;
- the positive and negative effects of the alternative actions or policies;
- the course of action that will produce the greatest overall utility.

There are two drawbacks to the utilitarian perspective on morality. First, implementation of the utilitarian perspective requires extensive knowledge of facts, and sometimes this knowledge is not available. If we do not know the long-term positive and negative consequences of an action or policy, we do not know how to evaluate it from a utilitarian perspective. Sometimes utilitarians are reduced to a best-guess approach. This is not very satisfactory. Utilitarianism also can lead to injustice for some individuals. Mining operations that cause black lung disease in some of the miners may produce more utility than harm from an overall standpoint, but would be unjust to the miners.

In making care-based decisions (following the Golden Rule), actions are right when they equally respect each human person as a moral agent. To consider the effects, you must place yourself in the position of those who could be affected by your actions. Philosophers have proposed a hierarchy of rights that should be protected through the application of the Golden Rule. The first is the most basic: life, physical and mental health. The second involves maintaining self-fulfillment through honest and truthful interactions. The third involves rights necessary to increase one's self-fulfillment, such as the right to property and to equal treatment.

Application of the Golden Rule morality involves these steps:
- Determine the audience for the action. (Similar to the audience whose rights are under the utilitarian analysis.)
- Evaluate the seriousness of the rights infringements each action will impose
- Choose the course of action that produces the least serious rights infringements

There are two principal difficulties with Golden Rule morality. First, it is sometimes hard to apply the rule in a way that leads to a clear conclusion. This is especially true if the rights violations are merely potential rather than actual, or if the action is only a slight infringement on a right. Also, Golden Rule moral philosophies can produce implausible results. To protect lives, cars can be made so safe that no one would be able to afford one.

Following rule-based analysis, or deontological principles, our actions must be translated into universal principles of action without regard for the consequences. For example, it is right for me to toss my biodegradable lunch leftovers out of the car window only if I believe it would be correct for everyone driving on this road every single day to do the same. Critics of this method of decision making argue that it can result in a mindless bureaucracy.

For most choices to be made by planners, the utilitarian model, with its emphasis on information, is the most useful. Let's return to the problem facing our planning director and briefly analyze the dilemma in terms of this theory.

End-based Decisions/Utilitarianism

Who is the audience for the conditional use approval? (Who will benefit and who may be harmed?)

Beneficiaries:
- Contractors who will build the plant
- Business owners from secondary and tertiary economic spending
- Residential property taxpayers as a result of an improved tax base that may reduce their burden
- Other companies that may now be able to locate in the community given that a precedent has been established
- Schools as a result of an increase in the tax base
- The unemployed and their families
- Purchasers of the product made by the plant
- The manufacturing company

Losers:
- Those with existing health problems that may be exacerbated or those who will have new health problems — primarily the elderly and children
- Adjacent property owners who may see the value of their property decline because of their proximity to a perceived health hazard
- Taxpayers who may have to cover the cost of increased health and social services to the ill, and the families of those who become sick
- Those who will pay higher taxes and utility rates to cover new infrastructure costs to support plant and related economic/residential development

Consider the positive and negative effects of the alternative actions:

	Positive	Negative
Approve	Jobs	Loss of reputation as clean community
	Tax base	Some air pollution
	Economic development	Probable health effects for some percentage of the population
Disapprove	Protected health for the most vulnerable members of the community — elderly & children	Loss of jobs
	Avoid increased public health care costs	Discourage future economic development of similar jobs
	Preserve and build upon reputation as clean community	Loss of investment and spin off opportunities

Decide which course of action produces the greatest overall utility. In this case, are there ways that the negative outcomes or costs can be shifted to the project and away from the community? If so, the end-based decision may be even easier, particularly if the plant were to offer to sign a legally-binding agreement with the community stipulating that it would:

• continue to look for new technologies that might, in the future, eliminate emissions of potential hazardous materials;

• fund annual physicals for those affected by the plant and be responsible for long-term health care for those individuals whose health is harmed by the plant;

• pay development impact fees to cover infrastructure improvements needed to support the plant;

• agree to operating stipulations that limit emissions during active daytime hours and permit them only during the night when children and the elderly are less likely to be outdoors.

With such an agreement in place, and considering the need for jobs in your community, it would be much easier for you as the planning director to recommend the approval of the conditional use permit for the manufacturing plant.

THE SOURCES OF OUR ETHICS

An ethical framework for decision making helps us respond to the feelings we have of being responsible to someone or something. We acquire such sentiments through the process of socialization. These feelings are manifestations of values and beliefs that we have acquired from family, friends, religious affiliations, professional training, and organizational involvement. Values are the most basic kinds of belief and they help determine how we behave. Over time, our values become more systematized and create within us a predisposition toward courses of action.

Internal

Our most basic orientation to what is right and wrong is not derived from reading the AICP Code of Ethics. It comes, instead, from the conscious and unconscious lessons we were taught as children by our parents, our religious institutions, and our schools. We were instructed as to how people should treat one another. We were chastised when our behavior was inconsistent with the norm. Gradually, we adopted the values of our family, society, and country. Those values endure as we practice planning, and may account for our choice of planning as a profession.

In the planning culture of the United States, morals and ethics are distinct even though they are related. Morality is personal and in many cases private; ethics is professional and public. Moral codes, however, can influence our professional work. For example, growing up in a multi-generational family could pre-dispose one to examine the consequences of a proposed plan or project in terms of its impact on the elderly.

This publication approaches most judgments carefully. The AICP Code of Ethics clarifies your responsibilities to those you serve and to those with whom you share your profession. Your behavior will be judged as to how you perform in your role of planner.

External

Our Democratic Society. Planners are properly concerned about public involvement and community goal setting. Legislation and case law directly define the expanse and limitations of planning.

The Organization. Organizations vary, but in one area they are all alike — they demand loyalty to their rules. The rules and expectations that govern work life in a public agency may be quite different from those in a private business. Planners must make sure that the inward-looking demands of an employer do not overwhelm the outward-looking expectations of the profession.

Professional Training. A first important contributor to your sense of planning ethics is the professional training and the formative experiences of the early years of your career. Planners educated in accredited planning schools throughout the United States share a common set of assumptions, outlooks, and expectations about one another and their field.

Professional Standards. By joining AICP, planners choose to belong to a group with uniform standards for acceptance, experience, quality, and behavior. AICP members accept a higher level of personal responsibility for their actions.

A Summary of the AICP Code of Ethical Conduct

For planners who have joined AICP, the adopted "Code of Conduct" establishes a set of community norms for guiding behavior. Key elements of the code appear below. For the full text, refer to Attachment II. The code has been in force since 1978, when first adopted by AICP. Since then, the code has been refined and enhanced through the adoption of amendments and advisory rulings. Adherence to the code is one requirement of membership in AICP. Procedures exist to provide counseling, to judge alleged misconduct, and to discipline members in the case of misconduct.

Code Elements

A. Serve the public interest
    1. Have special concern for long-range consequences
    2. Pay special attention to inter-relatedness of decisions
    3. Provide full, clear, accurate information
    4. Give opportunities for meaningful citizen participation
    5. Expand choice and opportunity
    6. Protect the integrity of the natural environment
    7. Strive for excellence of design and conserve the heritage of the built environment
B. Perform work competently and independently
    1. Exercise independent, professional judgment
    2. Accept decisions of employer or client
    3. Do not perform work when there is a conflict of interest

   4. Do not represent a client for a year after leaving public employment on a matter over which you had some influence
   5. Do not solicit clients or employment through false claims
   6. Do not sell services by implying ability to influence through improper means
   7. Do not improperly use your power of office to seek a special advantage
   8. Do not accept work you cannot perform
   9. Do not accept work beyond your level of competence
   10. Do not reveal information
C. Contribute to the development of the profession
   1. Protect and enhance the integrity of the profession
   2. Accurately represent views of colleagues
   3. Review work in a professional manner
   4. Share the results of experience and research
   5. Establish the appropriateness of solutions
   6. Contribute time and information to the development of others
   7. Strive to increase opportunities for women and minorities
   8. Do not commit an act of sexual harassment
D. Strive for high standards of integrity, proficiency, and knowledge
   1. Do not commit a deliberately wrongful act
   2. Respect the rights of others
   3. Strive to continue one's education
   4. Accurately represent one's qualifications
   5. Analyze ethical issues
   6. Contribute time to groups lacking planning resources

Rulings

1. Sexual harassment is unethical
2. Public planners should not have a stake in private development
3. Outside employment or moonlighting should not conflict with loyalty, energy, and powers of mind owed to one's primary employer
4. Information should be used honestly
5. Planners who know of unethical conduct must report it
6. Illegal conduct should be reported, even if it means revealing confidential information

The APA Statement of Ethical Principles and Its Relationship to the Code

The APA Board of Directors first adopted a "Statement of Ethical Principles" in 1987 as a guide to all APA members. It complemented the AICP Code, but did not include all of the same elements. The statement was more specific in identifying ethical behavior for public planning officials. Over the next several years, the members of AICP and APA worked to craft a single statement of ethical principles. The American Planning Association adopted a "Statement of Ethical Principles in Planning" in May 1992. The full text of the statement appears in Attachment I. The statement, as distinct from the code, serves as a guide to ethical conduct for everyone who participates in the process of planning as advisors, advocates, and decision-makers. The introduction sets forth its intent by presenting a set of principles to be held in common by certified planners, other practicing planners, appointed and elected officials, and others who participate in the process of planning.

The code and principles contain many common elements. It is important to keep in mind that the code, which is a component of the ethical principles document, is formally subscribed to by each certified planner and includes enforcement procedures. The APA principles are advisory and members of the organization are expected to adhere to the standards although there is no enforcement mechanism. Nonetheless, there is significant value in having a unified statement. The aspirational contents of the planning professional's code are made clear to all and the standards that should inform the behavior of all participants in the planning process are set forth. For the reference of the reader, codes applicable to others in positions related to the planning process are provided including:

• The Social Responsibility of the Planner adopted by the American Institute of Planners

• ICMA Code of Ethics with Guidelines adopted by the ICMA Executive Board

The Role of the Planning Commission in Establishing the Ethical Climate

The citizen who expects fair treatment from the "planning process" will not distinguish between the activities of the planning commission and the planning staff in making an assessment of the ethical nature of the work. Therefore, it becomes incumbent upon the community's volunteer and paid planners to work together to establish a climate that supports high ethical standards.

The members of the planning commission can help to reinforce a high standard of public confidence by:

• having open minds and exploring creative solutions;

• operating by adopted by-laws and rules of procedure that establish the legal minimum that all participants have a right to expect;

• discussing and adopting APA's Statement of Ethical Principles in Planning;

• respecting codes of ethics that govern the conduct of professionals;

• taking advantage of training opportunities to improve one's ability to do the job.

Citizens today are asking more questions of and expressing less confidence in their appointed and elected officials. Planning commissioners and planners together can help make the planning function in any community an example of how things ought to be done. Full, frank, and cooperative efforts are essential. Without the support of the planning commission, the planner is unlikely to be able to establish and nurture an ethical environment regardless of her or his personal intentions.

HOW TO RECOGNIZE AN ETHICAL PLANNER

The ethical planner is rational. Such a planner can reason, judge, and decide with respect to the quality of behavior.

The ethical planner is self-determining. Despite the influences of others, the ethical planner is accountable for her or his actions.

The ethical planner recognizes errors in judgment. Despite society's propensity to promote self-esteem and its refusal to judge, an ethical planner is capable of acknowledging that a course of action was either contrary to his or her nature or unjust to others. The planner adjusts his or her behavior in response to this new information.

The ethical planner lives in a community. As a member of the family of planners in service to the public, an ethical planner embraces obligations to others.

The ethical planner seeks to avoid doing bad things, and acts in a constructive fashion to do good. For the ethical planner, the emphasis is on the affirmative dimension of his or her conduct. Ethical obligations extend beyond legal compliance because many types of impropriety, such as unfairness, deception, and hypocrisy, cannot be effectively prevented by enforcing rules.

If, after reading the above paragraphs, you recognize yourself as the ideal ethical planner, you can either stop reading or plan to be the instructor for local ethical training programs. For those who wish to educate themselves further, we will now examine how this book can help you learn more about and practice ethical problem solving.

TOOLS FOR LEARNING ABOUT ETHICS

There are many ways of learning planning ethics — reading, attending lectures, and listening to the experiences of others. Ever since the first fires were built in caves, storytelling has been a powerful teaching tool. This publication relies on parables, stories about problems and how they can be solved. Each scenario presents one or more ethical issues for consideration. These ethical issues are the author's interpretation of the dilemma based on the information provided in each scenario. In the belief that a strengthened ethical awareness can develop through an understanding of colleagues' views, these scenarios were developed to encourage discussion. It is vital that planers talk to one another about ethical dilemmas. While many parables have the answer included in the story, the scenarios used in this document do not. Instead, the reader must decide what to do.

Reading and Responding to the Scenarios

Planners are challenged to consistently and systematically analyze situations to develop a basis for informed ethical judgment. Rarely will planners be confronted with a dilemma such as the one described above whereby a plant that may emit carcinogens wants to locate in town. Much of the ethical conflict will be of a more basic variety that is guided by the code. In these situations, planners must first recognize what the ethical issues are. Next, they must examine and rank their values with respect to a particular decision. Planners perform their work in an environment that allows for a broad range of administrative discretion. As a consequence, planners need some benchmarks for relating the various, and sometimes competing, claims of different values that can enter into official actions. There are steps that lead to practical moral reasoning by which planners can evaluate the appropriateness of a particular course of action. These steps will help the planner develop a keener moral imagination. The steps allow a planner to integrate internal sources of values with external demands while maintaining a sense of integrity.

1.   Define the problem. This sounds obvious, but it is nonetheless crucial. Think about the issue. What are the critical issues posed? Where is the conflict with the code? For example, the difficulty may lie with the administrative procedures of an agency that preclude adequate public

review and comment. These procedures create a process that you deem to be unethical given the AICP Code's requirement for meaningful citizen input.

Next, consider who else is involved with the ethical issue? It could be your employer, your co-workers, the natural environment, the public or, as in the example noted above, multiple stakeholders. Identifying all of the relevant parties will help you think about what actions you might take, and what the consequences of those actions might be.

The ethical problem cannot be analyzed or resolved absent a clear written statement. The discipline required to take this first step will greatly facilitate completing the next elements.

2.   Clarify your primary goal. Look at the situation at hand and suggest where or how you might make a difference. For example, if your goal is to expose corruption among local elected officials, a far more public and emphatic course of action is required than might otherwise be the case.

3.   Examine all the facts in light of this primary goal and your problem statement. Focus upon the particulars most relevant to your goal. Be prepared to search out more information to improve your understanding of what may be pertinent.

4.   Brainstorm alternative courses of action that you might pursue. Develop ways you could improve the situation. During this phase of your ethical analysis it may prove helpful to consult with a colleague. The American Institute of Certified Planners maintains a list of members available and qualified to consult with you. You can access these individuals by contacting the AICP staff at 202-872-0611. Depending on the nature of the issue, local contacts may prove valuable. The professional development officer of your APA chapter will be able to identify appropriate individuals.

5.   Evaluate the alternatives and the consequences that may result from your course of action. Compare these alternatives to the code. It will help to organize the review process and highlight points you might have missed. You should understand the moral reasons for and against a course of action. Ethical dilemmas are complex, and different elements of the code may pertain to a single set of circumstances. You will need to do a conscientious balancing based not only on the facts and context of a particular situation, but also on the precepts of the entire code.

6.   Select the preferred course of action and give it another test: publicity. How would you defend this decision in public if asked to do so? Finally, subject your alternative to a gut check. Does it feel right?

7.   Implement your plan of action. The course of action you select must be one you can achieve. If you are not able to implement the preferred alternative, go back and re-examine your choices and select another.

These steps are similar to those undertaken in many types of planning analyses. They are recommended here because they work to help identify and analyze choices. The preferred course of action is the one most consistent with the requirements of the code, and that has the greatest potential for a personally satisfying decision. In the section that follows, the technique is described as it might be used on the job.

Sample Scenario: What Are You Willing to Do to Keep Your Job?

The following scenario is presented to allow the reader to test the techniques for ethical analysis suggested above. Extensive commentary is included to illustrate the thought process.

You're a newly hired planner and the boss drops by your office to chat one Friday afternoon. He mentions that a development review assignment will be on your desk early the following week. He says, "Mr. Jones has a small subdivision proposal. He was the treasurer of the mayor's last re-election campaign. The mayor just called to remind me of his support for good new development and his belief that Mr. Jones' subdivision would be an asset to the city. I told the mayor that I did not foresee any problems." As the director gets up to leave, he turns and, smiling, says, "Have a nice weekend. Relax and come back to work ready to do your job. See you first thing Monday morning."

Although new to the agency, you are not new to the profession. You believe that the director has ordered you to make a favorable recommendation on Mr. Jones' subdivision. You are extremely uncomfortable. You wonder what you should do next.

1.   Define the problem. The mayor's relationship with the applicant seeking development review is subverting the normal process of analysis and recommendation. Your boss has alerted you to the relationship and encouraged you to offer a favorable review.

2.   Clarify your primary goal. You would like to keep your job and to behave ethically. Given this goal, you will seek resolution without confrontation.

3.   Examine all the facts. In this case, you are missing several pieces of information. For example, the project might actually conform to all of the development requirements and the mayor is correct in his assessment

regarding the project's desirability. Also, what is the director's reputation? Is he usually a "good guy?" Or is there a history of staff coercion? This absence of information dictates your immediate course of action — collecting more data

4.   Brainstorm alternative courses of action. You consult with trusted colleagues. You eventually come to the conclusion that the director is asking you to make a finding unsupported by the facts of the case. You weigh the alternatives in terms of the requirements of the code. Five aspects seem most relevant. (See page 16.)

• **A.3** Provide full, clear accurate information. In full, clear and accurate information were to be provided, you could not recommend in favor of the project.

• **B.2** Accept decisions of employer. The code stipulates that when the employer is asking the planner to do something illegal, that does not serve the public interest, the planner is not bound to follow the decision of the employer. In this case, the code requirement would not apply.

• **D.1** Do not commit a deliberately wrongful act. If it is wrong, if you believe it to be wrong, you may not act on the option even if directed to do so.

• **D.5** Analyze ethical issues. You are required to make your decision within the framework of the ethical stipulations of your profession.

• **Advisory Ruling No. 5** Planners who know of unethical conduct must report it. Not only is the director asking you to do something unethical, you are charged to report this unethical conduct to the AICP (assuming the director is a member).

5.   Evaluate the consequences. (See page 16.)

6.   Select the preferred course of action and give it another test: publicity.

Based on all of the factors set forth, you decide that you will ask for a meeting with the director to explain your position and to ask for a response. If the director remains unmoved, you will decline the assignment. Adding the step of making absolutely sure there is no misunderstanding makes you feel comfortable with how you would explain or defend your actions if asked to do so.

Alternative Courses of Action	Possible Outcomes
Hear no evil. See no evil.	Keep job/lose integrity.
Do full analysis to see what the subdivision proposed is really like.	You have more specific info about whether or not the project is in compliance. By supporting your argument with facts, the likelihood of a favorable outcome increases.
Clarify what the planning director really wants.	You may find out that you misunderstood or overreacted.
Resign	Unemployed with a loss of income.
Prepare a memo to the file that outlines the assignment you have been given.	Establishes a paper trail in the event of future problems.
Confront the planning director.	Unclear. You will clarify your personal stance but may damage future working relations.
Consult with others.	Find out if the inference is standard operating procedure or whether you have misunderstood the conversation. You may find moral support as well.
Delegate upwards. Ask your boss to take the lead on this. Explain that, because of your new status, you are unsure of your ability to do the assignment.	The director might refuse and your days could be numbered. The director might accept and you would be off the hook. The director might chose to reassign the task to someone else.
File grievance.	You are likely to lose such a grievance. You may retain your integrity, but you will have to resign because the work environment will be extremely uncomfortable after a grievance procedure.
Check personnel policies for protection.	Understand your rights and responsibilities, and those of your employer.

7.   Implement your plan of action.

You call the director's office and make an appointment. You also begin reworking your resume understanding that you have embarked on a course of action that may well cost you this job.

HOW TO REACT TO A POSSIBLE ETHICAL LAPSE

What behavior is expected when you are notified, either officially or unofficially, that you may have violated the code? First, resist the temptation to argue. Your primary responsibility is to retain an open mind and respond only when you are able to do so calmly and thoughtfully. If there are points of confusion that may have resulted in a misunderstanding, you should make every effort to explain what has occurred. Be prepared to apologize for even having inadvertently created the appearance of unethical conduct. Second, turn to the code for guidance as to your general conduct when confronting an accusation.

• A planner must strive to provide full, clear and accurate information on planning issues...

• A planner should strive for high standards of professional integrity...

Suppose a cordial, conciliatory response has not resolved the matter? You should avail yourself of the ethical resources available to you through your APA chapter. Seek out the counsel of your chapter professional development officer. Explain the circumstances surrounding the issue and offer a scrupulously candid version of your role in the events. In an open manner, ask whether the behavior might be reasonably construed as having violated the code. Be prepared for bad news. Experience has shown that such accusations are rarely made unless there is a strong basis for the charge. When there is an aggrieved party, that person usually has deep-held personal feelings in addition to an understanding of the code. If the answer to your inquiry is affirmative — that you may have violated the code — you should begin immediately to prepare a more thorough and heartfelt apology. You also must seek ways to make restitution or to resolve the problem you may have created. A formal letter of apology acknowledging wrongdoing (even when not intentional) can help calm the waters. Consult with the professional development officer to brainstorm alternatives for redress.

Professionally, your goal in these difficult circumstances should be to resolve the matter before charges are filed with the AICP Executive Director. Once that has occurred, an apology may not stop an investigation and issuance of a formal complaint. An apology and attempted redress could substantially reduce the ire of the complainant and he or she might choose either to withdraw formal charges or to not file them at all.

Finally, even when an investigation yields a determination that there has been a code violation, the recommendation regarding what level of action should be taken by the AICP Commission will undoubtedly be influenced by a sincere effort to acknowledge wrongdoing and repair the damage you have created. A well-scribed mea culpa combined with aggressive actions to remedy a wrong will make your life easier and help restore your ethical posture.

The section below, which describes how an ethics charge is handled by AICP, provides other comments on your expected conduct in response to various phases of the ethics procedure.

PROCEDURES UNDER THE CODE OF ETHICS AND PROFESSIONAL CONDUCT: HOW TO SEEK ADVICE, AND TO FILE AND RESPOND TO CHARGES OF MISCONDUCT

The players who give life to the AICP Code of Ethics and Professional Conduct are the planners and members of the public who report violations; the AICP Executive Director; the AICP Ethics Committee (which has four members appointed by the AICP President, plus a chair who is a member of the Commission); and the AICP Commission.

Steps In the Procedures

Informal Advice. Requests for informal ethics advice may be made either to the executive director or a chair of a Chapter Professional Development Committee. Any advice given informally is not binding on AICP. Nevertheless, a planner who has sought and received such informal advice after making full disclosure of all relevant facts is unlikely to be severely disciplined, if disciplined at all, should it turn out that the advice was wrong.

Formal Advice. The executive director may issue formal advisory rulings on the propriety of a planner's conduct. Requests for advisory rulings must be in writing and must contain sufficient details, real or hypothetical, to permit a definitive opinion.

As a matter of practice, the executive director will issue a formal advisory ruling if the request is from a planner seeking advice about proposed future professional conduct. On the other hand, the executive director will decline to issue an advisory ruling if it is perceived that the request has been made instead of filing a formal charge of misconduct. The executive director reasons that the planner whose conduct is described in the ruling might be identifiable. The advisory ruling could thus be used to embarrass a planner who has had no opportunity to state a different version of the incident. When this occurs, the executive director will suggest that a formal charge of misconduct be submitted. If the person who made the request is a certified planner, the executive director may further stress an ethical obligation to file a charge of misconduct and refer the person to Advisory Ruling No. 5.

If the executive director issues an advisory ruling and the AICP Ethics Committee endorses it, the ruling will be published as commentary on the code and as a guide to its application. Even if it's not published, an advisory ruling is binding on AICP and may be relied upon, as long as there was full disclosure and the actual conduct does not vary. There is no requirement in the code that the AICP Commission approve advisory rulings.

Filing a Misconduct Charge. Any person, whether or not an AICP member, may file a charge of misconduct. Certified planners who have "certain" knowledge of "clearly unethical conduct" by other certified planners have a duty to file a charge of misconduct. The threat of filing a charge of misconduct may not be used as leverage in dealings with other planners.

Sending a Letter. A charge of misconduct should be made in a letter sent only to the executive director of AICP. The letter should identify the certified planner against whom the charge is being made and detail the conduct that allegedly violates provisions of the code. It should be noted that it is improper for a certified planner to send even a "courtesy" copy of the charge directly to the alleged offender. The executive director serves as the exclusive correspondent between the charging party and the respondent.

In the letter stating the charge, it is not necessary to cite the precise code provisions allegedly violated. Provisions of the AICP/APA Ethical Principles in Planning should not be cited, since they are not enforceable. The letter also should include documentation of the alleged misconduct. The documentation may be extensive, or it may simply be a newspaper clipping describing misconduct.

Anonymously filed charges also are permitted. Anonymous filing results in a number of disadvantages. An anonymous filer is not sent notification of the disposition of the charge, and has no right to appeal to the

AICP Ethics Committee if the executive director dismisses the charge. Anonymous filers have the option of furnishing an e-mail or post office box address in the event the executive director needs to reach them. There is nothing to prevent an anonymous charging party from later providing his or her identity. But the identity should be provided prior to the executive director's decision as to whether he will issue a complaint.

After receipt of the charge, the executive director will send a copy to the certified planner whose ethics are being questioned. That planner will now be referred to as the "Respondent." The executive director's cover letter will invite a general, informal response and may also request answers to specific questions. While the Rules of Procedure state no deadline for an informal response, the executive director customarily requests that it be submitted within 30 days.

Responding to the Charges. The respondent, upon receiving a charge of misconduct, should decide whether to seek legal representation. It is not necessary to be represented by an attorney. If, however, the respondent feels a need for legal advice, it's advisable to seek legal consultation as early as possible, certainly before submission of an informal response.

Advisory Ruling No. 5 requires respondents to cooperate fully with the executive director's investigation. Unless a respondent plans to surrender his or her certification, which is always an option, it's advisable to put forth all of the facts and arguments that address the charge. It also is important to identify all witnesses. No purpose is served by expressing outrage and attacking the motivation of the charging party. If, at any time, the executive director determines that the respondent is retaliating against the charging party or any other person who cooperates with the investigation, the executive director may issue a complaint against the respondent.

After the executive director receives the informal response, or the established deadline passes without a response, the executive director will decide whether an investigation is appropriate. If the charge appears without merit, the executive director will dismiss it and send a letter to the charging party, if identified, giving an explanation for dismissing the charge. The respondent will receive a copy. The dismissal is final, unless the charging party appeals the dismissal to the AICP Ethics Committee within 30 days.

Conducting an Investigation. If an investigation is warranted, the executive director will assign the complaint to staff. During the investigation, witnesses identified by the charging party and the respondent may be interviewed. Normally there will be a request to interview the respondent. The executive director, however, will not make credibility findings. If, for example, the charging party says that the planner against whom the charge is filed claimed to have a politician in his hip pocket and the planner denies the allegation, the executive director will not determine which version is factual. If the case turns on determining which version is correct, the executive director is likely to issue a complaint and have the ethics committee resolve the credibility dispute. Because Advisory Ruling No. 5 requires that respondents provide the executive director with all information relevant to the charge, records must be produced as soon as possible. The respondent also has a duty to encourage others with relevant information, whether favorable or unfavorable, to cooperate. Advisory Ruling No. 5 provides that if the ethics committee determines that allegations against a respondent cannot be proved because of a lack of cooperation, the ethics committee may determine that the allegations should be considered proven. The rationale is that planners owe a duty to their profession to assist in an investigation. As AICP has no subpoena power, a respondent's cooperation is crucial.

If the investigation leads the executive director to believe that a complaint will not be sustained, the executive director will dismiss the charge in a letter, giving a full explanation of the reasons. The letter will notify the charging party of the opportunity to appeal within 30 days to the ethics committee of AICP. If an appeal is filed, the ethics committee will sustain or reverse the executive director's decision, or send the charge back for further investigation and/or reconsideration.

Negotiating a Settlement. If it appears that the issuance of a complaint is likely and will be difficult to challenge, the respondent should consider an early settlement. There are several ways to settle an ethics proceeding in the early stages. If the charging party is personally aggrieved by the respondent's conduct, and a private resolution between the two would not be viewed as compromising code principles, the staff investigator may be willing to communicate reasonable settlement offers from the respondent to the charging party. The result could be a withdrawal of the charge with the blessing of the executive director.

Often, settlement discussions take the form of a negotiated "plea bargain." The code sets forth four levels of discipline. The mildest is a private reprimand. Because an identified charging party will be made aware of the private reprimand, there can be no assurance as to how private the reprimand will remain. A public censure, which is stronger than a reprimand, is published in an AICP publication, currently *Planners' Casebook*. Suspension and expulsion are the most severe forms of discipline. Notice of such actions are subject to publication by AICP. The goal of the respondent in negotiating a "plea bargain" is to convince the executive director and the ethics committee that they should settle for the mildest form of discipline appropriate to the alleged misconduct.

Issuing a Complaint. When issuing a complaint, the executive director keeps the focus as narrow as possible. A complaint consists of numbered paragraphs containing recitations of alleged facts. Following the facts are numbered paragraphs of alleged violations. These paragraphs cite provisions of the code that the executive director believes are implicated. All of the allegations in the complaint are based on the results of the executive director's investigation and may be additional to, or different from, those initially relied upon by the charging party.

Preparing a Response to a Complaint. The rules of procedure specify that an answer to a complaint is due 30 days from the date the complaint is received by the respondent. Unless the respondent can demonstrate extraordinary circumstances, the failure to deny any alleged fact within the specified time frame is deemed an admission of that fact.

In answering a complaint, a respondent is obliged to cooperate. It is neither sound nor acceptable to respond with what lawyers refer to as a "general denial." If the respondent does not know whether an alleged fact is correct, the respondent should say so, but only after making an effort to verify the truth. If a lack of knowledge prevents a respondent from conceding the truth of a fact allegation, the allegation will be considered in dispute. Unless specifically admitted, all allegations of violations are presumed to be denied. A respondent may explicitly deny the allegations of violations and state reasons why such violations cannot be sustained. Should he prefer not to, there will be a later opportunity for the respondent to send the ethics committee an argument as to why the code was not violated.

If an alleged fact is stated incorrectly in the complaint, the respondent should provide the correct version, if it is known. For example, assume that a respondent had become an investor, but not a partner, in a business venture. In a factual allegation in the complaint it is stated that: "Respondent became a partner in the business venture." The respondent should answer by denying that she became a partner, but acknowledge that she became an investor in the business venture. A candid answer would also disclose the details of the investment arrangement. For example, "my investment was $25,000 and, in exchange, I was given a contract promising me 3% of the annual net proceeds of the business." Moreover, the respondent is free to add facts to the response that she perceives as exculpatory, such as: "I held no office or employment with the venture, nor did I have any input in its business decisions."

When the executive director receives the answer, it is compared to the complaint to determine if there are any material facts in dispute. For example, if a complaint dealing with allegations of a conflict of interest contains a fact allegation that the planner received double compensation for the same work from two different clients, the denial of double compensation in the answer would result in a "disputed material fact." On the other hand, if the same complaint contains a factual allegation that the planner sent the same work product to both clients and the answer denies that the work was "sent" but claims that it was "hand delivered" to the clients, there is no dispute as to a "material fact" because the mode of delivery of the double payments is not an essential element of a violation.

The executive director has the option of amending a complaint to delete any disputed facts, whether or not material. The executive director also may amend the complaint to restate fact allegations by verifying and adopting the respondent's version of what occurred. Since the executive director has the burden of persuading the ethics committee that an ethical violation has occurred, the executive director cannot risk deleting any contested allegations of fact that may prove material to the outcome of the case.

Conducting a Hearing. If material facts are in dispute, the executive director must notify the ethics committee. The chair of the committee then may appoint one or more committee members to conduct a hearing. Normally, one member is appointed and is referred to as the "Hearing Member." A Notice of the Hearing is sent by the executive director who arranges the location and time of the hearing. The location is normally in the vicinity where the alleged misconduct occurred. The notice will contain a list of all disputed material facts to be resolved. The issues at the hearing will be confined to resolution of those facts.

Prior to the hearing, the executive director will furnish the respondent with a list of proposed witnesses and will respond to questions from the respondent as to the direct evidence to be produced. The respondent is expected to reciprocate. At the hearing, the hearing member will listen to and/or read the evidence submitted by the executive director and the respondent. The executive director has the burden of producing the witnesses and/or tangible evidence to establish that the disputed material facts are correct as stated in the complaint. Once the executive director has produced such witnesses and other evidence, the respondent will be given an opportunity to produce witnesses and/or tangible evidence that controverts the executive director's evidence.

It always is preferable to have witnesses testify in person. If any witness cannot be available, an affidavit will be accepted. If the credibility of a witness affidavit is challenged, the hearing member may continue the hearing so that the party issuing the challenge may have an opportunity to further examine the witness on videotape. The videotape can be sent to the hearing member who will then have an opportunity to observe the demeanor of the witness in responding to cross-examination.

A recording device is optional. The hearing member may prefer to take notes. At the conclusion of the hearing, the hearing member must make findings as to the disputed material facts. The hearing member has the option of asking the parties to submit proposed findings. The standard of proof for resolution of factual issues has traditionally been the "preponderance of the evidence" or "which version is more likely than not?"

Resignations and Lapses of Membership When Ethics Charges or Complaint Proceedings Are Underway. If an AICP member who is the subject of a charge of misconduct voluntarily resigns while a charge or complaint proceedings are pending, the charge or complaint (if issued) will be dismissed. However, the individual may not reapply for AICP certification. If membership lapses during an investigation due to non-payment of dues, the charge will be dismissed if issued. If a reinstatement request is made within the four-year period, the ethics matter will be reopened. If the former member does not apply for re-certification within the four-year period, application may not be made for re-certification.

Action by the Ethics Committee. Under the rules of procedure, the ethics committee determines if the code has been violated on the basis of the admitted facts and, if a hearing was held, the findings of fact. The deliberations, therefore, require a review of the complaint, the answer, and the hearing member's findings. In addition, the executive director and the respondent will be invited to submit written arguments for the committee's consideration. The committee members will discuss the facts and issues, and then vote. When the deliberations are completed, the executive director or a committee member will be instructed to prepare a draft written opinion for the committee's approval. Once approved, the opinion will be sent to the respondent, the charging party and the AICP Commission. If the opinion exonerates the respondent, the matter is closed. If the opinion concludes that there was blameworthiness, the ethics committee will issue concurrently its recommendation of discipline.

Action by the AICP Commission. If discipline is recommended, it cannot be imposed without the affirmative vote of two-thirds of the AICP Commission. The commission must vote on the discipline within one year after the complaint has been issued. An invitation to appear in person or submit information in writing is sent to the respondent at least 30 days prior to the scheduled vote. If the one-year deadline is approaching, the commission may vote on the issue of discipline via teleconference. A respondent who prefers direct eye contact with commission members might waive the one-year requirement in exchange for an opportunity to appear at the next in-person meeting of the commission.

The commission's vote is final and, as recorded by the secretary, is forwarded to the respondent and the charging party.

USING THE SCENARIOS

The next chapter includes numerous scenarios. Multiple scenarios are included for those portions of the code that practicing planners have identified as being major sources of ethical conflicts on the job. Note that the scenarios and commentary do not contain every possible response but, instead, put forth a number of possible approaches. The scenarios do not include an adequate level of detail to answer all questions. They are brief. They require a reader to make assumptions and select a course of action before getting on to the real work: sharing perspectives and insights with others.

The following section describes how to use the scenarios to learn more.

As a Reader

Carefully read the scenario, go through the process and then compare your choice to the discussion in the commentary.

In Workshops

Format. A primary objective in preparing this publication was to pull together information that could be useful to organizations interested in holding educational programs on ethics. The scenarios readily lend themselves to such use.

Two types of scenarios are included in this publication. Scenarios are short problem statements and several should be combined for a single program. Discussion scenarios are longer and one or two could be the basis of an entire event. The two types have been provided in the hope that they will appeal to the reader for use in different settings. In small groups, in chapter meetings, in local APA newsletters, the scenarios can be a springboard to discussion and an effective means of raising the profession's consciousness.

Chapters can present ethical scenarios for group discussion at professional development meetings. "Answers," in the form of commentary, are presented immediately following the scenario. The scenarios, commentary, and an answer sheet can be distributed to help organize the ethics program.

There are two ways the scenarios can be used in meetings.

Small group alternative

• Distribute copies of selected scenarios to members.

• Take ten minutes to study the material and gather responses from participants.

• Briefly restate the scenario and list the participants' responses to the ethical choices.

• Count the number of people selecting each response and record on a blackboard or a flip chart; calculate the percentage of responses by choice.

• Have the participants explain their choices. This is the heart of the exercise and the moderator must take care to make sure that the commentary is not dominated by just a few individuals.

Large group alternative

• Divide members into smaller groups.

• Assign each group a scenario to discuss and a recorder who will tabulate results.

• Allow for in-depth participation by individuals, but do not permit the group to force a consensus if one does not emerge naturally.

• Report back to the large group giving the major results and key reasons for the answers selected.

Discussion Scenarios. The discussion scenarios, in contrast to the shorter scenarios, have no suggested answers. They lend themselves to an interesting dialogue, provided the moderator is well versed in the requirements of the code and is prepared to lead the commentary development. Another way of using the discussion scenarios is to assign roles and ask participants to describe what they would do next and why.

Selecting Scenarios to Use in a Workshop. In choosing scenarios for a workshop, select ones that respond to topics of pressing concern. The Table of Contents is organized by the elements of the code so that you can easily identify the ones of interest and relevance. One way to identify provocative topics is to consult with local planners. Another is to use the Internet to scan the headlines or do a keyword search (ethics) of the major daily newspapers in the geographic area where the workshop will be held.

Appendix. The attachments in the appendix may serve as handouts for the workshop and can facilitate discussion or assist workshop participants who may not already be familiar with the code requirements. As a point of reference, ethical material from the International City Management Association is provided. This is included because conflicts with actions by city managers are often a source of ethical conundrums for professional planners. Having the ICMA Code in hand may assist in resolving those situations.

A Word about the Moderator

The role of the individual who presents the material is critical to a successful chapter program. Care must be taken to draw out all participants and not to permit a single individual to dominate the conversation. Equally important is maintaining an evenhanded approach to recording responses and prompting more detailed answers. The moderator must be non-judgmental. The group must expand upon the ideas as it struggles to identify the potential consequences of alternative courses of action. For example, groups often approve a combination of alternatives or identify a new course of action. Such ethical creativity is to be encouraged.

Moderators also are encouraged to distribute evaluation forms to assist chapter professional development officers in planning other sessions on ethical matters.

Sessions should conclude with a group brainstorming of things that can be done locally to help improve the ethical climate. Frequently made suggestions include:

- Articles in chapter newsletters
- AICP Code posted in the planing office
- Planning commission adoption of ethical principles and annual training for new commissioners
- Ethics workshops
- Ethics brown bag lunches in the office
- Coaching/job search help for planners who lose their jobs
- Letters to the editor of major newspapers

IS IT WORTH THE EFFORT TO TRY
AND UPHOLD ETHICAL PRINCIPLES?

Newspapers report a plethora of bad tidings when it comes to ethics:

• 58% of physicians would lie to an insurance company to ensure medical care for patients

• 62% of parents say it is acceptable for them to help a child with a class project that is supposed to be done by a child alone

• 17% of parents say it is acceptable for children to obtain test questions in advance; 11% would accept copying another student's work

• 65% of high-schoolers say they would cheat to pass a test.

The Journal of the American Medical Association admits that nearly half of the drug reviews published since 1997 were written by researchers with undisclosed financial support from companies marketing the drugs.

But research also encourages us to pursue opportunities to think reflectively. Behavior is affected by the communities we build. For example, colleges find that a focus on ethics can curb cheating. It is apparent that lax ethical conduct is partly the result of believing that such behavior constitutes the norm: everyone is doing it. In those instances when integrity is stressed and codes of conduct are formally adopted, behavior improves. If people believe that unethical conduct is socially unacceptable, they are less likely to cheat or lie. Similar results were found by Elizabeth Howe in her work, *Acting on Ethics in City Planning.* Planning is performed in communities with a particular ethical climate. But those climates can change for both better and worse. Teaching, reading, and thinking about ethics will improve the milieu in which planning is performed. Finally, those who are most satisfied with their resolution of ethical dilemmas are those who undertake self-inquiry. Thinking about core values to resolve conflicts helps us focus on our most fundamental principles. In turn, this renews a larger sense of purpose for all our work.

2
Scenarios

WHEN THE PLANNING DIRECTOR
WANTS AFFORDABLE HOUSING

You are the planning director in a small but growing upper-income bed-room suburb/city of a major metropolitan area. As part of the department's work program that was approved by the planning commission, you are preparing a report about housing opportunities in the city. New census data confirms your suspicions that there is a lack of land zoned for affordable housing. By analyzing the median income, current housing availability, and future trends, you have concluded that the amount of undeveloped land zoned for apartments should be doubled. You are not alone in this assessment. A team of planners has worked together on the analysis and the recommendations.

At the planning commission work session, you share the results of the team's efforts and outline your recommendations. You see that the commissioners are reacting negatively. You know that many citizens will oppose additional rental units and that your recommendations for more quadraplexes and triplexes will not be popular. Planning commission members raise questions about the level of community dissatisfaction such a report might cause. There seems to be no question about the validity of the analysis; planning commissioners just don't want to make waves. You feel provoked. You share with your commission components of the code that address the planner's responsibility to serve the public interest. While there has not been much public discourse on the topic, you know that many citizens will see such an initiative as bringing low-income people into the community. So far the news media has not asked any questions, but you know from experience that you are likely to get a phone call from the city editor before too long. As a planning director, how should you proceed?

Ethical Issues:

Planners (and planning commissioners) have a responsibility to broaden housing opportunities for a diverse range of income levels. They also have an obligation to expand choice and opportunity for all persons, not just those who complain.

Action Alternatives:

1.   Tone down the report by removing the specific recommendation that increases the amount of land zoned for multi-family housing. Plan to return at a later time recommending additional measures to add more apartment zoning.

2.   Re-title the report to add the words "preliminary, as a guide only" to the title and then recommend that the planning commission adopt the report in concept. Expect no implementation initiatives. Figure that you have at least laid the groundwork and that it will be up to future planning directors to follow through.

3.   Take a deep breath and move ahead. Encourage the commission to debate the analysis and recommendations thoroughly to understand the issues and the potential areas of compromise between the commission and the staff. Schedule a public hearing knowing that it will be painful. Push for increased housing opportunity in your community as far as you believe the data supports the need for such action.

4.   Other

Code Citations:

A.3   A planner must strive to provide full, clear, and accurate information on planning issues to citizens and governmental decision-makers.

A.4   A planner must strive to give citizens the opportunity to have a meaningful impact on the development of plans and programs. Participation should be broad enough to include people who lack formal organization or influence.

A.5   A planner must strive to expand choice and opportunity for all persons, recognizing a special responsibility to plan for the needs of disadvantaged groups and persons, and must urge the alteration of policies, institutions, and decisions that oppose such needs.

B.   A planner owes diligent, creative, independent and competent performance of work in pursuit of the client's or employer's interest. Such performance should be consistent with the planner's faithful service to the public interest.

B.1 A planner must exercise independent professional judgment on behalf of clients and employers.

C.5 A planner must examine the applicability of planning theories, methods, and standards to the facts and analysis of each particular situation and must not accept the applicability of a customary solution without first establishing its appropriateness to the situation.

D.6 A planner must strive to contribute time and effort to groups lacking in adequate planning resources and to voluntary professional activities.

Discussion:

Several ethical issues are raised here, beginning with housing diversity. Planners (and planning commissioners) have a responsibility to broaden opportunities for a diverse range of housing consumers. Here the planning director has noted this responsibility in a report and should follow through on it as strongly and as reasonably possible. In pursuit of such an objective, one may look for workable methods or even compromises.

One may be tempted to handle such a matter quietly to limit controversy and publicity. Indeed, negative publicity and public reaction may make it harder to realize the basic goals of housing opportunity. Nevertheless, one also must respect and invite citizen participation. Decisions or recommendations regarding major policies such as this certainly should be made with public input in a public meeting or hearing. Perhaps additional preparations will make this hearing a constructive one.

Re-titling the report, alternative 2, avoids responsibility. By choosing to move ahead, alternative 3, the director certainly will jeopardize his popularity with both the community and the commission. He should not do so lightly. The commission, however, should back his right to do so. Over the long run, such efforts by the director may turn around public opinion.

While each alternative has an element of appeal, the third one is most respectful of citizen participation, with no disrespect to other principles involved. The planning director should explain to the planning commission that increasing the amount of affordable housing is an important issue. The commission should be encouraged, at a minimum, to hold a public hearing to receive more input. You hope that some of the groups interested in affordable housing will be there and present a strong citizen-based case confirming your analysis. You may even wish to seek out such involvement and support. Other members of the team who worked on the report can be useful in this respect.

TEMPORARY TOILETS

You are the city's downtown development planner. Based on a recommendation from the Mayor's Task Force on the Homeless, you are placed in charge of a project to locate temporary toilets and showers in the downtown. Within the program budget, you arrange for eight port-o-potties and site showers to be placed in alleys and regularly serviced. A contract is signed with a commercial firm to maintain the facilities. They are well used and very popular with the homeless. However, the commercial tenants, whose businesses rely on the alleys for loading and unloading, have become upset. The homeless have begun loitering near the toilets and creating security problems. Numerous letters have been published in the local newspaper arguing against the project. "The homeless can use facilities provided by the Salvation Army," the letter writers argue. Local business owners think that aggressive panhandling and a perception of a lack of safety are keeping people away from downtown and hurting sales.

As a planner, you believe that downtown must be maintained in a way that makes it safe and comfortable for all citizens, including the homeless. Two months after the installation of the temporary sanitary facilities, you begin preparing your final report and drafting recommendations for action by the Task Force on the Homeless.

You have been directed by a member of the city council to conclude that the pilot project was a failure and to recommend immediate removal of the facilities. Your boss in the planning department would just prefer for the whole problem to go away. How should you write your report?

Ethical Issues:

Does a program that successfully meets the needs of one group of citizens take precedence over the needs of other groups who are adversely affected as a result? If the primary beneficiaries are disadvantaged, does it make a difference?

Action Alternatives:

1.   Tell the truth, the whole truth, and nothing but the truth. You were warned early in your career as a planning student that you would sometimes be pressured to "cook the numbers." You have always resisted such efforts and you will continue to do so.

2.   Knowing that you will get no support from your boss, decide to emphasize operational difficulties in the text as well as community opposition. Without recommending that the toilets be removed, stack the infor-

mation in a way that it would not be illogical for the elected officials to reach such a conclusion.

3. Meet with the chair of the Mayor's Task Force on the Homeless to discuss the project and steps that might be taken. See if the task force can step into a leadership role if the planning department will not. Be careful not to incriminate your boss or to name any names.

4. Rethink the final recommendations of the task force. Consider whether there may be other alternatives that meet the objectives of both the business community and the homeless. Perhaps a drop-in center funded by the business community could be established to provide showers, lockers, etc. Present these alternatives as part of your report.

5. Other.

Code Citations:

A.3 A planner must strive to provide full, clear, and accurate information on planning issues to citizens and governmental decision-makers.

A.5 A planner must strive to expand choice and opportunity for all persons, recognizing a special responsibility to plan for the needs of disadvantaged groups and persons, and must urge the alteration of policies, institutions, and decisions that oppose such needs.

B. A planner owes diligent, creative, independent and competent performance of work in pursuit of the client's or employer's interest. Such performance should be consistent with the planner's faithful service to the public interest.

B.1 A planner must exercise independent professional judgment on behalf of clients and employers.

B.2 A planner must accept the decisions of a client or employer concerning the objectives and nature of the professional services to be performed unless the course of action to be pursued involves conduct that is illegal or inconsistent with the planner's primary obligation to the public interest.

C.5 A planner must examine the applicability of planning theories, methods, and standards to the facts and analysis of each particular situation, and must not accept the applicability of a customary solution without first establishing its appropriateness to the situation.

Advisory Ruling:

4. "Honesty in the Use of Information" (see appendix for full text). As professional givers of advice — advice that may affect the well-being of communities and individuals for many years — we have a special obligation to cherish honesty in the use of information that supports our advice…. Yet many daily pressures do battle against honesty. We are pressed to be effective advocates for… an elected administration or a cause…. Do not cook the numbers.

Discussion:

The situation is all too familiar: elected officials asking planners to take the heat. It happens. Being asked to shade the truth is being asked to do something unacceptable. Public planners must not be seen adjusting reality to accommodate political will. However, a full and complete report also would have to acknowledge the opposition of local businesses and the probability that some members of the community at large have concerns about the proposal.

Nothing in the directive prohibits you from exploring options. But don't rule out your boss either. Your employer may dislike the temporary toilets, but may have some other ideas. Talk with your employer in enough detail to provide an overall framework for subsequent discussions with the task force.

Finally, keep in mind that you have an unavoidable responsibility to the homeless to recommend ways to meet their basic human needs.

Either alternatives 1 or 4 would be acceptable. Alternative 2 would not. Alternative 3 is a weaker approach because it attempts to shift the planner's responsibility elsewhere. It might, however, be acceptable as a first step.

USING THE ZONING ORDINANCE TO ELIMINATE FEEDING PROGRAMS FOR THE HOMELESS

You are the chapter professional development officer and the director of community development in a midwestern city of approximately 100,000. A colleague, who is the director of planning in a nearby city and who also is an AICP member, is taking heat from business owners because of the growing visibility of the homeless in the downtown. In response, he has declared all soup kitchens to be restaurants. None of the soup kitchens provide adequate off-street parking based on the number of seats in their respective "restaurants." The "restaurant" operators have been notified that they are in violation of their certificates of occupancy, which are now subject to revocation.

A major controversy erupts and lands at the feet of the planning commission. The commission, upon appeal by numerous churches and social service groups, has agreed to hold a special meeting. It appears that the commissioners may overrule the planning director.

Yesterday some of your planners asked to meet with you in your capacity as the professional development officer. "We are embarrassed by this fiasco," they say. They want you to do something about the circumstances whereby planners are being portrayed as cruel and heartless tools of the business community. They ask if it would be possible to bring charges under the AICP code against the planning director for failing to provide special attention to meeting the needs of the disadvantaged? What should you say to them?

Ethical Issue:

What is your responsibility to your colleague and to your profession when another planner makes a charge of unethical behavior?

Action Alternatives:

1. The decision of the planning director will undoubtedly be reversed, so no real harm was done. Further, the community debate has helped to raise public sensitivity to the issue and this is a long-term benefit.

2. You think that the director was wrong in ignoring his ethical responsibility toward the poor, and that you will assist the complaining planners in making a charge of unethical conduct.

3. You will look into the matter further, discussing it with the planning director and possibly with others. You would be glad to talk to them further after those conversations, but you do not wish to express an opinion on this specific case just yet.

4. The director appears to have been considering a balance of community interests and has done nothing obviously wrong.

5. Other.

Code Citations:

A.5 A planner must strive to expand choice and opportunity for all persons, recognizing a special responsibility to plan for the needs of disadvantaged groups and persons, and must urge the alteration of policies, institutions, and decisions that oppose such needs.

C.1   A planner must protect and enhance the integrity of the profession and must be responsible in criticism of the profession.

C.3   A planner who reviews the work of other professionals must do so in a fair, considerate, professional, and equitable manner.

D.5   A planner must systematically and critically analyze ethical issues in the practice of planning.

Advisory Ruling:

5.   A planner who has certain knowledge of clearly unethical conduct on the part of the certified planner has a duty to file a charge of misconduct.

Discussion:

Your role in this scenario is that of the professional development officer and you are being asked to review the ethical nature of a decision made by another. In this case, particularly because you were not party to the events involved, you need to gather additional information before you can answer any questions about whether such a controversial set of actions was ethical. This orientation on the part of the professional development officer would preclude giving the advice laid out in alternative 1, which proposes no further action. Alternative 1 also is a poor answer because it somehow implies that decisions, if unethical, are not the concern of other planners as long as some higher authority reverses those decisions.

Alternative 2, pursuing a complaint, is consistent with your responsibility as the professional development officer to help maintain good planning practice. Be prepared for the tension that will undoubtedly result between you and the planning director.

Alternative 3, having a discussion with the director, may be a reasonable intermediate choice because it provides an opportunity to gather additional information. Reporting wrongdoing is called for, but only when one has knowledge of a clear wrongdoing. That is not the case here. While the planning director may not be thrilled to have you express your concern, you may be able to act in the role of facilitator, helping to define alternative solutions to the problem of feeding the homeless. Strong resistance by the director would lead you to follow up with another alternative.

Alternative 4, concluding the director acted appropriately after careful consideration, implies a lack of wrongdoing. It might be the best response if you, as the professional development officer, had some personal knowledge of the facts. A more active role, as described in alternative 3, is preferred.

Background:

Note that in all of the alternatives offered, there is a presumption that failing to attend to the needs of the poor and the homeless represents a breech of one's professional ethics. Section A.5 of the code reminds planners of their special responsibility to plan for the needs of disadvantaged groups and persons, and to urge the alteration of policies, institutions, and decisions, which oppose such needs. To draw a conclusion, the professional development officer would have to find out what the planning director has done to provide for the kinds of facilities needed to serve the homeless and indigent population of the city. An approach that closes soup kitchens without regard to where else they might be located would not be ethical, no matter how loud the demand for such action might be.

PUBLIC DECISION-MAKING WITHOUT PUBLIC INPUT

As a new employee in the county planning department, your assignment is to prepare the department's recommendations for the capital improvements program (CIP). When you received the assignment, the planning director told you that all city agencies submit their requests to the planning department where they are assembled. Your job is to review the requests for consistency with adopted plans and policies, and prepare a formal report listing the requests and offering recommendations. The report then will be sent from the planning department to the planning commission and, finally, to the county supervisors for action. Although you have been given no explicit instructions regarding public comment, you assume there will be public hearings before the planning commission.

For several days you have been waiting for the list of projects. While at the copy machine one morning, you overhear a conversation about an in-house, informal review committee that "weeds out" unnecessary requests. You initially are startled, mostly because the director never mentioned the group. On the other hand, you tell yourself, this committee must be doing a pretty good job. After all, the other departments aren't squawking, and it certainly gives the county supervisors a more manageable list of projects. You ask how this system evolved and you are told that the supervisors needed a streamlined process and this scheme was devised.

In a sense, you feel as though the job has been taken away from you and from the planning commission. You are concerned that there is no public input to the process. Is there a problem?

> **Ethical Issues:**
>
> Has an important public planning process been subverted to gain efficiency? Are appropriate people making public policy?

Action Alternatives:

1.   There is no problem. You can't have a public hearing on everything or nothing would ever be accomplished. You probably just didn't understand the assignment. You were expecting something to work like a textbook description rather than the real world.

2.   There may or may not be a problem. Is the informal committee using reasonable planning standards or dividing the pie according to electoral districts? Find out if good planning rationale, consistent with adopted plans, is being followed.

3.   There is a problem because the public and the commission have been led to believe that the process allows them to comment on all the proposals, not a refined sub-list. Write your report to advise members of the community that they are looking at an edited version of the original requests made by all the departments.

4.   Decide that your director has a lack of confidence in you. Why else would you be given a meaningless task and not be told what you need to know? Consider resigning rather than serving as a "front" for a system in which you have no part.

5.   Other.

Code Citations:

A.3   A planner must strive to provide full, clear, and accurate information on planning issues to citizens and governmental decision-makers.

A.4   A planner must strive to give citizens the opportunity to have a meaningful impact on the development of plans and programs. Participation should be broad enough to include people who lack formal organization or influence.

A.5   A planner must strive to expand choice and opportunity for all persons, recognizing a special responsibility to plan for the needs of disadvantaged groups and persons, and must urge the alteration of policies, institutions, and decisions that oppose such needs.

B.   A planner owes diligent, creative, independent and competent performance of work in pursuit of the client's or employer's interest. Such performance should be consistent with the planner's faithful service to the public interest.

B.1   A planner must exercise independent professional judgment on behalf of clients and employers.

B.2   A planner must accept the decisions of a client or employer concerning the objectives and nature of the professional services to be performed unless the course of action to be pursued involves conduct that is illegal or inconsistent with the planner's primary obligation to the public interest.

C.   A planner should contribute to the development of the profession by improving knowledge and techniques, making work relevant to solutions of community problems, and increasing public understanding of planning activities. A planner should treat fairly the professional views of qualified colleagues and members of other professions.

Discussion:

Before consulting ethical guides, one must examine the relevant local government charter or enabling legislation to ensure that no specific or implied requirements for public review are being ignored. If such is the case, the planner should immediately inform others of the need to operate in compliance with the law. In this instance, assume that the issue is not one of failing to meet the legal requirements. The public has the right to participate in public decision-making. The code is explicit in urging that planners strive to provide full, clear and accurate information and to give citizens the opportunity to have meaningful impact on the development of plans and programs. The code does not, however, state when in the planning process public participation should occur. In some communities, there is little participation in CIP planning.

You should begin with alternative 2 and collect a more information about the process. Investigate the situation to see if there has been public participation in the past. Perhaps you could sit in on a meeting of the review committee and find out if the decisions being made follow good planning practice and publicly adopted plans. If so, there may be no ethical problems.

If you are not permitted to join the committee or if people are not forthcoming in their responses, you should raise this issue with your supervisor and be prepared to act upon alternative 3. This course of action needs to be undertaken within the context of your responsibilities to fairly treat the views of colleagues. In this case, your brief tenure may mean that you do not grasp that which is a well-understood and completely accepted process. On the other hand, your fresh perspective may be just what is needed to remind the planners that they have substituted their role for that of the commissioners in an effort to make the commissioners' job easier. There are other ways that community participation can be solicited absent the presentation of a laundry list of capital projects. A "call for projects" could be issued to all the relevant citizen boards and commissions. The planning commission meeting at which the CIP report is to be discussed should be advertised. You can suggest these and other alternatives to your director to help structure a more participatory process.

Reject alternative 4. This is hardly the type of problem that merits resignation. Being a newcomer may put you at a disadvantage in terms of understanding what is a completely accepted process within your community. You also may have learned an important lesson; not all the information you need to do your job will be handed to you. You need to be prepared to gather additional intelligence from your colleagues, files, and other records about how to do your job. Keep in mind that the code is not the place to seek information about how to "get the hang" of a new job. You should be cautious about jumping to conclusions. A conversation with a more experienced planner can help you work through such circumstances. You also could talk with the professional development officer of your local chapter.

PLANNER WONDERS IF COMMUNITY UNDERSTANDS DEVELOPMENT'S POTENTIAL IMPACT

You are an African-American planner on the city's small planning staff. You seem to have become the official minority ombudsman for all projects. Both the Minority Alliance Chamber of Commerce and the City Chamber of Commerce support a proposed redevelopment scheme presently before the planning commission. The minority community's support mystifies you. Mostly low-income housing would be lost during the initial phases of the redevelopment, and opportunities for job creation available to the minority community appear limited. The planning staff seems in favor of the project, partly because there is no community opposition. You know that the city council is not likely to approve the project without the minority alliance endorsement. What should you do next?

Ethical Issues:

You believe the minority community's support is based on incomplete information. You feel an obligation to provide additional data. At the same time, you do not want to be disloyal to your organization by encouraging opposition to an idea that does seem to enjoy some community support.

Action Alternatives:

1.   You accept the facts as presented and say nothing. No one has tried to withhold information.

2.   You make sure that the proposal is adequately advertised to minority community groups. This fulfills your responsibility.

3.   You talk to the director and try to figure out some mechanism for building a greater awareness of low-income concerns (minority and otherwise) into the evaluation process.

4.   You decide that the process is too far along for successful intervention and determine to work to improve future communications.

5.   Other.

Code Citations:

A.3   A planner must strive to provide full, clear, and accurate information on planning issues to citizens and governmental decision-makers.

A.4   A planner must strive to give citizens the opportunity to have a meaningful impact on the development of plans and programs. Participation should be broad enough to include people who lack formal organization or influence.

D.6   A planner must strive to contribute time and effort to groups lacking in adequate planning resources and to voluntary professional activities.

Discussion:

You want to help those communities that may not understand the impact of the proposed development. However, you need to balance that responsibility with your obligations to the city at large and to your employer. You would like to be helpful without creating political trouble.

By accepting the facts and doing nothing, you ignore the aspirational quality of the AICP code. The code requires you to go further and contribute time and expertise to those communities that are lacking in resources. Reject alternative 1.

Assuming that one particular group will represent all the interests of a community is, at best, risky. It is not likely that any chamber of commerce, whether minority or otherwise, will focus on the preservation of low-income housing as a primary objective. Further, you understand that you are placing a set of value restrictions on the minority chamber by expecting it to focus on the problems of jobs for minorities as opposed to economic development.

Successful planning departments have effective strategies for community involvement. Many public notice requirements in ordinances were formulated long ago when the newspaper was the primary source of community news. Since then, readership has declined and is often limited in low-income neighborhoods. While technician planners would argue that their job only requires them to follow the rules, a more politically oriented planner would focus on serving the public interest and would want to do more. Advertising does not ensure that the groups understand the consequences of the proposed redevelopment.

Alternative 3, building greater community awareness of the low-income community concerns, would be the best, providing you have a director open to what may be interpreted as criticism. It is the responsibility of all planners, not just minority planners, to be sensitive and responsive to those who are most dependent upon others to meet their basic living needs.

Alternative 4 is a well-rationalized version of doing nothing. While it would be preferable to ignoring the situation, it does not represent the best choice.

WHERE HAVE ALL THE AFFORDABLE RENTAL HOUSES GONE?

You are the planning director in Farmers Twig, a city of 200,000 in central Texas. In one neighborhood near city hall, the houses are aged but mostly well kept. The streets are cracked but serviceably patched. Along the older, tree-lined avenues of Farmers Twig, residents concede that maintaining middle class standards can be a struggle. Used car dealerships and dilapidated houses dot the area amid evidence of recent improvement efforts, such as a new city hall and redeveloped parks. For this neighborhood, the planning commission has been asked to review and endorse a proposal by the city's Department of Housing and Community Development to undertake suburban renewal. The project will cost $1.8 million over the next three years.

Major public improvements like traffic circles and neighborhood entryways are planned. The idea is to buy a few old homes and resell them to builders who will raze them and then replace them with bigger, more expensive houses. The city will arrange for low-cost renovation loans for residents who want to stay. Farmer's Twig will rebuild the streets and provide a new name for the neighborhood, preferably one with an excess "e" on the end, like The Residences at Downtown Parke. As a result, it is hoped that the free market will lift the rest of the area into affluence.

The mayor likes the plan and says, "This is a way to renew our city and keep the tax base from falling flat. This area will be our first success story." City officials make no bones about their desire to see properties improved and home values rise, but they insist that the program is benevolent and that no one will be forced to participate. "It's not urban renewal. It's stimulating private ownership," said Housing and Community Development Director Arvada Escalante. Escalante freely credits the nearby town of Bobwhite for the idea. "They were able to transform an old neighborhood into an affluent enclave," he said.

What about those who refuse to sell? "We'll be busy enforcing the cleanliness codes from now on," responded the mayor. The mayor has sent a letter to the planning commission urging its endorsement of the project, stressing that city staff held two meetings with residents to hear their ideas and no one objected.

You are beginning to write the staff report and you have questions in your mind.

Ethical Issues:

Should planners endorse projects that may have the effect of reducing the supply of affordable housing? How do you balance competing public goods? Does to duty to expand choice and opportunity for disadvantaged citizens supercede other code responsibilities?

Action Alternatives:

1.   Look at the need to improve the tax base as a legitimate, and ultimately primary, public policy and write a report sensitive to this, but do not recommend in favor of the project.

2.   Include in the staff report a discussion of housing affordability in your community and how the project will affect housing choice. Recommend in favor of the project and alternatives that can be implemented to ameliorate negative consequences.

3.   Recommend against the project until there is a companion local program in place to replace any lost affordable housing.

4.   Other.

Code Citations:

A.1   A planner must have special concern for the long-range consequences of present actions.

A.2   A planner must pay special attention to the inter-relatedness of decisions.

A.3   A planner must strive to provide full, clear, and accurate information on planning issues to citizens and governmental decision-makers.

A.4   A planner must strive to give citizens the opportunity to have a meaningful impact on the development of plans and programs. Participation should be broad enough to include people who lack formal organization or influence.

A.5   A planner must strive to expand choice and opportunity for all persons, recognizing a special responsibility to plan for the needs of disadvantaged groups and persons, and must urge the alteration of policies, institutions, and decisions that oppose such needs.

A.7   A planner must strive for excellence of environmental design and endeavor to conserve the heritage of the built environment.

B.   A planner owes diligent, creative, independent and competent performance of work in pursuit of the client's or employer's interest. Such performance should be consistent with the planner's faithful service to the public interest.

Discussion:

There are two competing public goods between which the planner must decide: economic revitalization leading to an enhanced tax base versus preservation of a decaying housing stock which is affordable. Both are legitimate ends to be pursued. That's why it presents a true dilemma. The planner must, however, make a final decision. Such a decision would be made in the context of a number of variables about which the scenario is silent. Nonetheless, operating based on the information offered, you consider whether two public meetings were adequate. Based on the generally high quality work done in Farmers Twig, you believe the meetings were carefully planned and that you must accept the fact that those who attended the meetings chose not to object. Planning to improve a deteriorating neighborhood will benefit low-income homeowners who stay in the community, even if some renters will have to move as rents increase.

Making public improvements to the neighborhood will undoubtedly trigger private investments in individual homes. Such investment will, over time, help conserve the existing housing stock and, as a result, the heritage of the built environment. All these consequences are to the good.

Consideration of the inter-relatedness and long-range consequences of decisions requires one to acknowledge that almost any form of intervention/improvement of a neighborhood can, over time, enhance the values of property and, thereby, diminish the availability of affordable units. In fact, a few low-income housing advocates in Houston, Texas systematically eliminate public improvements, such as paved potholes and repaired sidewalks, in an effort to discourage interest in their neighborhood. In San Francisco, other neighborhoods zealously guard the remaining blue-collar industrial buildings which, because of noise and associated blight, help to reduce the desirability of nearby housing.

Alternative 2, recommending options that will help to increase the supply of affordable housing while at the same time supporting the project is the preferred choice. Alternative 1, while not unethical, is silent on the critical test of balancing competing interests. Further, your decision is likely to have little or no impact. While that should not determine what you do, it is worth bearing in mind that if you wish to influence events, this alternative won't help. Alternative 3, rejecting the project, might appeal to some. It is certainly an ethical action. As noted in the first sentence of the commentary, both objectives are public goods so either choice can be supported. However, alternative 3 is unduly harsh, unless the planner is convinced that this project is part of a larger and systematic effort to exclude lower-income residents from Farmers Twig.

Source: The Dallas Morning News, *June 16, 1998 with some names and details changed.*

BEING RESPONSIVE TO HISPANIC COMMUNITY VALUES

You are a consultant planner recently engaged by a city with a forty-percent Hispanic population. Most of the Hispanic community arrived as immigrants over the past decade. The entire city council and the city manager are Anglos.

Your job is to devise a zoning plan that will reduce future densities resulting from in-fill development in an older residential area. On the surface, the consulting engagement seems reasonable, particularly in light of the city council's professed desire to balance the population, and the availability of public services.

Your first meeting with community groups offers a different perspective. The neighborhood targeted for the rezoning is overwhelmingly Hispanic. Proposals to reduce future densities through mechanisms such as limits on overnight, on-street parking and restrictions on the number of bedrooms in a residential unit are denounced as discriminatory against Hispanic families. Data from the Census Bureau confirms that Hispanic families tend to be larger than Anglo families. The residents believe that the city is trying to force them out of the community. You are deeply disappointed by the tone of this meeting. You schedule a meeting with the planning staff to secure additional background information. After talking with the planners, you conclude that the Hispanic community's accusations may be well founded. What should you do?

Ethical Issues:

What is your responsibility when the minority community's interests may not be well served by your employer's goals? How do you balance your loyalty to an employer and the need to accept the client's definition of the work to be accomplished against your responsibility to serve the needs of the disadvantaged?

Action Alternatives:

1.   Hold a series of community meetings to develop an alternative acceptable to the most directly affected residents. You have had only one community meeting and those who attended it may not be entirely representative of the larger community or other points of view within the Hispanic community.

2.   Review with the planning director and the city manager the results of your first meeting and report your concerns about housing opportunities for the Hispanic community. Ask for additional informa-

tion that the city might have on the topic. Inquire as to the previous history in working with residents in this area.

3.   Recommend to the mayor that you pursue additional alternatives that maintain the potential for higher densities. Let the elected officials know that you understand their concerns, but emphasize the problem with the single approach identified in your contract.

4.   Explain to the mayor that zoning is not the best tool to resolve a broad conflict over community values. Suggest that the contract be terminated and that you be compensated for the value of services provided to date. You identify the general types of consultant services you think the community could benefit from at the present time.

5.   Other.

Code Citations:

A.4   A planner must strive to give citizens the opportunity to have a meaningful impact on the development of plans and programs. Participation should be broad enough to include people who lack formal organization or influence.

A.5   A planner must strive to expand choice and opportunity for all persons, recognizing a special responsibility to plan for the needs of disadvantaged groups and persons, and must urge the alteration of policies, institutions, and decisions that oppose such needs.

B.   A planner owes diligent, creative, independent and competent performance of work in pursuit of the client's or employer's interest. Such performance should be consistent with the planner's faithful service to the public interest.

B.1   A planner must exercise independent professional judgment on behalf of clients and employers.

B.2   A planner must accept the decisions of a client or employer concerning the objectives and nature of the professional services to be performed unless the course of action to be pursued involves conduct that is illegal or inconsistent with the planner's primary obligation to the public interest.

B.8   A planner must not accept or continue to perform work beyond the planner's professional competence or accept work that cannot be performed with the promptness required by the prospective client or employer, or that is required by the circumstances of the assignment.

Discussion:

This scenario suggests a clash in values: those of the community versus those of the elected officials. It would appear that the fears of the Hispanic community might be justified. Often a planner confronts situations in which competing values must somehow be reconciled. The code provides a good frame of reference for analyzing what should be done.

Look back at the process for determining ethical actions. Identify your view of the public interest, and the specific goal or objective you would like to achieve. Examine the facts, which in this scenario are sketchy. A situation such as this calls for additional research as to the values and opinions behind the contract and the facts that may or may not support those values and opinions. (Presumably a competent consultant wouldn't be caught in this situation because the appropriate research would have been done before accepting the engagement.) This research may help the creative planner to more fully understand the controversy. Consider the alternative courses of action listed in the scenario and look to the code for guidance. The code clearly identifies one basic theme as underlying most others: serve the public interest. Who, however, defines the public interest in this case? Is it the community, the elected leaders, or the consulting planner? How are those versions of the public interest balanced? The code places that final responsibility squarely at the feet of the planner in the course of carrying out the engagement.

The scenario places you as a consultant rather than a staff planner. The difference is a relevant one as the consultant usually works on a more narrowly defined task. The consulting planner must usually focus work on objectives defined by the hiring agency. The need to complete the work in a timely fashion may constrain the consultant from broadly questioning the client's determination of public interest. The governmental staff planner, on the other hand, may have a more complete knowledge of history and background and be in a better position to clarify the public interest, and to function as more of an advocate.

Suppose the consultant was having difficulty because the engagement required a different set of technical skills than the consulting firm could offer? The consultant would be bound, in that circumstance, to report the need for additional assistance.

Alternatives 2, 3, and 4 all have merit and indicate a thoughtful effort on the part of the planner. However, 2 is the weakest and suggests no independent thought or judgment, both of which are needed in this instance. Alternative 1, which implies changing the scope of work without consulting with the employer, may be the most appealing course of action. It holds out the possibility for achieving an accommodation of all points of view. It is unlikely, however, that the contract could financially support a major new outreach. Unless the consultant can see a way to accomplish this alternative without losing her or his shirt, alternative 4, seeking to conclude the engagement, might be the next best choice.

A SIMPLE OFFICE CONVERSION

You are the newly hired and only planner in a small community of several neighborhoods with a variety of housing conditions. This is your first meeting. The petitioner in a proposed zoning map amendment is seeking office zoning to convert a residential rental unit into a real estate office. His rental unit is in poor condition as are some of the nearby properties. He claims that low residential rents prevent him from making improvements, but an office use would permit the necessary renovations. Standard notification procedures were followed. No residents have spoken at the hearing. A motion has been made and seconded to approve the request. You have been asked to offer a staff recommendation. You are concerned about setting a precedent. What should you do?

Ethical Issues:

How do you balance the need for a range of affordable housing types in a community against the desire of an individual property owner to maximize the rate of return on property?

Action Alternatives:

1.   Recommend that the request be approved because the petitioner appears earnest and should have a chance to do what he wants, particularly because no residents complained.

2.   Request that you be granted additional time to review the files to see if other cases like this have had their proposals approved. If so, then you would recommend approval for this one.

3.   Recognize that such rental properties are needed in the housing stock to provide an adequate variety of choices. Also recognize that in the long range, if every rental unit were converted to office use, your community would be sadly deficient in offering the necessary housing opportunities. Recommend that it not be approved.

4.   Encourage further commission discussion before presenting your recommendation. Bring up concerns about citizen participation, housing

opportunity and the long-range impact of such a decision. Base your recommendation upon the comments made by commissioners.

   5.   Other.

Code Citations:

   A.1   A planner must have special concern for the long-range consequences of present actions.

   A.7   A planner must strive for excellence of environmental design and
endeavor to conserve the heritage of the built environment.

   B.   A planner owes diligent, creative, independent and competent
performance of work in pursuit of the client's or employer's interest. Such
performance should be consistent with the planner's faithful service to
the public interest.

   B.1   A planner must exercise independent professional judgment on
behalf of clients and employers.

Discussion:

Ideally, you would not attend a planning commission meeting unless
fully prepared to participate. However, some planners, especially in small
agencies, find themselves faced with the expectation that they are instant
experts. Such is the case in this scenario.

   Planners can make effective arguments supporting redevelopment
through changes in land use. It is commonly stated that a new infusion of
income will allow conservation of property. While not a factor to be
ignored, it is simply not a strong enough point to carry the entire weight
of the argument.

   There is a pro and con to each alternative. The first alternative, recommending approval, has the appeal of letting someone act freely as long as
no one is harmed. As a planner, however, you must recognize that the
people who would endure the negative impacts of a project are not
always vocal or present. You must temper free use of the land with consideration of all long-range impacts.

   The second alternative points to equitable treatment of the land. If two
pieces of property have identical characteristics and similar circumstances
surrounding them, they generally should receive the same treatment. You
must, however, set limits and occasionally, based on new and better information, change an unwise but common practice.

   The third alternative states a few of the long-range considerations that
should come in to play. You must look to the future impacts of each pos-

sible decision and state any concerns during the hearing. In a zone change hearing, you must base your recommendation upon the information presented at the hearing. If you have concerns and are inclined to base your recommendation upon those concerns, you must state them. However, a recommendation to deny must be based on accurate and complete data.

Alternative 4 would be the least desirable. It implies that the newly hired planner would immediately abdicate a responsibility to provide independent judgment. The best choice would be a combination of alternatives 2 and 3. Request additional time, and consider a broad range of issues before preparing a recommendation.

ANNEXATION ANALYSIS BLUES

You are a newly hired junior staff planner assigned to prepare recommendations on petitions for municipal annexation. You work for a large mid-western city and you are pleased to have this important assignment. Your boss tells you that only annexations that generate net revenue to the community should be recommended to the city council. You wonder whether other criteria should not also be evaluated, such as improvements to the quality of life that may result from a higher level of public service when annexation occurs. For example, you believe that areas with failing septic systems should be prime targets for annexation and the extension of municipal wastewater systems even though they are likely to be low-income neighborhoods. You see a pattern of annexing high-income residential or commercial areas while skipping over low-income neighborhoods. What should you do?

Ethical Issues:

Do you have a responsibility to speak out against public policies that work to the disadvantage of low-income groups? Do you have a duty to report behavior that may be unethical?

Action Alternatives:

1.   Suggest that a special study be undertaken to carefully address costs and benefits of several typical annexations. Propose to base future recommendations on the results of this study.

2.   Seek to relate annexation to other policies, such as the comprehensive plan, and/or visioning efforts for the municipality. Comb such documents for support and write a paper suggesting new annexation policies.

3.   Talk to residents in areas you believe appropriate for annexation. Look for publicity and support for broader annexation efforts. Invite the newspaper to prepare articles supporting your point.

4.   Talk to other city staff, seeking support for changes to the current policy. Encourage your boss to see what she can do to change the policy. Offer to help with the analysis and other supporting documentation.

5.   Other.

Code Citations:

A.   A planner's primary obligation is to serve the public interest. While the definition of the public interest is constantly evolving, a planner owes allegiance to a conscientiously attained concept of the public interest, which requires special obligations.

A.1   A planner must have special concern for the long-range consequences of present actions.

A.2   A planner must pay special attention to the inter-relatedness of decisions.

A.3   A planner must strive to provide full, clear, and accurate information on planning issues to citizens and governmental decision-makers.

A.4   A planner must strive to give citizens the opportunity to have a meaningful impact on the development of plans and programs. Participation should be broad enough to include people who lack formal organization or influence.

A.5   A planner must strive to expand choice and opportunity for all persons, recognizing a special responsibility to plan for the needs of disadvantaged groups and persons, and must urge the alteration of policies, institutions, and decisions that oppose such needs.

C.5   A planner must examine the applicability of planning theories, methods, and standards to the facts and analysis of each particular situation and must not accept the applicability of a customary solution without first establishing its appropriateness to the situation.

Advisory Ruling:

5.   A planner who has certain knowledge of clearly unethical conduct on the part of the certified planner has a duty to file a charge of misconduct.

Discussion:

The code strongly supports planners' efforts to expand choice and opportunity. This scenario shows a method communities can use to make neighborhoods exclusive and to restrict opportunities for access to public services. While the primary public motive may be fiscal responsibility, the effect can be a form of economic segregation. Certainly you should discuss this work with your boss, and attempt to persuade her of planners' ethical responsibilities.

Will any or all of the four stated alternatives help you persuade her or help you both work with the city council to change its policies? Although alternative 1 sounds appealing, don't expect the analysis to be easy to perform or the results easy to interpret. The perception of the current policy is probably that the costs of providing municipal services to most residential development are greater than tax benefits, particularly when a jurisdiction is without impact fees. This may be confirmed in the study.

Alternative 2 is the best answer from a planner's perspective, but many communities either have no plan or the plan does not comment upon such issues. Without becoming subversive you may be able to pursue other aspects of alternatives 3 and 4. The best combination of alternatives depends on the local situation. Clearly the planner should encourage some consideration of changes. The question of whether the actions to limit annexations constitute clearly unethical behavior is open to debate in this instance.

Section C.5 of the code requires you to consider what alternatives, besides annexation, are appropriate. You need to find out what the authorizing legislation says must be included in the analysis. Are these petitions received by the city seeking annexation, or petitions that the city generates? What kinds of recommendations have been prepared in the past, and what has the history of the city been in dealing with these recommendations? Additional effective guidance may be derived from some of the answers. For example, the city may have other ways to assist low-income communities in need of utilities other than through annexation.

Consideration of the duty to report is always appropriate, but in this case would be an extreme over-reaction on your part.

SENDING THE SEX SHOPS NEXT DOOR

You are the economic redevelopment director for the City of Dale, which is working on a plan to reuse the Dale Naval Air Station. Imagine your surprise when you pick up the newspaper to see that the adjacent city, Grand Fromage, has voted to require all sexually oriented business to operate in a concentrated area along the east side of the air station as part of a new ordinance to regulate sexually oriented businesses.

The newspaper quotes one of the Grand Fromage council members as saying, "I don't see anything wrong with putting this up on the site near the air station. It's so far away from the downtown that people won't even think it's in Grand Fromage. They'll think it's in Dale. They will say, 'Hey let's go to the dirty movies in Dale.'"

The vote of the council was not unanimous. "I oppose what we're doing. It's like putting a knife in the back of any kind of redevelopment out there," opined another council member.

You pick up the phone and call the Fromage planning director who explains, "We had to protect the city from the adverse secondary impacts of those businesses. Plus our moratorium on establishing sexually oriented businesses was about to expire so time was running out."

The planning director tells you that there is not much for you to worry about. Under the new ordinance, businesses operating in the area will be required to meet strict health and safety guidelines, as well as comply with new sign restrictions. Plus, he adds, there are new landscaping and lighting provisions. "Look, maybe it's not your idea of the perfect land use; but we did write into the ordinance that the sexually oriented businesses are not allowed to serve alcohol. Maybe that will deter the growth of such businesses," says the planning director.

You're outraged at the planning director's willingness to dump this on your project area. You wonder how he could do this. The planning director says he had no problem in recommending this to his Council. You decide to:

Ethical Issue:

Is it ethical to deliberately seek to relocate unwanted land uses so that they minimize their impact on your community and increase their impact on another?

Action Alternatives:

1. Do nothing because the sexually oriented businesses (SOBs) are still within the boundaries of Grand Fromage.

2. Talk to the Dale police chief about cooperative efforts with Grand Fromage to ensure compliance with the law.

3. Write a letter to the Grand Fromage planning director complaining about the lack of warning and inviting the director to join your city's Economic Development Technical Advisory Committee and support efforts to ameliorate the impact of the relocation of the SOBs.

4. Write a letter to the editor of the local newspaper complaining about the lack of cooperation.

5. Other.

Code Citations:

A.1 A planner must have special concern for the long-range consequences of present actions.

A.2 A planner must pay special attention to the inter-relatedness of decisions.

A.4 A planner must strive to give citizens the opportunity to have a meaningful impact on the development of plans and programs. Participation should be broad enough to include people who lack formal organization or influence.

A.7 A planner must strive for excellence of environmental design and endeavor to conserve the heritage of the built environment.

C.5 A planner must examine the applicability of planning theories, methods, and standards to the facts and analysis of each particular situation and must not accept the applicability of a customary solution without first establishing its appropriateness to the situation.

D.5 A planner must systematically and critically analyze ethical issues in the practice of planning.

Discussion:

The planning director of Grand Fromage has ignored his responsibility to serve the public interest. The public interest is not defined by municipal boundaries. While a different recommendation from the planning director might not have changed the outcome of the city council's action, it would have helped the community understand what constitutes a sound basis for making planning decisions. Specifically, the director's stance seems to be one of looking out for oneself to the exclusion of considering the inter-relatedness and long-term consequences of such decisions, or other alternatives.

As a practical matter, the Grand Fromage planning director seems to have forgotten the adage of "what goes around, comes around." Other communities in the area will, undoubtedly, sit up and take notice. A short-range "gain" for the Fromagians may result in a long-term loss when matters arise requiring the cooperation of others to benefit Grand Fromage.

Each of the alternatives being considered by the redevelopment director is ethical with the exception of "doing nothing." The AICP code requires the careful consideration of ethical issues. Taking action when you have identified an ethical lapse also is expected.

In the short term, working to ensure the adequate enforcement of the new standards is important. In the long run, seeking to establish a more effective collaborative environment for land-use decision making is likely to have the greatest impact.

Source: The Fort Worth Star Telegram, *June 16, 1998. Names and details have been changed.*

STREET VENDORS VS. CORPORATE AMERICA

You are the planning director in a large urban area. Many residents are immigrants from developing nations. The mayor recently appointed a Task Force on Vending. This was done at the request of the Chamber of Commerce and the police department. Both entities have identified problems associated with the proliferation of vendors. You were assigned to provide staff support to this task force. At the first meeting of the task force numerous points are made.

• Street vending is a traditional toehold on the economic ladder for immigrant groups.

• Vending is an honorable means of survival for workers unable to secure employment in the formal sector of the economy.

• Illegal street vending encourages a lack of respect for the law, mostly because prosecuting illegal street vendors is not a priority for the police department.

• When there is enforcement, the police are likely to imprison a mother of six making $20 a day selling fruit. The result is enormous hardship to the family and little improvement to the public urban landscape.

• Vending can be seen as a way of celebrating the city's ethnic diversity.

• Authorizing vending would permit the health department to oversee food sales.

• Street vending represents competition for business owners who pay a variety of taxes that support public services.

• Vending, even if regulated, creates an atmosphere that many taxpayers find distasteful.

It is obvious to you that the task force members are maintaining open minds. You have been directed to draft a policy statement that would provide a context for the analysis of alternatives and final recommendations. You are to present the policy statement at the next meeting. What should you consider in preparing your response?

Ethical Issues:

How can you fulfill your responsibility to balance the needs of all the residents of the community when maintaining the status quo would work to the disadvantage of new residents? Should the needs of new immigrants take precedence over a traditional community desire for a neat and orderly public street and sidewalk system?

Action Alternatives:

1. Street vending should be viewed as a positive aspect of the culture and the role of government should be to facilitate micro economic enterprises. The only restrictions that should be placed on such activity would directly relate to the public health and safety.

2. Street vending, while it has some benefits, also has some drawbacks to the community. The task force should seek to structure a compromise in which vending should be strictly limited to certain "street market areas" to be designated in the community.

3. You do not yet have enough information to prepare the assignment. Instead, you plan to explain that you will prepare a survey and administer it to task force members to assess their values before presenting a philosophical framework.

4. Other.

Code Citations:

A. A planner's primary obligation is to serve the public interest. While the definition of the public interest is constantly evolving, a planner owes allegiance to a conscientiously attained concept of the public interest, which requires special obligations.

A.1 A planner must have special concern for the long-range consequences of present actions.

A.2 A planner must pay special attention to the inter-relatedness of decisions.

A.3 A planner must strive to provide full, clear, and accurate information on planning issues to citizens and governmental decision-makers.

A.4 A planner must strive to give citizens the opportunity to have a meaningful impact on the development of plans and programs. Participation should be broad enough to include people who lack formal organization or influence.

A.5 A planner must strive to expand choice and opportunity for all persons, recognizing a special responsibility to plan for the needs of disadvantaged groups and persons, and must urge the alteration of policies, institutions, and decisions that oppose such needs.

A.7 A planner must strive for excellence of environmental design and endeavor to conserve the heritage of the built environment.

C.5 A planner must examine the applicability of planning theories, methods, and standards to the facts and analysis of each particular situation and must not accept the applicability of a customary solution without first establishing its appropriateness to the situation.

D.2 A planner must respect the rights of others and, in particular, must not improperly discriminate against persons.

D.5 A planner must systematically and critically analyze ethical issues in the practice of planning.

D.6 A planner must strive to contribute time and effort to groups lacking in adequate planning resources and to voluntary professional activities.

Discussion:

Firstly, congratulations are due to you as the planning director. The mayor must have a lot of confidence in you and your abilities to have placed you in this position. A review of the topics discussed at the first meeting would imply that a fairly broad constituency is represented on the task force. It is not made clear, however, whether a specific time frame and work assignment have been given to the vending task force. Such factors would, of course, help in the selection of the most ethical course of behavior.

To answer the questions posed in the scenario, you need to be able to clearly identify what professional role you see yourself playing. This definition of role will affect your understanding of what constitutes the most ethical behavior. While few planners would argue with the need to serve the public interest, there is not universal agreement on how that interest is defined. For many planners, the public interest is the result of public debate. Their role, then, becomes one of facilitating a full discussion of all of the issues by all of the key parties. Whatever recommendations arise from such a debate, they are, by definition, an expression of the public interest. Consequently, many planners would, in this scenario, view their job as soliciting a broad range of input from all of the task force members. Equipped with such a philosophy, you would prefer alternative 2, seeking a compromise.

If you view the planner as someone responsive to the public interest, and who seeks to change institutions, policies, and decisions that oppose the needs of disadvantaged groups and persons (Section A.5 of the AICP code), then you would arrive at a different conclusion. In this mode, you would consider that one should not adopt a policy position that discourages people from trying to support themselves. Concerns about cleanliness and safety are legitimate, but shouldn't define acceptable economic activity. It is true that some people think vending is unattractive and that the vendors compete with stores. You can face that second argument head on. After all, libraries compete with bookstores. Regional urban parks compete with theme commercial parks. There are things that are public goods and should be promoted, even if they represent competition for the private sector. Responsiveness to the task of serving the disadvantaged as a primary role and responsibility would lead to the selection of the first alternative. And the code is written based on an activist-leadership role for planners.

Alternative 3, while written to incorporate language that implies the solicitation of views, is really nothing more than a carefully worded cop-out and should be avoided as your response. Alternative 2, a compromise, may be the outcome of the deliberations of the task force, but it should not be a starting point in your preparation of a position paper.

BALANCING COMPASSION AND ENFORCING THE SIGN ORDINANCE

You are the recently hired planing director. Before you moved to the town, the community adopted a new sign ordinance that includes provisions banning temporary banners from being strung across major roadways. Former basketball great Magic Johnson is coming to your town to appear at an AIDS research benefit and an illegal banner sign has been placed at a key intersection. You saw the banner when you drove to work. You called in a staff member to gather more information. The facts are that:

• According to your staff, the sign is exactly the same in dimension and color as those former baseball star Pete Rose used a few years ago when he promoted car dealerships and fast food franchises. Rose's signs prompted the new ordinance.

• The ordinance was designed by staff to eliminate such banners partly at the request of the electric department which was concerned about wear and tear on the electric poles when the signs were being erected and removed.

• Several community leaders apparently requested the ordinance, although you are not clear as to the basis of their opposition to the banners.

No one has complained to you about the temporary banner, but you know about it. You think it likely that the mayor will get phone calls from one of the neighborhood associations, which thinks all banner-type signs look tacky. There also are likely to be requests from individuals unsympathetic to the cause who will demand enforcement of the sign ordinance. You assume that this fund-raising event has the support of elected officials and many residents or else it would not have been planned for your community. What should you do?

Ethical Issues:

What do you do when you feel that your administrative responsibilities as a planner conflict with your basic human desire to help others who are in need?

Action Alternatives:

1. You personally believe that the sign ordinance is defective because it does not provide special exemptions for temporary signs. You decide to help the city attorney draft such language and to stall all callers by explaining that additional legal research is underway.

2. Proceed with enforcement, at a snail's pace, knowing that, with any amount of luck, the event will be over before a certified letter can be delivered. To make sure there are no problems later, prepare a memo documenting all of your actions and the overwhelming administrative burden of all the other complaints and investigations currently pending.

3. Pretend that you did not see the sign and wait to see if any phone calls materialize. If they do, you will place the item on the agenda for the next planning commission meeting for general discussion.

4. You are charged with enforcing the law, whether you like it or not. You begin that process and proceed with due diligence, although perhaps with little enthusiasm. You promptly investigate, prepare the complaint, and deliver a copy to the event organizers giving them a few hours to remove the offending sign.

5. You assign a staff planner to listen to all of the tapes of the discussion that occurred at the planning commission and city council meetings when the sign ordinance was adopted. The tapes may provide guidance for use in this case.

6. Other.

Code Citations:

A. A planner's primary obligation is to serve the public interest. While the definition of the public interest is constantly evolving, a planner owes allegiance to a conscientiously attained concept of the public interest, which requires special obligations.

A.1 A planner must have special concern for the long-range consequences of present actions.

A.5 A planner must strive to expand choice and opportunity for all persons, recognizing a special responsibility to plan for the needs of disadvantaged groups and persons, and must urge the alteration of policies, institutions, and decisions that oppose such needs.

B.1 A planner must exercise independent professional judgment on behalf of clients and employers.

C. A planner should contribute to the development of the profession by improving knowledge and techniques, making work relevant to solutions of community problems, and increasing public understanding of planning activities. . ..

C.5 A planner must examine the applicability of planning theories, methods, and standards to the facts and analysis of each particular situation and must not accept the applicability of a customary solution without first establishing its appropriateness to the situation.

D.1 A planner must not commit a deliberately wrongful act that reflects adversely on the planner's professional fitness.

Discussion:

This scenario was crafted to eliminate some of the more obvious grounds for making exceptions to the sign ordinance. For example, there was a clear public welfare need to restrict the banners (protect public property). It was not an attempt to repress speech. Apparently, there have been no legal challenges to the validity of the ordinance.

Many planners define the public interest in terms of the fairness of the process and less in terms of the fairness of the outcome of the process. Process planners tend to view the choice as fairly clear-cut. The law was written to cover such signs. The only problem seems to be that the specific cause is stirring compassion or political posturing. Process type planners would stress that any planning agency must have a reputation for even-handedness, especially an agency with enforcement powers. Procedures must be established and followed for such cases. If you concur with such an orientation to planning, alternative 4 would be your best choice.

Process oriented planners, however, are not the majority of the public planning profession. In general, concern for the results of the process weighs more heavily in the minds of public-sector planners. Compassion as a personal value is an important underlying credo to the code. Character is built when your professional responsibilities conflict with your deepest values, such as when your daughter's league-championship baseball game falls on the afternoon of your major budget presentation to the city council (and the city manager is nervous about your proposals and his tenure).

The code would be a shabby tool if it became a refuge for those who wanted to oppress and deny rights to others. Alternatives 2 or 3 (processing enforcement slowly or waiting for complaints) would be consistent with a more value-laden approach to planning. Alternative 1, undertaking legal research, will not solve the problem. Alternative 5, researching the meeting tapes, looks to be an interesting exercise, but not necessarily relevant to the decision that must be made more immediately. There is not a single correct answer. The best choice is the one that most closely fits your personal and professional identity.

Background:

This scenario raises an interesting side issue in terms of zoning enforcement. How does a planning department set priorities among zoning investigation cases? Is it based on receiving complaints from influential people, from staff observations, or a formal program emphasizing various aspects of the zoning ordinance. Your staff should consider and agree upon operating procedures for zoning enforcement and inspection activities.

MOVING THE AIRPORT

You are a member of the city planning department staff. One Sunday, during coffee hour after church, a representative of Community Ministries (CM) approaches you. CM is an ecumenical coalition working to establish greater political accountability between locally elected officials and their minority constituents. You are asked what you can do to stop the progress of a study evaluating the feasibility of expanding the airport at its current site. You know that a consultant already has been hired and is working for the airport authority. The area adjacent to the airport includes a municipal golf course. That land was designated as the site for future airport expansion thirty years ago. CM strongly opposes expanding the airport at its current site because the noise will impact nearby low-income Hispanic and African-American neighborhoods. The CM board is urging that the airport be relocated to an adjacent suburban county.

You wonder how beneficial it would be to move the airport. You weigh the loss of the tax base. The proposed location is too far from downtown to be conveniently served by mass transit. Will the nearby residents who have airport related jobs be able to retain them? What would happen to the current airport site? The economy wouldn't support any redevelopment in the near future, you think. You keep reading in the newspaper that the next generation of airplanes will be quieter. But that isn't much consolation to the people who would experience an increase in noise because of today's aircraft. Besides, you know that the current airport noise problem is severe. You also are puzzled by efforts to expand the airport now. The number of passenger and cargo flights has been stable for the past several years. You do recall the theme of the current chamber of commerce president is "A first class airport for a first class city."

Keeping in mind that you have been approached by a fellow church member and asked for help, what should you say to the CM representative?

Ethical Issues:

When asked for help, is it unethical to assist citizens in opposing what you believe to be a good planning proposal? Do personal relationships overrule your professional judgment?

Action Alternatives:

1.   Explain that while you understand the nature of the concern, the work is outside the jurisdiction of the planning department because the consultant was hired by the city to work for the airport authority.

2.   Offer to formally discuss the topic with members of the Community Ministries board at their next meeting. Explain that you will be glad to detail how the study process works and what the opportunities are for public involvement.

3.   Suggest that the Community Ministries board state its concerns during the citizen communication time at a city council meeting and ask for direct input into the study process.

4.   Explain that the job of the planning department is not to stop development even though it may be unpopular. The commission must give all parties a fair hearing and decide what is in the best interest of the entire community after receiving recommendations from the planning staff.

5.   Offer to help CM find the right people to obtain information immediately. Take the representative's name and telephone number and call her with the best source of information.

6.   Other.

Code Citations:

A.   A planner's primary obligation is to serve the public interest. While the definition of the public interest is constantly evolving, a planner owes allegiance to a conscientiously attained concept of the public interest, which requires special obligations.

A.2   A planner must pay special attention to the inter-relatedness of decisions.

A.3   A planner must strive to provide full, clear, and accurate information on planning issues to citizens and governmental decision-makers.

A.4   A planner must strive to give citizens the opportunity to have a meaningful impact on the development of plans and programs. Participation should be broad enough to include people who lack formal organization or influence.

A.5   A planner must strive to expand choice and opportunity for all persons, recognizing a special responsibility to plan for the needs of disadvantaged groups and persons, and must urge the alteration of policies, institutions, and decisions that oppose such needs.

D.6 A planner must strive to contribute time and effort to groups lacking in adequate planning resources and to voluntary professional activities.

Discussion:

When you are known as a public planner, individuals and organizations will ask for information or assistance on a variety of matters. Often planners will be asked about matters outside the normal jurisdiction of the planning department. In this scenario, you also have reasons to doubt the wisdom, or at least the comprehensiveness of consideration, given by the Community Ministries board. All these factors make it likely that you might wish to avoid involvement.

Nonetheless, you should not avoid commenting merely because of the difficulties involved. The AICP code urges planners to provide full, clear, and accurate information to citizens. This category of citizens includes friends and social acquaintances as well. You should do more research, if necessary, and give some response to your fellow church member. After all, as a planner, you know the process best. Your role should be to make connections. Keep in mind that you have not been asked to reveal any information that is not already a matter of public record. Alternative 5 is preferred.

The code also urges that planning officials strive to expand choice and opportunity for all persons, recognizing a special responsibility to plan for the needs of the disadvantaged. This would suggest that the planning department could, based on the research about the airport authority's plan, take the initiative in making sure that the low-income communities have the necessary information about the consultant study. The CM board may not be the only, or the most appropriate, conduit of data. Perhaps a status report could be made at a meeting of the planning commission. Of course, all of the research and discussion of information you conduct should be done in a completely open fashion. After you respond as set forth in alternative 5, alternatives 2, 3 or 4 would be acceptable follow-up. Alternative 1 is a bureaucratic dodge and should be avoided.

ANNUAL BIRTHDAY DINNER

For the past year you've been an employee of the city's planning department. You are a member of the city committee charged with selecting a consultant to update the comprehensive plan. Your best friend since high school, Frank Jordan, has called to schedule your annual birthday dinner.

Your wives are good friends and, for the past ten years, Frank and his wife have taken you and your wife to dinner at a nice local restaurant. Frank owns the largest architectural firm in the city and his firm is a strong contender for the contract to update the plan.

You don't immediately accept Frank's invitation to dinner. You wonder if it is ethical for you to accept his offer given the possible contractual relationship. What should you do?

Ethical Issues:

Does accepting any favor from any person raise serious questions about your ethics? How big does a "favor" have to be before it becomes significant?

Action Alternatives:

1. Accept the offer, but make sure that the restaurant is similar in expense to where you have eaten in the past.

2. Decline the invitation until after the contract is awarded. You would not want anyone to see you together and draw the wrong conclusion.

3. Agree to dine together, but suggest that it be a Dutch treat because you are now a city planner.

4. Other.

Code Citations:

A.3 A planner must strive to provide full, clear, and accurate information on planning issues to citizens and governmental decision-makers.

B.3 A planner shall not perform work if there is an actual, apparent, or reasonably foreseeable conflict of interest, direct or indirect, or an appearance of impropriety, without full written disclosure concerning work for current or past clients and subsequent written consent by the current client or employer. A planner shall remove himself or herself from a project if there is any direct personal or financial gain including gains to family members. A planner shall not disclose information gained in the course of public activity for a private benefit unless the information would be offered impartially to any person.

B.7 A planner must not use the power of any office to seek or obtain a special advantage that is not in the public interest nor any special advantage that is not a matter of public knowledge.

D.5 A planner must systematically and critically analyze ethical issues in the practice of planning.

Discussion:

To avoid even the appearance of a conflict of interest, must one sacrifice all friendships on the altar of public service? The answer is no. Community service does not require you to sever all ties to the community. A planner must not seek or offer favors, but in the case of a long-standing friendship, you are not seeking any form of hospitality designed to influence or reward your behavior. What is required is that at any point in the future when your friend's business is involved, you disqualify yourself from influencing the decision in any way. That means, in this instance, while you can go out to dinner together, you ought to resign from the committee making the consultant selection. If you are not willing to do that, then alternative 2, declining dinner, is the only acceptable course of action.

DEVELOPER OFFERS SUMMER EMPLOYMENT TO PLANNER'S CHILDREN

You are a planning director in a resort community in the Rocky Mountain region. During a break in the planning commission meeting, you chat with commissioners about the difficulty of finding summer jobs for your two children in this small town. A local developer overhears the conversation and seeks out a conversation with you. The developer mentions that he often hires teenagers for the summer to work at his lodge. He encourages you to have your son and daughter drop by for an interview. What should you do?

Ethical Issues:

Is it a conflict of interest if you have family members employed by someone whose development proposals are reviewed and evaluated by your public agency?

Action Alternatives:

1.   Surely your children should not be deprived of summer employment because you are a planner. You decide to send your children down for an interview. You assume that if hired, it will be based solely on merit.

2.   You consult with other members of the staff who assure you that the developer often extends this common courtesy to the town's appointed and elected officials. You are told that the developer will not expect any special treatment. You decide to send your children to the interview.

3.   While thanking the developer for his offer, you decline on the grounds that it would be improper to accept favors from someone who has to submit projects to you for approval.

4.   You clarify in your own mind that you did not specifically seek this favor. The developer made the offer of his own free will. You evaluate the suggestion and decided to send your children for an interview.

5.   Other.

Code Citations:

B.3   A planner shall not perform work if there is an actual, apparent, or reasonably foreseeable conflict of interest, direct or indirect, or an appearance of impropriety, without full written disclosure concerning work for current or past clients and subsequent written consent by the current client or employer. A planner shall remove himself or herself from a project if there is any direct personal or financial gain including gains to family members. A planner shall not disclose information gained in the course of public activity for a private benefit unless the information would be offered impartially to any person.

B.7   A planner must not use the power of any office to seek or obtain a special advantage that is not in the public interest nor any special advantage that is not a matter of public knowledge.

Discussion:

The job offer was made in a context that is related, however indirectly, to your role as a planner. Reasonable people would easily infer that you would feel a debt, however slight, to your children's employer. Therefore, you should not accept the offer. Reject alternative 1.

The code does give you the option of making a full public declaration of the situation and asking for permission from your employer to have your children work for the developer. A possible extenuating circumstance may be if your children had previously worked for the developer and were merely continuing a practice that pre-dated your tenure as the planning director. You would detail this information in your request for approval. However, if this is a new offer of employment, it should be declined inasmuch as the director should not have to regularly declare a conflict of interest related to proposals from a local developer.

Alternative 3 is the preferred course of action. It most clearly complies with the code. If, in fact, it is common for members of the planning staff to receive similar offers, you, as the director, may wish to establish new policies to maintain your ethical credibility or to conduct a workshop on ethics for your planning staff.

Alternative 4 is not acceptable. You cannot avoid your responsibility by claiming that temptation offered itself and that you did not seek out the favor.

Background:

Discussion of family matters in public settings could make a planner appear to be soliciting help. If a planner is seen by some as manipulating the public setting to advance personal interests, it will undermine public trust in the planning process. As planning director, you should exercise more discretion.

BEING OFFERED CONFIDENTIAL INFORMATION

You are a county planner in the high desert country. During a recess in a planning commission meeting, you are approached by a long-time acquaintance. You believe this individual to be a person of great integrity. He tells you that he has information about one of the applicants appearing before the planning commission later that evening. The applicant will be seeking approval for several variances and a conditional use permit for a planned unit development. The acquaintance says that, although the information is confidential, it is of such a serious nature that your staff recommendation on the application would likely be swayed. You gather that your friend doesn't have anything complimentary to say about the applicant. He asks you to step out in the hall so that he can briefly convey his concerns to you "in the interest of protecting the community." What should you do?

Ethical Issue:

Is it unethical to receive information on a confidential basis when it may bear on a planning-process applicant's fitness?

Action Alternatives:

1.   Recognizing that this is a reputable individual, listen long enough to ascertain whether the information is actually material to the case. If it isn't, politely end the conversation.

2.   Explain that this isn't the kind of conversation one should have in the halls. Provide your phone number and remind your acquaintance that you are always glad to receive calls from the community about matters of general interest.

3.   Explain that material evidence, which might affect the commission's decision, needs to be presented to all of the commissioners. Invite the friend to address the commission during its executive session.

4.   Advise the friend that while you appreciate his concern, information that could influence the public decision-making process needs to be presented in the public hearing.

5.   Other.

Code Citations:

A.3   A planner must strive to provide full, clear, and accurate information on planning issues to citizens and governmental decision-makers.

A.4   A planner must strive to give citizens the opportunity to have a meaningful impact on the development of plans and programs. Participation should be broad enough to include people who lack formal organization or influence.

Advisory Ruling:

6.   Illegal conduct should be reported, even if it means revealing confidential information.

Discussion:

Those who believe they have the inside scoop often approach planners. In many cases they may have better information than does the planner. In other instances, they have different opinions, experiences and values that affect their judgment and result in varying perceptions of "what is really going on." In general, a planner who is well informed regarding the breadth of a community's interests and needs is a planner who is likely to make better decisions. The challenge to the planner is how to arrive at a broad understanding.

The code requires that information pertinent to a decision be made available to the decision-makers. The problem with receiving confidential information in a secretive manner, even from a reliable source, is that the other party will have no opportunity to respond to the comments and to refute them if they are negative. A planner should not be making decisions based on half-truths, yet that may be all one has when one hears a single side of a story. Alternatives 1, 2, and 3 are unacceptable. They all involve accepting information that should be part of the public record in a non-public setting.

There are particular problems with alternative 3. State law generally limits the purpose and conduct of executive sessions.

Because you do not know whether the information being offered relates to a violation of law, Advisory Ruling No. 6 is not relevant to determining your final course of action.

Alternative 4 is preferred. There should be full disclosure at the public hearing. Suppose, even after requesting that the comments be made public, the person pressures you to continue to listen? You should explain that what is said to you must be disclosed. There is a crucial difference between informing and seeking to unreasonably and unfairly influence decisions. Encourage him to sign up to testify at the public hearing on the proposed planned unit development. You can acknowledge that this might be difficult. Nonetheless, it is the only appropriate thing to do.

WHEN AN APPOINTED OFFICIAL SEEKS PERMIT APPROVAL

You are the planning director in a mid-western city of almost 100,000. Tonight the planning staff will present a request for rezoning to the planning and zoning commission. The case involves a single-family home located in a residentially zoned neighborhood. Over time, the adjacent commercial zone has been allowed to expand. The house is now located on the edge of the commercial zone. The owner wishes to convert the house to a gift shop and has requested a change to commercial district.

Immediately before the meeting begins, a commissioner mentions to you that, contingent on the approval of the application, he has already offered to purchase the home as an investment. He also tells you that he originally suggested to the property owner that the zoning change be requested from the planning and zoning commission. Additionally, the commissioner says he has been working with the city staff to determine what conditions would be placed on the property. It appears that the commissioner intends to participate and vote when the commission hears this matter. What should you do?

Ethical Issues:

Do you have an obligation to make certain the entire planning process is as free of conflicts of interest as possible? What constitutes a public declaration of a conflict of interest?

Action Alternatives:

1.   Advise the commissioner that you believe this to be a conflict of interest and suggest that he disqualify himself from future discussion of the proposal with the staff or the board.

2.   Informally raise the issue with the chair of the planning commission and ask that she clarify the conflict of interest standards for the entire commission. This should be done in a matter-of-fact manner.

3.   Do nothing. After all, the commissioner isn't making any secret of his intention. So there couldn't be anything unethical as long as the commissioner is willing to advise you of his interest.

4.   Consult with staff during the first recess to secure additional information regarding what influence the commissioner may have exercised over the staff recommendation. If it appears there was any impropriety, ask the commission to postpone action.

5.   Other.

Code Citations:

B.   A planner owes diligent, creative, independent and competent performance of work in pursuit of the client's or employer's interest. Such performance should be consistent with the planner's faithful service to the public interest.

B.1   A planner must exercise independent professional judgment on behalf of clients and employers.

D.5   A planner must systematically and critically analyze ethical issues in the practice of planning.

The code does not address the specific issue in this scenario. However, the AICP/APA Ethical Principles in Planning (see attachments) does include pertinent language. Planning process participants should make public disclosure of all "personal interests" they have regarding any decision to be made in the planning process in which they serve.... They should abstain completely from direct or indirect participation as an advisor or decision-maker in any matter in which they have a personal interest, and leave the chamber in which such a matter is under deliberation, unless their personal interest has been made a matter of public record... and the public official, public agency, or court with jurisdiction on ethics matters has expressly authorized their participation. Planning process participants should not participate... as a decision-maker on any... project in which they have previously served as an advocate.

Discussion:

Alternative 1 would be the best course of immediate action. In this scenario, the commissioner is in conflict with several portions of the statement of ethical principles. The disagreements include those related to a conflict of interest, and using an official position to secure information for personal financial gain. It is just as much a conflict of interest to be reserving for one's self a future benefit as to be receiving an immediate one. It can never be acceptable for a public planning official to identify potential investment opportunities and then encourage property owners to seek permission from that same planning official.

As planning director, you have a responsibility for the entire planning process, even those decisions not directly under your control. You must speak out to protect the integrity of the planning commission from allegations of conflicts of interest in its decision making.

In addition to alternative 1, alternative 2 should be pursued. Bring the matter to the attention of the chair of the planning commission as soon as possible. In private, prior to the meeting, remind the chair that it would be in the best interest of the commission to have the member with the conflict dismiss himself from the discussion as well as the vote. To address the immediate problem, suggest that the chair review the conflict of interest rules that govern the commission's behavior. At the start of the meeting, have the chair ask for disclosures of conflict of interest. Remind the chair that the public needs to know about the conflicts, and the disclosure must be made in a public setting. You or the chair may persuade the commission member not to participate in the decision.

Your role in the meeting is to present a staff report. While you need not refrain from presenting a recommendation just because of this discussion, you should speak clearly on this, lest someone thinks the commissioner was successful in trying to influence your staff position.

For the longer term, if the planning commission has no laws, administrative rules, or policies that govern its actions regarding conflicts of interest, have the commission review and adopt the AICP/APA Statement of Ethical Principles in Planning. Ask the city attorney to determine what state or local requirements may pertain as well.

Alternative 3, taking no action, is a poor option and is inconsistent with the aspirational direction of the code.

Of course, you should follow up after the meeting with your staff (alternative 4). However, this would be an insufficient response if it were to be your only initiative. It should concern you that your staff seems insensitive to a breach of ethical conduct and is not keeping you informed.

PLANNER SUSPECTS DEVELOPER
INFLUENCE ON PLANNING COMMISSIONERS

You are part of the professional planning staff working for the planning commission. In your town, procedures call for you to submit your recommendations in writing to the commission before public hearings. The process does not allow for presentations by the staff at the public hearing. Only the applicant and the public make remarks. A copy of the staff report is entered into the record. Often applicants and citizens make comments and claims that you feel are not supported by the facts. It is obvious to you that this jurisdiction views the role of the planning commissioner as one of helping the developer get the job done.

Your lack of public influence and inability to provide accurate data to the commission frustrate you. You know that members of the planning commission have close ties to the local development community. Far from abstaining on these cases, the commissioners often vote to overturn your recommendations in favor of development proposals. What should you do?

Ethical Issues:

You feel that you are being denied the opportunity to fulfill your responsibility to serve the public interest by providing accurate and impartial information and the long-term perspective. At the same time, you are bound to respect the decision of your employer regarding the definition of the work to be performed. How do you balance these different aspects of the code?

Action Alternatives:

1.   Meet informally with the commission to express your concerns in a general way. After carefully explaining the importance of complete information, offer to draft a new set of procedures for public hearings that would provide for a staff role.

2.   Talk with the chair of the planning commission. Separate your concerns about collusion from your concerns about the process. Ask for the chair to address the latter. Assume that the meeting format is a long-standing community tradition. You only can begin to chip away at it.

3.   Begin a file documenting incidents where you believe the commissioners' judgement may have been unduly influenced. Plan to review your concerns with your chapter's professional development officer.

4. Stay frustrated and do nothing because circumstances aren't likely to change and, realistically, you could end up unemployed if you rock the boat on this issue.

5. Other.

Code Citations:

A. A planner's primary obligation is to serve the public interest. While the definition of the public interest is formulated through continuous debate, a planner owes allegiance to a conscientiously attained concept of the public interest, which requires special obligations.

A.1 A planner must have special concern for the long-range consequences of present actions.

A.2 A planner must pay special attention to the inter-relatedness of decisions.

A.3 A planner must strive to provide full, clear, and accurate information on planning issues to citizens and governmental decision-makers.

B.1 A planner must exercise independent professional judgment on behalf of clients and employers.

B.2 A planner must accept the decisions of a client or employer concerning the objectives and nature of the professional services to be performed unless the course of action to be pursued involves conduct that is illegal or inconsistent with the planner's primary obligation to the public interest.

Discussion:

Planners sometimes are employed by a jurisdiction that views the role of the staff as being limited in terms of providing guidance to decision-makers. The scenario is written to imply that if the commission had better or different information, it might be making other decisions. Such is not always the case. In fact the commission may have created the process that the planner finds frustrating because it is consistent with the commission's vision. Also of concern is the possible collusion between members of the planning commission and the development community. Such collusion, if it were to occur, would seriously damage the public's faith in the planning process.

Either alternative 1 or 2 would allow the planner to share frustration in a positive way, and to see if any progress can be made. Perhaps the planning commission does not understand your concerns because it always has done things a certain way. Commissioners' actions may reflect a community philosophy that more jobs and business activity are desirable. A conversation regarding these matters would be in order.

Alternative 2 is preferred in that it represents "going through channels" and is consistent with the planner's concern about establishing a credible process. Keep in mind that the planner's diminished role may result from a failure to establish credibility or good working relations with commissioners and reflect the commission's overall level of confidence. You would do well to consult with other colleagues and try to secure some specific advice about what to do.

Developing a file and consulting with the chapter's professional development officer sounds as if you are thinking about filing an ethics charge. The AICP Code of Ethics and Professional Conduct applies only to AICP members, not planning commissioners. You probably are wasting time with this approach.

Alternative 4, staying frustrated, will lead to worsening relations. This will do little to advance planning in the minds of the commissioners or to advance your career.

The scenario, while framed in the context of the frustrations of a planner, gets at the heart of a complicated question. What happens when the planners and the planning commission have different concepts of serving the public interest? Commissions that conduct themselves inappropriately get a reputation that can affect their ability to attract and retain the best staff. The same is true of the planners.

NO HOME FOR GROUP HOMES

You are the planning director working for a planning and zoning commission. Your community is an older industrial area struggling to recover from the loss of several key employers. The housing stock is aging. The population is becoming increasingly dependent on government programs and services. State planning enabling legislation has changed. Group homes must now be permitted as a matter of right in all residential zoning categories. You know that your community's zoning ordinance is out of compliance.

You are aware that your community has failed to provide its "fair share" of group home opportunities. In response to this new window of opportunity resulting from the state legislation, a number of county service agencies have contacted you about the availability of affordable houses that could be converted to group homes. In anticipation of a future request, you have drafted the changes required to bring your local zoning ordinance into conformance. After a bitter debate, the planning and zoning commission rejects the proposal. You are told to forget the idea. "If we are sued, then, and only then, will we consider making changes to the ordinance," said the planning commission chair.

The city's attorney is present at the meeting, but offers no comment or objection. As a future candidate for the city council himself, he is in no hurry to burn bridges or make rash statements.

Soon thereafter, an applicant requests approval of a building permit in compliance with the language you had recommended. You think that state law mandates approval of the permit. However, as planning director you have to sign off on the building permit certifying consistency with the local zoning code. The applicant makes it clear that with the help of legal services, he intends to make a test case of your jurisdiction. What should you do?

Ethical Issues:

Once your planning commission has made a decision, especially one that is not in compliance with a new law, what is your obligation to the commission? How far can you go in encouraging more socially responsible decision-making by appointed officials after they have rejected your overtures?

Action Alternatives:

1.   Meet with the planning commission chair to explore the commission's reasoning. Be prepared to explain your position in terms of proper planning, state law, and ethics.

2.   Deny the permit. It does not comply with your local ordinance.

3.   Accept your employer's decision and explain the current position of the planning commission to the applicant. While not withholding information, volunteer no encouragement and avoid expressing a point of view that shows you to be at odds with the commission.

4.   Contact the municipal attorney for advice. See if the attorney can intervene on your side with the stated purpose of ensuring that the city complies with state requirements, if only to avoid a lawsuit.

5.   Contact a trusted media representative. After securing a commitment of confidentially, explain what is going on.

6.   Other.

Code Citations:

A.5 A planner must strive to expand choice and opportunity for all persons, recognizing a special responsibility to plan for the needs of disadvantaged groups and persons, and must urge the alteration of policies, institutions, and decisions that oppose such needs.

B.2 A planner must accept the decisions of a client or employer concerning the objectives and nature of the professional services to be performed unless the course of action to be pursued involves conduct that is illegal or inconsistent with the planner's primary obligation to the public interest.

D.1 A planner must not commit a deliberately wrongful act that reflects adversely on the planner's professional fitness.

Discussion:

This is an occasion when being clear about your goal is essential to proposing and acting on alternatives. You can go public and lose your job. If the economy is good, and there are jobs in more enlightened jurisdictions, this would be an easy course of action. However, in this scenario, your goal is to act ethically and also keep your job. Because of the economic circumstances described in the scenario, it would be difficult to find another job.

The ethical planner certainly should present arguments for expanded choice and opportunity. You should work with the commission, the applicant, and legislative bodies to encourage changes. However, in this case, the ethical planner also needs to be nimble. The code is clear that in the case when the course of action is illegal, then the planner is freed from the obligation to accept the decisions of an employer. To ignore the requirements of state law would be a deliberately wrongful act. You must devise a means by which your jurisdiction can make progress towards compliance with state law. Ethically speaking, you also should help the applicant, as much as reasonably possible, according to the law.

Alternative 1 is not a bad step, particularly if you can steer the conversation toward a more appropriate resolution in terms of state legal requirements. At the initial planning and zoning commission meeting, you were correct in presenting the ordinance changes and arguing for expanded choice and opportunity. Although the commission rejected the proposal, you still have a responsibility to continue to work with the commission, the applicant, and legislative bodies to encourage changes. You have an active role to play. But you don't want to make this a case of the lone planner versus the planning commission.

The ethical planner would want the public to know that its interest, as represented by a new state law, is being subverted. Alternative 5, contacting the media, would get the ball rolling towards resolution in advance of the first applicant showing up at your office. With public scrutiny, the elected officials can direct that the necessary ordinance be written. They no longer have any discretion.

Alternative 2 sounds as if you may be provoking a lawsuit (assuming the commission will turn down the permit). It may be somewhat satisfying on a gut level, but it is not the most productive long-run strategy. Resources will be diverted to a lawsuit, and the reputation of your community and its citizen planners will suffer.

Alternative 3 is neither legal (under state law) nor ethically responsive to the aspirational components of the code. It does offer bureaucratic cover. In this case, you are caught between conflicting requirements of state and local law. Because this is a new state law, you could call around and consult with other local planning directors and perhaps glean some ideas from their attorneys.

One feasible course of action is alternative 4. This case clearly calls for expert legal advice. Denial of permits is an area where an attorney should become involved. Following the law is a fundamental basis for planning ethics. The attorney may advise you regarding the permit at hand and may advise the commission regarding the importance and validity of your proposed ordinance. Keep in mind that, just as there are unethical planners, there are unethical city attorneys. The lawyer may be a political appointee who is happy to commiserate but has no interest in solving your problem. Exercise the same reasonable care you would in confiding to any colleague who could be of help.

Bernie Dworski, Legal Counsel for APA and AICP, provided assistance in developing this scenario.

MAKING TIME FOR PLANNING ON THE PLANNING COMMISSION AGENDA

You are the newly-hired planning director in a metropolitan area in the Southwest. Your community is experiencing a moderate rate of growth. When you arrived, you studied the files of recent planning commission meetings. You saw that entire meetings were devoted to development review. In the past eight months, no planning-related matters have been brought before the commission. Given the rate of growth, and the absence of a comprehensive framework for decision making, you are anxious to revise the planning commission's agenda.

At one of the commission's two monthly meetings, you place items on the agenda to start addressing the backlog of neighborhood and special studies. You recommend to the commission that beginning next month, one monthly meeting will be devoted to processing development applications. The other will address planning issues. The next day, the president of the Homebuilders' Association hears about this and reacts angrily. He calls you to complain about unnecessary delays in reviewing new development. How should you handle the situation?

Ethical Issues:

Should the "everyday" demands on planning commissions consume all of the planners' and the planning officials' time to the exclusion of other planning concerns? Does a planner have a responsibility to make sure a commission understands and responds to all of its responsibilities as set forth in the APA Statement of Ethical Principles in Planning?

Action Alternatives:

1.   Stick to your guns. A lack of long-range planning can result in poor short-term decisions. If you don't do something soon, you'll be trapped in a cycle that puts planning on the back burner.

2.   Offer to meet with the homebuilders and explain your decision. In the long run, you will tell them, an adopted plan will lead to greater stability in the planning process. You agree to include discussion of this as the first item on the agenda of the planning-oriented meeting.

3.   Withdraw your decision. A new planning director can't afford to risk alienating the president of the local homebuilders. You have always had good relations with the development community and you need to recover from a bad first step.

4.   Call the planning commission chair and ask her to respond to the homebuilders. After all, the planning commission ought to take a position supporting planning. In addition, she knows the personalities involved.

5.   You decide that your decision is the right one, but that you need to build support for it. You contact commissioners to explain your perspective on the need for a more balanced agenda and learn more about the history of the current system.

6.   Other.

Code Citations:

A.1   A planner must have special concern for the long-range consequences of present actions.

B.   A planner owes diligent, creative, independent and competent performance of work in pursuit of the client's or employer's interest. Such performance should be consistent with the planner's faithful service to the public interest.

B.1   A planner must exercise independent professional judgment on behalf of clients and employers.

C.   A planner should contribute to the development of the profession by improving knowledge and techniques, making work relevant to solutions of community problems, and increasing public understanding of planning activities.

Discussion:

While the need for planning may be obvious to a professional planner, not everyone else understands the necessity. Clearly the homebuilder belongs to that group. Perhaps the commission and others do not share the perspective of the new planning director. There is no question that a lack of comprehensive planning deserves attention. The AICP code requires in Section A.1 that attention be given to the long-range consequences of present action. Without a plan in place, commissioners and staff are ill equipped to assess possible long-term results. A planner must work to increase the commission's understanding of the full range of planning responsibilities.

While alternative 1, sticking to your guns, is within the context of ethical behavior, it certainly would not be effective. One of the purposes of ethical decision-making should be to identify fruitful and ethical strategies. This alternative does not meet the dual test.

Alternative 2, meeting to explain your thinking, has limited value. Meeting alone with the homebuilders does not address the need for support from your own commission and staff. Besides, the homebuilders are only one constituent group for planning. In general, meeting with different groups to explain your decisions will be less productive than seeking input for your decision-making from the beginning.

Withdrawing your decision for the reasons cited, alternative 3, is unacceptable. First, it ignores your ethical responsibility to promote decision-making with attention to long-range consequences. Second, you probably would lose all credibility as a director if you followed this course of action. Third, you would send a message that you are reluctant to make the right decision if it has the potential to alienate a powerful interest group. (This should not be construed as counseling against a change of opinion when you have made a mistake due to incorrect data or similar circumstances.)

Telling the planning commission chair that she should do your job is another poor choice. Reject alternative 4. You cannot, at this late date, attempt to shift the responsibility for your actions to another party. It is your mess; now you clean it up!

In evaluating the desirability of alternative 5, it is important to note that the decision to undertake comprehensive planning was apparently made independently by you as the director, absent discussion with the commission and, perhaps, without consultation with other staff. There are specific ways to address this problem that are less confrontational and likely to be equally effective in the long run. The issue is as much one of strategy as it is of ethics. The commission and staff must be involved in change, even while the director leads that change.

Every community needs an annual work program. As the newly hired director you are in the best position to draft one for review by the planning commission. The discussion surrounding the adoption of a work program can help the commission broaden its view. Therefore, alternative 5, supplemented with a more deliberate and consultative change process, is the most desirable alternative.

A good follow-up step for alternative 5 would be a meeting with the Homebuilders' Association president and other community groups to explain the long-term benefits of the new scheme.

Note: In using this scenario, "other" may be the preferred choice as individuals craft a response similar to the paragraph above in which alternative 5 is supplemented by other actions.

OFF-THE-JOB SOCIAL RELATIONSHIPS
AFFECTING ON-THE-JOB PERFORMANCE

You are the director of a community development agency. Among other things, this organization is charged with preparing applications for state and federal empowerment zone funding. Sandra Marks, a senior planner under your supervision, has the responsibility for recommending which of several competing proposals will be supported by the city.

Three months after beginning her work, Marks meets Mike Katz at a party. Later she learns that he is the local real estate representative for a major hotel chain interested in locating in your city's empowerment zone. After several dates with Katz, Marks has become fond of him.

Today, Marks asks to speak with you. She says she realizes that their respective professional responsibilities have created a potential conflict of interest. Marks says that she intends to continue her relationship with Katz. She insists that she is mature enough to separate her professional and private lives. What should you do?

Ethical Issues:

Is maintaining a social relationship that overlaps with a professional role unethical even if the parties involved try not to influence any decisions? Is it more important to avoid even the appearance of unethical conduct by your staff, or to support an employee's right to her private life?

Action Alternatives:

1.   Direct Marks to stop seeing Katz until she completes her responsibilities for reviewing the proposals. In that way, a clear line will have been drawn.

2.   Assign Marks to a different set of responsibilities in the planning department. You have to make sure your department is not vulnerable to allegations of conflicts of interest.

3.   Discuss the matter with your supervisor, the city manager, and decide to hold a workshop for staff dealing with ethical issues including conflict of interest.

4.   Trust Marks to do her job professionally without being biased by the relationship. After all, she has never given you any reason to doubt her integrity.

5.   Other.

Code Citations:

B.3   A planner shall not perform work if there is an actual, apparent, or reasonably foreseeable conflict of interest, direct or indirect, or an appearance of impropriety, without full written disclosure concerning work for current or past clients and subsequent written consent by the current client or employer. A planner shall remove himself or herself from a project if there is any direct personal or financial gain including gains to family members. A planner shall not disclose information gained in the course of public activity for a private benefit unless the information would be offered impartially to any person.

C.3   A planner who reviews the work of other professionals must do so in a fair, considerate, professional, and equitable manner.

D.   Strive for high standards of integrity, proficiency, and knowledge.

Discussion:

Your first concern is to make sure that you follow good office procedures in terms of basic fairness. You have to ask yourself: Would I handle the situation differently if it involved a male member of the staff dating the secretary to the real estate representative? After you have answered this question, you can decide how to deal with Marks.

Alternative 1 appears to resolve the potential conflict of interest problem, but does not address the fact that there will continue to be the appearance of the conflict. Besides, realistically, you cannot stop people from dating even though you might make such a request. It is best to accept the nature of the personal relationship, which is really not your business except as it affects the integrity of the staff's analytical work. Instead, you should focus on the professional relationship, which is your concern. Marks, if an AICP member, may, upon reflection, end the relationship.

Alternative 2 is best. Marks has taken the important first step in addressing the situation by coming to you. The code requires that the disclosure be placed in writing, and that she formally asks for permission to continue both the social relationship and her current work responsibilities. After Marks submits the request to you, the code directs you to deny it. If you are unwilling to deny her request, then you could stipulate, that any time Marks reports on a project or is involved in a decision, that she publicly acknowledge her social relationship. This acknowledgment should be made within the department and at public meetings. This would be a cumbersome process, but might work depending on the attitude of the parties involved.

Discussing the matter with the city manager, alternative 3, could be viewed as a breach of trust. It could discourage future disclosures by other staff members. If you honestly feel that the issue is likely to be brought to the attention of the manager by other parties, you might wish to discuss it. But you should do so in a general context that avoids names and stresses that the situation has been resolved. The ethics workshop suggestion is good and might be employed as a logical addition to alternative 2.

Alternative 4 is unacceptable. Public employees have a right to a private life, but only to a certain extent. Recent investigations surrounding public figures have created a new sensitivity to the basic premise that everything you say and do can and will be held against you in the court of public opinion. Even if Marks performs in an even-handed fashion, the department's credibility may be eroded. There is the appearance of a conflict of interest. You do not have the option of ignoring the situation.

SENIOR PLANNER QUESTIONS COMPETENCE OF DIRECTOR

You are a newly-hired senior planner in a fast-growing suburban community adjacent to a metropolitan area in Georgia. Lately, you have become increasingly disenchanted by the performance of your boss, the director, who is a member of AICP as are you. Because of the director's unfamiliarity with recent computer applications, staff members cannot use current tools and techniques in their work. The director will neither initiate nor support requests for new computers, printers or software. No software other than word processing is available. The Department of Public Works, not planning, developed and maintains the city's GIS system, again because of the director's lack of interest.

The problem is compounded by your boss' managerial style, which is very dictatorial. Entry-level staff planners rarely stay for more than a year. Although the city manager speaks with the director, the mayor ignores the director entirely and will only speak with other planners on the city's staff. Lately things have gotten worse. At meetings, the director has difficulty focusing on the topic at hand and is avoiding all work that requires sustained mental activity. You wonder what bad judgments, actions, or inactions on the part of the director may cause harm to the community? What is your ethical responsibility to the public, your colleagues, and your boss?

Ethical Issue:

How do you show respect for the decisions of your employer when you do not believe that the decisions are well founded in fact or current practice? What responsibility do you have when a supervisor fails to continue his/her professional development and can no longer render the best planning advice?

Action Alternatives:

1.   You decide to focus on the real issue — does the community suffer as a result of the director's incompetence? To that end, you decide to assess the types of plans and ordinances in effect as compared to other places of similar size with similar planning resources. You begin making discrete inquiries.

2.   You wonder whether other colleagues share your perceptions. However, you don't want to start discussions like this at the office. You invite other key members of the planning department to your home for dinner and raise the topic for general discussion among colleagues.

3.   You begin to take notes on actions and make copies of documents that you feel indicate problems. You make no judgment now, but plan to review the file at the end of six months and determine the next step then.

4.   You wonder if all of this might be a medical problem. You describe the symptoms you are observing to a doctor. A medical problem that affects on-the-job performance could account for some of the problems you recently have observed.

5.   Talk to the personnel director and the city manager about the problem. You don't think they are particularly capable of offering a good solution, but you think they are in positions where they should be asked to help. They may already be aware of the issue.

6.   Other.

Code Citations:

A.3   A planner must strive to provide full, clear, and accurate information on planning issues to citizens and governmental decision-makers.

B.2   A planner must accept the decisions of a client or employer concerning the objectives and nature of the professional services to be performed unless the course of action to be pursued involves conduct that is illegal or inconsistent with the planner's primary obligation to the public interest.

B.8   A planner must not accept or continue to perform work beyond the planner's professional competence or accept work which cannot be performed with the promptness required by the prospective client or employer, or which is required by the circumstances of the assignment.

C.   A planner should contribute to the development of the profession by improving knowledge and techniques, making work relevant to solutions of community problems, and increasing public understanding of planning activities. A planner should treat fairly the professional views of qualified colleagues and members of other professions.

C.1   A planner must protect and enhance the integrity of the profession and must be responsible in criticism of the profession.

C.3   A planner who reviews the work of other professionals must do so in a fair, considerate, professional, and equitable manner.

C.5   A planner must examine the applicability of planning theories, methods, and standards to the facts and analysis of each particular situation and must not accept the applicability of a customary solution without first establishing its appropriateness to the situation.

D.   A planner should strive for high standards of professional integrity, proficiency, and knowledge.

D.3   A planner must strive to continue professional education.

Discussion:

> The scenario really happens. It may be relatively rare, but it does occur and we need to be right in our answers. One issue is that it can cause planing staff to jump the chain of command in order to get it resolved, and that presents them with an ethical dilemma in itself. In the end, you have to look at the bigger picture and go with that: How is the behavior of the director impacting the community?
>
> Letter to Planners' Casebook
Name Withheld

Issues of personal feelings must be set aside in sorting through the alternatives. You feel as if you are caught between aspects of the AICP code that appear to be in conflict: fairly treat the views of a colleague, accept the views of the employer, enhance the integrity of the profession, improve knowledge and techniques, and review the work of other professionals in a fair and considerate manner. Ultimately, the test is whether the director is serving the public interest. To respond to this test, you must be able to assess whether the problem here is one of style or substance.

If you believe the problem is primarily one of style, your course of action is limited. Even if you judge the director's manner to be ineffective, the decision about whether this style is or is not appropriate to your community is in the hands of the local elected officials and the city manager.

If the matter is more one of substance, you need to assess whether the community's planning is materially suffering as a result, or whether it is just the mental health of the employees. (Note that this is not an insignificant issue, just one that is not most effectively addressed by a code of ethics.) If it is, you might suggest a staff retreat for all planning employees which could focus, in a non-judgmental way, on what needs to be done in the department and how staff resources can be most effectively allocated.

Alternatives could vary if you were a friend of the director. You could talk to your boss on a personal basis to explore health issues, long-term employment options, etc. If it does seem to be health related, you could then speak with several of the planner's long-time friends to see if perceptions match.

This is one of the scenarios where your goal or underlying intention has to be clear in your mind. If you want to protect the community, you may be able to take on more of the director's work and shield him. If you just want to get rid of someone whom you think is not capable of doing a very good job, that would suggest an entirely different course of action. Assuming a fair analysis of the problem, each of the alternatives would be acceptable.

DO YOU HAVE A DUTY TO REPORT AND PUBLICIZE SUSPICIOUS CONDUCT?

You are a long-time supervising planner in a small city. The director recently retired. After a thorough personnel search, the city manager offered the position to an external candidate. In explaining his choice to you, the manager expressed his interest in a fresh perspective. He also tells you he expects your full cooperation and support for the new director. You nod your head and the meeting ends cordially.

A month later the new director is on board. After several months, you begin to struggle with what you see. The director is unusually cozy with developer representatives and regularly accepts invitations to lunch, dinner, weekend golf outings, and other miscellaneous social events. Although you haven't seen the director make a decision unsupported by data, the entire staff is uncomfortable over the apparent conflict of interest, and the other employees have met with you as a group to express their concerns. Things have gotten so bad that planning commissioners have started making jokes about it at their subcommittee meetings.

You arrange a meeting with the director who dismisses your suggestion that the integrity of the entire department is being compromised. Each of the specific instances you raise evokes only a chortle and an indirect suggestion that the real issue is your jealousy and disappointment over not having been promoted.

At the conclusion of the meeting, you resolve to give your new boss the benefit of the doubt for another few months before taking any action. In the interim, you watch what's going on with an increasing sense of dismay. The final blow to your pride, and the honesty and integrity of staff, comes when the director engages in obvious and pointed backslapping and handshaking in the back of the room, only with applicants, before the planning commission meeting. To you, it is not a matter of personal style but a demonstration of preferential treatment that convinces everyone in the audience that the planning staff is neither fair nor impartial.

That night you compose a letter to the executive director of AICP citing several instances of what you believe to be unethical conduct and you mail a copy to the newspaper as well. The letter, in its entirety, is printed in one of the regular features, titled "City Files." You receive several phone calls from other local planners congratulating you. Then comes an e-mail from the chapter's professional development officer (PDO). He tells you that your director has contacted the PDO regarding procedures for filing a complaint with AICP, and that your director has stated his intention of charging you with unethical conduct for having released to the press what should have been confidential information. In fact, the director even suggested that the PDO call you and provide you with this information.

Ethical Issue:

Should you report suspicious conduct? If so, how do you do proceed in a way that demonstrates both moral stature and respect for the rights of others?

Action Alternatives:

1.   Do nothing. To protect the integrity of the other staff, everyone in town needed to know there are ethical principles for planners. Just because the director didn't adhere to them didn't mean that planning staff members had lost their ethical compasses.

2.   Write a follow-up, pre-emptive strike letter to the executive director making your case about the "duty to report" and the absolute urgency of the case, which required public disclosure before any further damage could be done.

3.   Meet with your boss and express your belief that his actions are merely retaliatory and nothing more than an example of how he "just doesn't get it."

4. Write a letter to the editor with a copy to the executive director of AICP in which you argue that the need for confidentiality serves only to protect miscreants.

5. Other.

Code Citations:

B.2 A planner must accept the decisions of a client or employer concerning the objectives and nature of the professional services to be performed unless the course of action to be pursued involves conduct that is illegal or inconsistent with the planner's primary obligation to the public interest.

B.3 A planner shall not perform work if there is an actual, apparent, or reasonably foreseeable conflict of interest, direct or indirect, or an appearance of impropriety, without full written disclosure concerning work for current or past clients and subsequent written consent by the current client or employer. A planner shall remove himself or herself from a project if there is any direct personal or financial gain including gains to family members. A planner shall not disclose information gained in the course of public activity for a private benefit unless the information would be offered impartially to any person.

C.1 A planner must protect and enhance the integrity of the profession and must be responsible in criticism of the profession.

C.3 A planner who reviews the work of other professionals must do so in a fair, considerate, professional, and equitable manner.

Advisory Ruling:

5. States (in part) that (1) A planner who has certain knowledge of clearly unethical conduct on the part of the certified planner has a duty to file a charge of misconduct. A corollary obligation is that a planner should never use the threat of filing an ethics charge relating to current or past misconduct in order to gain, or attempt to gain, an advantage in dealing with another planner. (2) A planner should not make public allegations of code violations against another planner, but rather should trust the processes of the Institute to determine if a violation has occurred and, if so, the sanctions to be applied.

Discussion:

The behavior of the planning director is raising problems with the credibility and confidence of the entire planning staff. Elements of the code (B.2

and B.3) are being ignored. Affable behavior, when displayed only to some of the participants in the planning process, calls into question the fairness of the entire deliberative process. However, the problems in this scenario go beyond backslapping. The director is regularly accepting favors of significant material value.

But the question here is your behavior, not that of the director. Writing a letter to the AICP executive director is clearly called for, especially in light of Advisory Ruling No. 5, in which planners have a duty to report unethical conduct. That same ruling, however, calls for planners to trust the processes of the institute and not make public their charges. Further, you are expected to be both fair and responsible in your criticism (C.1 and C.3). Hence, the director is within his rights to make his countercharge.

Alternative 1 is not unethical. It simply acknowledges the status quo and restates your rationale for the actions taken.

Alternatives 2 and 4 are not precluded by the code, but writing letters explaining your misconduct does not excuse it. Likewise, a meeting with your boss is permissible and may prevent him from filing countercharges, but not if you use a didactic tone or fail to acknowledge your own shortcomings. Nor would such a meeting make your letter publishing acceptable. You cannot persuasively argue that the filing of the countercharge was retaliatory as it resulted from your going to the media with the original charge.

DOING OUTSIDE PROFESSIONAL WORK ON OFFICE TIME

You are the supervisor of long-range planning in a twenty-person office for a growing city in a major metropolitan area. In a friendly way, you drop into an employee's office and mention that she seems to be spending a lot of office time on outside work. By now, everyone in the office is aware that she is teaching a planning course at the university as an adjunct professor. You are both members of AICP and she says that she often sees you working on your computer on a publication for AICP. "What is the difference?" she asks. In your mind there is a difference. She is receiving remuneration for teaching and your work for AICP is being done as a volunteer. Is there a difference? What should you do next?

Ethical Issues:

During planning office operating hours, must all work be directly related to in-office assignments? Should supervisors worry about how time is spent provided the job gets done? If planners are required to contribute time for the betterment of the profession, does that mean contribute personal time or office time or a combination?

Action Alternatives:

1.   Check the city's personnel manual for a formal policy and look for a tactful and indirect way to report your colleague to the director.

2.   Back off fast. Messing with office relationships could cause a much greater interruption to the workflow than whatever she is doing.

3.   Consider again your own personal comfort level with the way you conduct your business.

4.   Other.

Code Citations:

B.8   A planner must not accept or continue to perform work beyond the planner's professional competence, or accept work that cannot be performed with the promptness required by the prospective client or employer or that is required by the circumstances of the assignment.

C.4   A planner must share the results of experience and research that contribute to the body of planning knowledge.

C.6   A planner must contribute time and information to the professional development of students, interns, beginning professionals, and other colleagues.

D.5   A planner must systematically and critically analyze ethical issues in the practice of planning.

D.6   A planner must strive to contribute time and effort to groups lacking in adequate planning resources and to voluntary professional activities.

Advisory Ruling:

3.   "Outside Employment or Moonlighting" (see appendix for full text). A planning staff member must take no employment outside official duties unless such employment creates no conflict with those duties either in the interests to be served or in competition for time and energy. If the planner decides that there will be no such conflicts, then outside employment must receive the explicit approval of the employer. No out-

side employment must be undertaken if its performance will reduce the quality or dispatch with which the staff member executes primary responsibilities.

Discussion:

Whether or not you receive remuneration for a planning activity accomplished on office time is a significant issue. If you are being paid, then you are moonlighting and you need the permission of your employer. You also need to make sure that your moonlighting work does not interfere with your primary assignment. There are likely to be prohibitions on using office equipment and supplies, as well as office time, for personal gain.

In this case, as the supervisor, you know that the employee failed to seek and receive your permission. If you believe that her teaching keeps her from completing her work on time, you should be prepared to report this to the planning director. You would make such a report to your supervisor about any employee who was failing to adequately perform his or her responsibilities. After all, if you saw a fellow employee stealing the office microwave oven, you surely would intervene. A planner's time is just as much public property as a desk or computer. It would be worthwhile to check to see if there is departmental policy. In this case, you should advise the employee of your ongoing concern in such a way as to make it clear that your next step will be to raise the matter with the director. Then follow through with alternative 1.

Alternative 2 may seem like the easy way out, but it represents an ultimately unacceptable course of action. If nothing is done, you may be establishing informal office policy that encourages moonlighting even when it seems to conflict with the timely completion of work assignments.

Alternative 3 is something you should do anyway, but does not substitute for more specific action to resolve the stated problems. An ethical planner always is willing to examine his or her behavior in the light of the code.

A PLANNER WORKS PART TIME IN REAL ESTATE SALES

You are the planning director in a small city. An AICP planner on your staff apparently has hung out his shingle as a real estate salesperson. You discover this when he starts taking business calls at the office. You are appalled. You call him into your office and tell him that such work is a conflict of interest. You give several examples, such as the fact that he shares an office with a planner who assists with long-range regional transportation planning and utility siting. He explains that the majority of his work will be done outside the city where he is employed and, therefore, he does not see any conflict. He does note that on a case-by-base basis he would like to occasionally sell residential real estate inside the jurisdiction. He says he would avoid involvement in any case where there had recently been or in the near future might be any planning or zoning action by the department. He agrees to curtail use of the office phone during his workday. What should you do next?

Ethical Issues:

Is it a conflict for a public planner to engage in real estate sales? Is the conflict based exclusively on where the sales occur?

Action Alternatives:

1.   Place a warning memo in his personnel file and tell him that he will be dismissed if he fails to give up his real estate practice in its entirety. Then do it if necessary.

2.   Monitor his use of the telephone and make sure he lives up to his end of the bargain. Withhold permission to sell inside the city until you see how things are going to work out.

3.   Report his behavior to the professional development officer of your chapter and pursue placing charges with the executive director of AICP. You are outraged at his arrogance.

4.   Permit him to continue his real estate activity outside the jurisdiction, but warn him that no such activity will be permitted inside the jurisdiction. Also stress that public property such as phones should not be used for private gain.

5.   Other.

Code Citations:

B.3   A planner shall not perform work if there is an actual, apparent, or reasonably foreseeable conflict of interest, direct or indirect, or an appearance of impropriety, without full written disclosure concerning work for current or past clients and subsequent written consent by the current client or employer. A planner shall remove himself or herself from a project if there is any direct personal or financial gain including gains to family members. A planner shall not disclose information gained in the course of public activity for a private benefit unless the information would be offered impartially to any person.

Advisory Rulings:

2.　　"Conflicts of Interest When a Public Planner has a Stake in Private Development" (see appendix for full text). Conflicts of interest are reasonably foreseeable when a planner attempts to serve a real estate development client while serving a public agency that may have a role in reviewing or approving projects of the client.

3.　　"Outside Employment or Moonlighting" (see appendix for full text). A planning staff member must take no employment outside of official duties unless such employment creates no conflict with those duties either in the interests to be served or in competition for time and energy. If the planner decides that there will be no such conflicts, then outside employment must receive the explicit approval of the employer. No outside employment must be undertaken if its performance will reduce the quality or dispatch with which the staff member executes primary responsibilities.

Discussion:

Planners' basic activities affect the way land can be used and, therefore, affect the price that people are willing to pay for land. Planners are privy to information not generally available to others that affects the future development potential of various parcels. Work in a planning agency regularly involves contacts with other agencies and levels of government, all of which are involved in the same basic system. Reasonable people, in looking at this issue, would find it unlikely that the planner could neatly separate his moonlighting and regular job.

The ethical response is to demand that the planner cease his real estate business as stated in alternative 1. It should be understood that any firing must comply with the requirements and notification procedures of a public agency.

You also should be willing to pursue alternative 3 as events dictate. Reporting unethical behavior to others, alternative 3, without taking any action on your part is less supportable as an approach to problem solving.

While alternative 4 may appear to be a compromise, since the most obvious conflicts are removed, it is not acceptable. First, a planner's primary interest must be the public interest, which does not always limit itself to the geographic boundaries of the employer's jurisdiction. Secondly, coordination is a primary purpose of planning. This gives a planner occasional inside knowledge and certain responsibilities related to adjacent jurisdictions as well as one's own community. Finally, the appearance of a conflict of interest is possible when one is paid privately for a service that is related to employment by a public agency. Such appearances, particularly in real estate, must be avoided.

Finally, this scenario illustrates the importance of a public policy on moonlighting. Many government agencies do have such policies. They often state that one must secure permission from a supervisor (or at least inform the supervisor) before initiating a new venture. Had such a requirement been in place, the controversy might have been avoided. The AICP's Advisory Ruling No. 3 contains such a provision.

CAN YOU BE A CONSULTANT TO THE PUBLIC AGENCY WHERE YOU ONCE WORKED?

You are the head of long-range planning in a small city in a Great Plains state. The planning director asked you and the zoning enforcement officer to examine the feasibility of computerizing the present zoning code, and to make recommendations for streamlining administration. Your report to the director was positive and you both asked to be assigned to carry out the work. The director decided, however, that doing the work in house would be too disruptive to existing activities and, instead, had you prepare a request for proposals (RFP).

The proposal and fee were advertised in a number of publications. No one responded to the RFP. You and your colleague have been kicking around the idea of quitting your jobs and setting up a consulting firm to take on the project. Another planner in the department suggests that this would be a conflict of interest. You strongly resent this suggestion inasmuch as no one in the private sector seemed interested in doing the work. If you don't do it, it probably won't be done. Furthermore, you think that having a streamlined system for administering the zoning code would benefit the public welfare. What should you do next?

Ethical Issues:

Should working as a private consultant for a public agency where you were recently employed be construed as a breach of ethics?

Action Alternatives:

1.   You should talk to the city attorney. If she says there is nothing illegal about your leaving and setting up a firm to immediately bid on city business, go ahead and do it.

2. Discuss the matter with your chapter professional development officer. Stress the fact that the work is in the public interest and, because no one else is interested in doing the job, you can't be accused of unfair competition.

3. Abandon the idea of setting up a consulting firm just to work on this one project. Besides the fact that there will be the appearance of a conflict of interest, you are going to go broke pretty soon with only one client in place.

4. Other.

Code Citations:

B.3 A planner shall not perform work if there is an actual, apparent, or reasonably foreseeable conflict of interest, direct or indirect, or an appearance of impropriety, without full written disclosure concerning work for current or past clients and subsequent written consent by the current client or employer. A planner shall remove himself or herself from a project if there is any direct personal or financial gain including gains to family members. A planner shall not disclose information gained in the course of public activity for a private benefit unless the information would be offered impartially to any person.

B.4 A planner who has previously worked for a public planning body should not represent a private client, for one year after the planner's last date of employment with the planning body, in connection with any matter before that body that the planner may have influenced before leaving public employment.

B.7 A planner must not use the power of any office to seek or obtain a special advantage that is not in the public interest nor any special advantage that is not a matter of public knowledge.

D.5 A planner must systematically and critically analyze ethical issues in the practice of planning.

Discussion:

Lawyers cannot prescribe planning ethics. Attorneys can inform you of the laws and administrative rules that apply to departing public employees. Talking to the attorney is a good first step, but will not resolve whether the establishment of a consulting firm to do this job is an ethical course of action. Reject alternative 1 as incomplete.

Alternative 2, talking with the chapter professional development officer, should lead to the best course of action, set out in alternative 3 (do not undertake the work). There is no way you can avoid the appearance of or an actual conflict of interest when, as a public planner, you propose a project that you will be hired to do on a consulting basis. This is an era of heightened sensitivity regarding these types of matters. The code, which specifically directs one not to represent a client for a year after the last date of employment, sets a benchmark for a period of time that would generally be recognized as a "cooling off" period. The implication is that it is unethical to work for your former public employer on a project over which you had influence for 365 days following your departure. The fact that no one in the private sector responded to the RFP does not make it okay. Nor can you resolve the issue by offering to moonlight to do the work.

If private practice appeals to you, review your interest with your supervisor and see what options exist. Seek work within the department that would minimize the appearance of a conflict of interest when you leave. For example, supervising GIS map preparation or demographic analysis of census data would cause fewer conflicts if you were to eventually leave and begin work consulting on zoning codes. At least one year should pass before accepting employment as a consultant from your former employer.

PRIVATE ENTERPRISE SEEKS A PUBLIC OFFICIAL

You are the development code supervisor. You have worked in that position for many years in a large city planning department in a jurisdiction with a very complicated development code. The land development ordinances grant you fairly wide latitude in administering approvals and exceptions from the details of the property development standards. You have managed to exercise your responsibilities firmly but with few controversies or complaints. You are well respected by both the public and private sector.

A major land-consulting firm offers you a position as a development approval expediter with a substantial salary increase.

Ethical Issues:

Are you precluded from taking skills you learned in the public sector to the private sector where you will be more adequately compensated? Would problems arise if, as an applicant for approval, you have to deal with your former colleagues? Will it look as if you "cultivated" your new job by making certain discretionary decisions in a way that favored your new employer?

Action Alternatives:

1.   Accept the new position and begin work immediately after clearing up loose ends around the office. You have served the public well for many years and you leave with a clear conscience.

2.   Decline the position because it might appear to be a conflict of interest. You have tried to establish your role in the community as being beyond reproach. Now is not the time to throw your reputation to the wolves.

3.   Try to negotiate and secure a commitment from the planning firm that will provide for a one-year lag between the time you cease work for the city and begin work on behalf of any project that you had previously reviewed.

4.   Negotiate with current and prospective employers for a lengthy transition period while the city secures and trains a replacement. You can stipulate that only after such a transition will you begin fulltime, regular work for the developer.

5.   Other.

Code Citations:

B.3   A planner shall not perform work if there is an actual, apparent, or reasonably foreseeable conflict of interest, direct or indirect, or an appearance of impropriety, without full written disclosure concerning work for current or past clients and subsequent written consent by the current client or employer. A planner shall remove himself or herself from a project if there is any direct personal or financial gain including gains to family members. A planner shall not disclose information gained in the course of public activity for a private benefit unless the information would be offered impartially to any person.

B.4   A planner who has previously worked for a public planning body should not represent a private client, for one year after the planner's last date of employment with the planning body, in connection with any matter before that body that the planner may have influenced before leaving public employment.

B.6   A planner must not sell or offer to sell services by stating or implying an ability to influence decisions by improper means.

B.7   A planner must not use the power of any office to seek or obtain a special advantage that is not in the public interest nor any special advantage that is not a matter of public knowledge.

B.9   A planner must not reveal information gained in a professional relationship which the client or employer has requested be held inviolate. Exceptions to this requirement of non-disclosure may be made only when (a) required by process of law, or (b) required to prevent a clear violation of law; or (c) required to prevent a substantial injury to the public. Disclosure of confidential information, pursuant to (b) and (c), must not be made until after the planner has verified the facts and issues involved and, when practicable, has exhausted efforts to obtain reconsideration of the matter and has sought separate opinions on the issue from the other qualified professionals employed by the client or employer.

D.5   A planner must systematically and critically analyze ethical issues in the practice of planning.

Discussion:

Planners who have moved between the public and private sector caution that the ethical considerations arise from the point one decides to consider the offer, not just accept it:

> If the offer will be seriously considered, one should immediately inform the appropriate planning department superior and recuse oneself from any applications involving the consulting firm until reaching a decision. So long as an offer is on the table, there is a real risk of the appearance of a conflict.
>
> Another factor is the form of the offer (verbal implied, verbal firm, written). Most consultants will approach making an offer to a public official with great care because of the possible negative interpretations and misperceptions... Until an offer is "real," there is no need to advise one's superior, but most offers are not made "cold" and it is when discussions are underway that the potential for problems is greatest.
>
> Michael T. Lambert, AICP
Pittsburgh

Many public agencies have policies governing transition from the public to the private sectors. Additionally, the AICP Code contains specific guidelines. For a year after leaving public employment, the planner must not represent a client before any body that the planner may have influenced when in the public's employ.

Reviewing the alternatives, you may find good and bad aspects in each. First ask, can one claim that such a job offer is the result of previously improper influence? Has there been such a close relationship with the private company that one might interpret the job offer as a reward? If the answer is yes, then a variation on alternative 2 is best. In taking this action, the planner should tell the supervisor that the offer was made and rejected. Full disclosure becomes important.

More likely there is no major conflict. Accepting the job is a fine alternative, once some of the details are resolved. Alternative 1, however, offers no details. Alternative 3 provides specifics, such as the one-year guideline from the AICP code.

Alternative 4 shows some positive consideration of the current employer's concern for orderly transition. If the consulting firm has no projects within the city's jurisdiction and will not have any during the transition period, this alternative may work. The one-year provision, however, must still apply for work with the new employer. Keep in mind that long transition periods can lead to the perception that your loyalties have shifted.

DEALING WITH ALLEGATIONS OF SEXUAL HARASSMENT

You have just been hired as the planning manager for an engineering firm. People are pretty friendly. As you are introduced to each of the principals, you hear several comments about your good fortune in working with an exceptionally attractive assistant and an equally good-looking draftsperson. The latter term is used with obvious derision.

During your first week on the job you overhear an off-color joke and lots of hearty laughter. You notice that the field crew manager has posted a calendar of bathing beauties. The young male computer whizzes have downloaded female nudes from the Internet and are using them as screensavers. Your boss calls your secretary "honey," as he introduces her to clients who come to the office. You remind yourself that the female receptionist in the front office has picture postcards of musclemen interspersed with ones from her favorite vacation beaches.

At the end of your first week your boss compliments you on "fitting in," and tells you that he already thinks of you as "one of the team."

During your second week on the job, the lone female planner assigned to work for you complains about the "atmosphere" at the office. She says that the company is a good one to work for in terms of salary and benefits, but she and other women have experienced harassment in various forms. Currently she is dating an engineer who works for another company, but co-workers used to tease her about her private life before this stable relationship developed. To illustrate what she calls a pattern, the planner says that the female draftsperson (whom you supervise) confided in her that engineers in the firm frequently ask her to go out. When the draftsperson explains that she prefers not to date people with whom she works, the engineers become disagreeable. "What's the matter?" and "Do you prefer women?" are the kinds of comments she's heard. She's asked that they refrain from these innuendoes to no avail.

You become more concerned and look through your predecessor's files. There is nothing on the subject — no policies, no files or notes on the topic, no comments on evaluations or letters from employees. You do find, however, a three-page listing of "dumb blonde" jokes that had apparently circulated around the office recently.

You carefully raise the topic with you boss and he replies, "That's interesting. I've never heard any of this before." After some discussion he suggests that you, as a manager, look into the situation and report back to him. You trust his sincerity and think he would be receptive to a well-considered report and useful recommendations. How should you proceed? And what would you emphasize in recommendations based upon the information to date?

Ethical Issues:

Is sexual harassment taking place? If so, what action needs to be taken to stop the harassment?

Action Alternatives:

1.   You can see there is a problem in the office and it needs to be addressed. Before making recommendations, however, you decide to gather additional evidence of unacceptable behavior on which to base your recommendations. After all, your report needs to address the complete range of problems.

2.   You decide you simply haven't been on the job long enough to have acquired the credibility necessary to do a thorough investigation. Therefore, you defer all action for six months. In the meantime, you decide you will carefully observe what is going on and then make a determination yourself whether to proceed.

3.   Without doing any further investigation, you decide not to pay attention to what's past but, instead, to focus on creating a better atmosphere. You institute a series of mandatory brown bag lunches to provide employees with a better understanding of the nature of harassment in the work place and to draft a company policy on the subject.

4. You feel that management has decided not to see the problem. You think it might be giving you the same message and you decide to drop the issue, at least temporarily. You can't afford not to do well on this job. Maybe in the future, if things go well, you could reconsider what, if anything, should be done.

5. Other.

Code Citations:

C.7 A planner must strive to increase the opportunities for women and members of recognized minorities to become professional planners.

C.8 A planner shall not commit an act of sexual harassment.

D.1 A planner must not commit a deliberately wrongful act which reflects adversely on the planner's professional fitness.

D.2 A planner must respect the rights of others and, in particular, must not improperly discriminate against persons.

Advisory Ruling:

1. "Sexual Harassment," (see appendix for full text). Joking or bantering about sexual subjects, comments suggesting sexual attractiveness, and comments disparaging women or men or their abilities generally may constitute petty harassment. If any such behavior is found offensive, offended persons should so say. The offensive behavior becomes harassment if continued after the offender is notified…. Negligence or omission on the part of an employer who is dismissive of a complaint of sexual harassment, and encourages the complainant to be tolerant of the offense is itself a form of harassment.

Discussion:

Alternative 1 is the preferred course of action. Obviously a problem exists in the office. Your own eyes and ears have confirmed the presence of "an intimidating, hostile, or offensive work environment." On the other hand, secondary parties have reported some of the evidence. Some planners have expressed concern about the office environment. Shouldn't it be enough to take action in your department since you have authority to demand that employees remove objectionable photographs or be spared unwelcome advances and disrespectful behavior? The answer is no. Your employees should not feel that the only "safe" work environment is under your watchful eye. Their ability to perform successfully for you is also dependent on their relationship with co-workers throughout the organization.

In preparing your report, you can use the code to define the problem and then list examples of how actions — whether intentionally harassing or not — lead to an atmosphere of hostility and intimidation for some employees. You also should list options for dealing with the problem, including the adoption of a company policy, and training.

Doing nothing, alternative 2, is a weak choice. While it is true that you probably lack personal respect and authority to carry out cultural reforms on your own, you are nonetheless required to be an example and demonstrate a willingness to speak out on behalf of your employees.

Instituting a training program, alternative 3, is a good idea but such training needs the commitment and participation of senior management if it is to be successful.

Alternative 4, a different version of doing nothing, is another poor choice. As an ethical planner and as a compassionate human being, you would not choose this option.

Background:

When written, the scenario was crafted not to identify the sex of the newly hired planning manager. Yet, when used in presentations, audiences have generally assumed that the manager has to be a male, since the employer is an engineering firm. This assumption is an interesting commentary about the stereotypes still found among members of the profession. These stereotypes are part of the reason some women continue to experience hostility in the workplace.

After Clarence Thomas' Supreme Court confirmation hearings, a new standard for judging office behavior began to emerge. Dubbed by legal commentators as "the reasonable woman" standard, the test of acceptable behavior has to do with whether women would find it to be appropriate. Prior to this, the courts applied more of a "reasonable man" criteria: if most men wouldn't find the behavior to be sexist, demeaning or harassing, then it wasn't.

This change in standards demands that both women and men in the office be held accountable for their behavior, and that both be open in establishing their personal comfort levels for social and professional interchange. This means that women must be able to advise men of dialogue or actions they find objectionable instead of suffering in silence or complaining to supervisors. Men must change their behavior in response. "I didn't mean anything by it" was a feeble excuse when we used it as children, and it is no more impressive when used in the work place. In the short run, there will continue to be mutual levels of befuddlement. In the long run, improved communication will lead to more effective and efficient work styles, which can only enhance the quality of professional products.

Section C.8 of the code says that a planner shall not commit an act of sexual harassment. Yet female planners report being the victims of inappropriate sexual conduct at the office. Why? Though women have been highly visible as a percentage of the planning work force for more than a decade, the gaps between men and women remain in terms of language, style, and attitude. The two sexes struggle to find middle ground. The reality that many women encounter in the planning agency is that men still hold most of the power. Some women are trying to get some of that power. This leads to situations charged with fear and anger. Women must learn to deal with harassment in the context of feeling less powerful. Still, as long as most women know they must depend on men for their jobs and future advancement, they are less likely to try to stop the offensive behavior.

Research shows that the problems and realities of sexual harassment are greater in smaller offices than larger ones because supervisors tend to wield greater power. For planners, the same is likely to hold true. Small work environments lack personnel systems, employee guidelines, in-house legal counsel, and outsider observation, all of which tend to curb the potential for abuse. For the many women planners who work in small- to medium-sized private firms or planning agencies, the reality of sexual harassment may be different from that experienced in the big city firm or department.

In all instances, professional planners, regardless of gender, have a responsibility to their colleagues to assure that the work environment is free of all forms of discrimination and harassment. Those who observe harassing behavior by others, and who do nothing, enable the harasser to carry out a campaign. A more proactive response is needed. Simply refraining from the offensive behavior is not enough.

Finally, all sexual harassment, whether of the same or opposite sex, is prohibited.

WINDOW DRESSING MINORITY CONTRACTING

You are a public agency planner who is managing a consultant study that includes a ten-percent "set aside" for women and minority contractors. As contract manager, you have direct responsibility for the outcome of the contract. In that capacity you have to authorize payment of invoices that list hours of work accomplished by the subcontractors. The proprietor of a woman-owned business (a planner) has complained to you that she is doing no real work, but being paid for just showing up at an occasional meeting. She wants to actually do the work for which she is being compensated. You talk with the planning director who advises you that, if you raise this matter with the Purchasing Department's Office of Minority Business Affairs, you will be seen as undercutting the city's social objectives. The planning director encourages you to do what you think is right, but warns you to be prepared to accept the consequences, whatever they may be.

The official city policy views the minority contractor's role seriously. The purchasing department took into account the qualifications of all the contractors (both prime and sub) at the time the award was made. The city assumes that the minority subcontractors will do the work as outlined in the proposal.

You then speak about the matter, somewhat indirectly, with the prime contractor. You are informed that nothing is amiss. The contractor pointedly and emphatically rejects your suggestions as "way out of line." From the conversation, you wonder if the issue is one of quality control. Maybe the minority contractor's work doesn't meet the prime contractor's standards. You are suspicious about the intentions of the prime contractor. Having received additional points in the ranking system for including minority subcontractors, he then does not use them to accomplish the work. What should you do?

Ethical Issues:

This scenario raises several problems. The AICP code urges fair treatment of the professional view of colleagues. And you have two colleagues with different views — the female planner and the prime contractor. The views of the planning director also are to be accorded respect. One of your responsibilities, according to the code, is to increase opportunities for women and minority planners. Finally, although not spelled out in the code, as a public employee you need to make sure that taxpayers pay only for work that is actually done in conformance with the contract requirements.

Action Alternatives:

1.   Do nothing. The subcontractor has a problem with the contractor. Your responsibility as a contract manager does not extend to such relationships.

2.   At the next progress meeting, in the presence of the prime contractor, specifically request several work items (within the scope of the contract) from the subcontractor.

3.   Put your concerns in writing, for the record, and send a copy to the director. This may have the effect of prodding some additional thinking on the part of your boss.

4.   Agree with your boss who seems to be saying that you should keep a low profile. He probably is right in warning you about the possible negative consequences.

5.   Other.

Code Citations:

A.   A planner's primary obligation is to serve the public interest. While the definition of the public interest is constantly evolving, a planner owes allegiance to a conscientiously attained concept of the public interest, which requires special obligations.

C.   A planner should contribute to the development of the profession by improving knowledge and techniques, making work relevant to solutions of community problems, and increasing public understanding of planning activities. A planner should treat fairly the professional views of qualified colleagues and members of other professions.

C.3   A planner who reviews the work of other professionals must do so in a fair, considerate, professional, and equitable manner.

C.7   A planner must strive to increase the opportunities for women and members of recognized minorities to become professional planners.

Discussion:

In this scenario you have several sets of responsibilities that seem to be in conflict with one another. The AICP code urges fair treatment of the professional view of colleagues. A fellow planner who feels her views are not being given a fair hearing has approached you. You have a responsibility to increase opportunities for women and minorities and, as the project manager, you have direct responsibility for the outcome of the contract. In that capacity you have to authorize payment of invoices that list hours of work accomplished by the female planner. Official policy takes the minority contractor's role seriously. So should you.

By doing nothing, as in alternative 1, you offer no help to the subcontractor who has complained to you about the situation. You know that her expectations regarding your role as contract manager are reasonable. You have a responsibility to make sure that the contract provisions are followed. Also, you could be making a mistake in thinking that just because you choose to do nothing, she will follow suit. If, instead, she chooses to complain to someone else, they will first come to review the situation with you. How will you defend your choice?

Alternative 2 would allow you to intervene without threatening your relationship with the prime contractor, and also would provide you with additional information to help you decide whether further action is required.

In contracting matters, it is wise to put everything in writing. So, alternative 3 is a good beginning, but it doesn't go far enough. This will provide some administrative cover in the event of future problems. However, an action alternative that does little more than "Cover Your Rear" is hardly the kind of ethical stance that the code hopes to inspire.

Alternative 4, lying low, is one that your boss will like, but it shares most of the shortcomings of alternative 1.

PLANNING DIRECTOR BROWBEATS CONSULTANTS

You are the senior staff planner in a department where revisions to the comprehensive plan are underway. In addition to supervising extensive planning staff work, the planning director is managing several different consultant contracts for the comprehensive plan. The director needs to get everything wrapped up before the upcoming election because several council members friendly to the process are not running for re-election. The director believes that he has a good chance of getting the revised plan adopted if presented to the current council. Conversely, it seems unlikely that members new to the council would vote to support a plan developed by their predecessors. In your opinion, the planning director has gone beyond strongly encouraging the consultants to meet all of the deadlines to threatening them with the loss of future city business and ruining their reputations within the planning community. You have talked to the director and expressed your concerns. He says you should remember what is really important, the comprehensive plan, and that no one will remember these little tussles once the plan is adopted. Is he right? Do you have any alternatives?

Ethical Issues:

When working toward an important goal like the adoption of a comprehensive plan, is it acceptable to use questionable tactics that may be unfair to some individuals?

Action Alternatives:

1. Prepare a memo to the director, for the record, stating your concerns about the threats.
2. Confidentially advise the planning commission chair of your concerns.
3. You have already exercised your most likely option: talking with the director. Just sit back and watch.
4. Other.

Code Citations:

B.2   A planner must accept the decisions of a client or employer concerning the objectives and nature of the professional services to be performed unless the course of action to be pursued involves conduct that is illegal or inconsistent with the planner's primary obligation to the public interest.

C.   A planner should contribute to the development of the profession by improving knowledge and techniques, making work relevant to solutions of community problems, and increasing public understanding of planning activities. A planner should treat fairly the professional views of qualified colleagues and members of other professions.

C.1   A planner must protect and enhance the integrity of the profession and must be responsible in criticism of the profession.

C.3   A planner who reviews the work of other professionals must do so in a fair, considerate, professional, and equitable manner.

D.   Strive for high standards of integrity, proficiency, and knowledge.

D.2   A planner must respect the rights of others and, in particular, must not improperly discriminate against persons.

Advisory Ruling:

5.   Planners who know of unethical conduct must report it. (See appendix for full text.)

Discussion:

It should not be necessary for the director to threaten dire consequences simply to get the consultants to meet deadlines which, presumably, were mutually agreed upon. If consultants fail to meet critical deadlines, then that should be used as criteria for determining if the city would wish to use their services again.

Threatening to ruin someone's reputation is out of line. The AICP code calls for the fair review of colleagues' work. Intimidation hardly can be conceived of as fair. Technically, it is the work that is to be reviewed fairly and not the individual. If one combines a reading of C.3. and D.2., one would be hard pressed to conclude that threats constitute ethical behavior. You also have a responsibility to your employer that would preclude you from complaining outside of the department because the public interest is not directly threatened by your boss' actions.

The advisory ruling, which requires you to report unethical conduct, is reserved for activities of a more substantial concern, i.e. misrepresenting or changing the consultant's finding. Therefore, among the choices presented in the scenarios, alternative 1 is the preferred course of action. A planner in Ohio offered a reasonable "other":

> I would state my concerns regarding the plan and the upcoming election, honestly, to the consultants. No planning consultant likes to see his or her work left incomplete...The memo could backfire for both planners if hostile individuals gain control of the council and use it against them.
>
> Kelly E. Templin, AICP
> Oxford, Ohio

WHAT HAPPENS WHEN A CONSULTANT TAKES ON TOO MUCH WORK?

You are the owner of a new and flourishing consulting firm. Not only does your firm do excellent work, but there isn't much competition from other firms. It's a heady time for you; the business and clients seem to be rolling in the front door. You recently purchased several pieces of expensive office equipment and signed a lease for larger quarters. But you haven't spent much time checking on "the nut," the amount of income required every thirty days to meet fixed expenses. Now your cash resources are depleted, and the nut looks huge. You aren't worried though. You decide that with enough creative management of existing staff, you'll survive and prosper. Your strategy is to hold off on producing contracted deliverables and throw all staff resources into procuring new work. From now on, you'll require a down payment when contracts are signed rather than waiting for payment after the first deliverable. For a while, things work well. However, two of your three staff members meet with you privately. They express concern that you are continuing to accept payment for work with deadlines that you know the firm cannot meet. You are shocked at their naïveté. Isn't this how all businesses grow into success? Yet they may be right.

Ethical Issue:

Is it ethical for a consultant to accept new clients when the firm knows it will be unable to meet the contractual deadlines for deliverables?

Action Alternatives:

1.   Dissolve the firm and send letters to clients informing them of your financial demise.

2.   Retrench. Find another tenant to sublease the new office and relocate to more humble quarters. Acknowledge, in writing to clients, that products will be delayed.

3.   Continue as you have been doing and hope for the best.

4.   Devote a limited amount of staff time to producing a few work products with directives to employees to create something to "get by."

5.   Other.

Code Citations:

B.   A planner owes diligent, creative, independent and competent performance of work in pursuit of the client's or employer's interest. Such performance should be consistent with the planner's faithful service to the public interest.

B.8   A planner must not accept or continue to perform work beyond the planner's professional competence or accept work which cannot be performed with the promptness required by the prospective client or employer, or which is required by the circumstances of the assignment.

Discussion:

The code is explicit. The planner should not accept work that the firm is unable to perform. The injunction applies to delay as well as areas of work outside the competence of the firm. And the reality is that most clients ask for references. The owner's initial strategy was extremely short sighted.

Alternative 1 gets the firm off the hook by dissolving the entity. But this may cause significant hardship among the clients and leaves unaddressed the issue of fraudulent conduct in terms of products/studies already paid for but not delivered. It also will result in difficulties for the current employees.

Alternative 2 is preferred. By taking action to solve the problem you created, you are behaving responsibly.

Alternative 3, crossing your fingers and hoping things work out, is both unethical and unproductive in terms of the future of your firm. Producing work consistently late will cost you valuable client references.

Providing poorly conceived work, alternative 4, is sleazy as well. It also raises the problem of how you will be able to retain your clients and turn them into repeat business.

THE CONSULTANT'S NEW STAFF

You are the chief of long-range planning in your Kentucky city. You also are currently the project manager for an extensive multi-year engagement. A consultant responded to your city's request for proposals (RFP) to prepare new land development ordinances and citizen involvement programs. The RFP emphasized the requirements for a staff with extensive experience and a history of workable innovation in these fields. A firm was selected on the basis of the experience and prior performance of its staff. Soon thereafter several key people left the consultant to establish another firm. The consultant notified the city that new staff of equal competence had been hired. You know of significant experience gaps in the new staff. Normally, you would discuss this issue at a regular senior staff meeting with the planning director and the city administrator. However, you know that the principal in charge of the project for the firm is a close friend of the city administrator. You fear this will make a difference in how you are perceived. What should you do next?

Ethical Issues:

How do you treat a difference of opinion with a professional colleague when you believe that the other person may have more public credibility? How do you determine when a difference of opinion is serious enough to require direct action even at some personal risk?

Action Alternatives:

1.   Advise the consultant of the suspected shortcomings. Ask for a response.

2.   Challenge the consultant's conduct and seek an opinion from the AICP Executive Director.

3.   Advise the planning director and the city administrator.

4.   Do nothing now and monitor the contract to ensure the quality of work does not slip.

5.   Other.

Code Citations:

B.8   A planner must not accept or continue to perform work beyond the planner's professional competence or accept work which cannot be performed with the promptness required by the prospective client or employer, or which is required by the circumstances of the assignment.

C.1   A planner must protect and enhance the integrity of the profession and must be responsible in criticism of the profession.

C.2   A planner must accurately represent the qualifications, views, and findings of colleagues.

C.3   A planner who reviews the work of other professionals must do so in a fair, considerate, professional, and equitable manner.

D.4   A planner must accurately represent professional qualifications, education, and affiliations.

Discussion:

Assuming that the gap in experience is enough to seriously jeopardize the consultant's ability to deliver the work product, the issue cannot be ignored. Care should be taken to comply with applicable city administrative procedures. The planner should review the language in the RFP addressing the qualification requirements. The planner then should request copies of resumes for the new personnel and compare them to the requirements of the RFP. If there are experience gaps, the consultant should be advised in writing. This is alternative 1, with a notable exception. Research must first be done; you would not wish to be perceived as making accusations based on assumptions. Alternative 1 also is the most ethical as a first step because it provides a professional colleague with the opportunity to address your concerns and to defend the changes in personnel. If, however, the consultant's justification is inadequate, additional action is called for.

Alternative 2 seems like overkill given that there may be a high degree of subjectivity associated with reviewing resumes. Ultimately, the planner retains the power of the purse and should be able to achieve a successful resolution of the problem.

Alternative 3 would be appropriate as a follow-up course of action. As the project manager, you should eventually advise the planning director and city administrator of your concerns and together devise a joint course of action which will best serve the public interest.

Alternative 4, doing nothing, fails to aggressively protect the public interest. It might work out, but only if you can assure yourself that if there are problems with contract deliverables, you will be able to effectively manage for a successful outcome in a very limited period of time.

Source: Robert S. Baldwin, AICP, and the Oregon Chapter of APA

THE CONSULTANT'S BROCHURE

You are a consulting planner is a large southern city. A colleague, who is also an AICP member and a consulting planner, teaches at the State University. The governor appointed your colleague to chair the State's Critical Areas Task Force. The group is selecting the criteria for designating critical areas. A month after the appointment, you see a brochure from your colleague's firm. It has been designed to reflect this most recent accomplishment. The brochure narrative notes the valuable expertise gained as a result of the task force service. The brochure further suggests that potential clients evaluate the competency of their current planning consultant. The narrative implies that competency is defined as a personal knowledge of the critical areas program and personal relationships with key state officials who will implement the critical areas program. The caption accompanying a photograph in the brochure points out that the relevant employee serves on the Critical Areas Task Force.

You currently are competing for the same business as your colleague. You feel that the brochure may be unethical because it implies an ability to influence decision through improper means. What should you do?

Ethical Issues:

Is it unethical to advertise your access to political power as part of your marketing strategy?

Action Alternatives:

1.   Complain about the faculty member to the AICP. Follow the rules of procedure published in the code beginning with a letter of complaint to the AICP executive director.

2.   Consult with the chapter professional development officer (PDO) and request that an article be prepared for the chapter newsletter on the subject of marketing materials and the need to avoid assertions that could cause someone to question a consulting firm's ethics. Request that the article be general in tone and hope for the best.

3.   Discuss the matter informally with several other colleagues to solicit their perspectives. Make your phone calls out-of-state, if possible, to avoid naming names. Instead, just discuss the overall negative impression you and others have of your colleague's conduct.

4.   Other.

Code Citations:

B.5   A planner must not solicit prospective clients or employment through the use of false or misleading claims, harassment or duress.

B.6   A planner must not sell or offer to sell services by stating or implying an ability to influence decisions by improper means.

C.1.   A planner must protect and enhance the integrity of the profession and must be responsible in criticism of the profession.

D.4   A planner must accurately represent professional qualifications, education, and affiliations.

Advisory Ruling:

5.   Planners who know of unethical conduct must report it. (See appendix for full text.)

Discussion:

Advisory Ruling No. 5 was written to help planners act upon the ethical principles in the code. It sets a standard for when action must be taken to report unethical conduct.

A planner who has certain knowledge of clearly unethical conduct on the part of the certified planner has a duty to file a charge of misconduct with the Executive Director.

By implication, if you do not have certain knowledge of clearly unethical conduct, you do not have a duty to report. However, when you believe that the information you have is reasonably compelling, reporting is a good choice. In this case, you feel that your colleague has violated the AICP code. The brochure has been prepared with the following lesson in mind: whom you know is more important than what you know. There is a clear effort to suggest the ability to influence planning decisions. This is not to suggest that it would be inappropriate to mention the work done for the state. The fact is that you believe that the consultant went too far. It is the kind of a problem — drafting self-congratulatory language — where conversations with colleagues before, rather than after, the fact can be illuminating.

What you decide to do partly depends on how strongly you feel. This may be an issue where reasonable people disagree. Therefore, it would be important to test your views with others before undertaking a report. Alternative 3, talking to colleagues, would be an appropriate first step. After those conversations, you would be better able to judge which next step would make sense: an article in the chapter newsletter addressing how to write ethical advertising materials or a letter to the executive director.

If you were annoyed, but not grievously offended, alternative 2 would be appropriate. Now would be a good time to talk with the chapter professional development officer.

PRESERVING INDIAN ARTIFACTS

You are a public agency planner concerned with the protection of several Native American artifact sites. A major public works project is planned for nearby and you have hired a consulting firm to identify the best construction practices for minimizing impact on the site. The consultant report hedges its bets and identifies a range of measures. The consultant acknowledges that there is no clear single choice since there is little practical experience comparable to these circumstances. Under pressure from your supervisor to get the job done, and from your peers to protect the history of the community, you select the most extensive, expensive practices and cite the consultant as the source. The consultant sees your version of the final report and is truly distressed. He feels that his work was misrepresented. He fears loss of future employment because he will be perceived as taking an extreme approach. He also believes that it may discourage communities from even acknowledging the problem if the only solution is gold-plated. You feel as though your approach, conservative in nature, was the most appropriate given the fragile and irreplaceable nature of the resource. The consultant wants to meet with you to discuss his concerns and see how you can address them.

Ethical Issues:

From the public agency planner's point of view: How do you respond to a request for a simple, straightforward recommendation when the issues don't lend themselves to that kind of a resolution? Is taking the most conservative approach the best approach when data is inconclusive?

From the consultant's point of view: How do you react when you believe that your work has not been fairly and accurately represented?

Action Alternatives for the Public Planner:

1. Decline to have the meeting. What's done is done. Talking won't change the recommendation you already made.

2. Agree to meet in the interest of damage control.

3. Submit a "refined" recommendation that elaborates on your first recommendation and that covers some of the consultant's concerns. Then meet with the consultant.

4. Agree to meet but bring others into the session who will support your decision.

5. Withdraw your recommendation and refine your work based on a meeting with the consultant.

6. Other.

Code Citations:

A.3. A planner must strive to provide full, clear and accurate information on planning issues to citizens and governmental decision-makers.

A.6. A planner must strive to protect the integrity of the natural environment.

A.7. A planner must strive for excellence of environmental design and endeavor to conserve the heritage of the built environment.

C.3. A planner who reviews the work of other professionals must do so in a fair, considerate, professional, and equitable manner.

C.5 A planner must examine the applicability of planning theories, methods, and standards to the facts and analysis of each particular situation and must not accept the applicability of a customary solution without first establishing its appropriateness to the situation.

Advisory Ruling:

4.   "Honesty in the Use of Information" (see full text in the attachments). There should be no need to explain what the code requires is full, clear, and accurate information. Half-truth, deceptions, and undocumented assertions don't pass. A half-truth is a whole lie.

Discussion:

The misuse of information is a serious breach of conduct. In this case, there was a failure by the public planner to disclose complete information. Information must be "full, complete, and accurate." One could urge decision-makers to adopt a conservative approach to conservation based on data provided. This is different from presenting only a single approach as scientifically based.

In terms of what can be done now, every attempt should be made to provide a more complete picture, even if that means submitting a revised recommendation. Either alternative 3 or 5 (changing the recommendation) would be appropriate. Whether the revisions to the staff report are made before or after the meeting with the consultant depends on when other decision-making meetings are scheduled. The correction must be made in time to influence the final decision.

Alternative 1, doing nothing, violates your responsibilities under the code. While you may not mean to behave unethically, you would be doing so if you ignored the issue after it was brought to your attention.

Alternative 2, agreeing to a meeting, is fine; but it is not sufficient. Likewise, alternative 4 is little more than a group version of alternative 2. It still doesn't hold water.

NEGATIVE COMMENTS ABOUT CONSULTANT WORK

At a recent national planning conference, you hear negative things about the quality of work done by a well-known consulting planning firm. Some of the comments are from people who may not have first-hand information. However, a former client made one of the critical statements. The firm, by coincidence, has submitted a proposal to do work for your community. You call all of the references supplied by the consultant. They are fine. What should you do next?

Ethical Issues:

How do you make sure that you don't pass on gossip, but do respond to legitimate issues affecting the expenditure of public dollars?

Action Alternatives:

1. You have checked the references and they are positive. The folks with whom you spoke are reasonable and had direct knowledge of the consultant's work. You want to avoid the appearance of looking to make trouble for yourself or anyone else. You decide no further action is necessary.

2. When spending public money, you have a responsibility to make sure that the public gets the best value. This requires you to be zealous in determining whether there are any reasons for not hiring the consulting firm. After all, consulting firms do not list clients who might give a bad reference. You do additional research and check with names not on the list provided by the firm.

3. Other.

Code Citations:

C.1 A planner must protect and enhance the integrity of the profession and must be responsible in criticism of the profession.

C.2 A planner must accurately represent the qualifications, views, and findings of colleagues.

C.3 A planner who reviews the work of other professionals must do so in a fair, considerate, professional, and equitable manner.

Discussion:

You want to be fair in your treatment of a colleague while at the same time making sure that you do not engage a consultant who will be unable to fulfill the requirements of the professional services agreement.

Alternative 1, doing nothing more, saves you work, but it ignores the fact that you have information that calls into question the qualifications of one of the respondents. You would not be in direct violation of the code by doing nothing because you would have followed all of your community's standard procedures for hiring. You would, however, have failed to be attentive to the aspirational intent of the code.

Alternative 2, expanding the reference check, is the most desirable. It is most consistent with the code requirement to fairly treat the views of a colleague. In this case you wish to treat fairly the views of those who have disparaged the consultant, as well as the views of the positive references. Unless you specifically have stated in your RFP that the only references you will check are those provided by the consultant, you are free to seek out additional information. To be fair, you should mention to the consultant that you will be checking with other colleagues. If you have major unresolved issues as a result of further checking, the consultant should be given an opportunity to respond.

GIVING CREDIT WHERE CREDIT IS DUE

Two county planners, David Bell and Christine Ewing, labor long and hard on the new Muirlandia County Subdivision Ordinance. Taking into account the latest bells and whistles derived from research, they also have added a large dose of community sensitivity. With their respective backgrounds in biology and engineering, their subdivision ordinance is an artful weaving of problem-solving alternatives. Both receive congratulations from their immediate supervisor when the county board of supervisors adopts the ordinance.

Not long after, Ewing's husband gets a job elsewhere and she relocates to another part of the state where public planning jobs are scarce. To keep herself busy, she writes to her friends at the local county planning office. She offers her services as a consultant and picks up a little work here and there.

A year later, Bell attends the State Conference of the American Planning Association. At the Awards luncheon, Ewing is awarded the Chapter's Annual "Master Planner" citation for her work on the Dry Creek County Subdivision ordinance. His curiosity piqued, Bell visits the displays of the award winning programs. He is shocked to discover that the Dry Creek ordinance is almost a verbatim replication of that of Muirlandia. Yet no mention is made of his contributions. He is, at first, disappointed and then he becomes angry. Why should she get the credit for work that he has done?

Bell talks to his former colleague and expresses his dismay. Ewing dismisses his concerns by pointing out that planners have always borrowed from the work of their predecessors and that planning reports are often issued under the name of the planning director with no attribution to the staff which prepared the document. Bell is not mollified. He wonders if Ewing has violated the AICP Code of Ethics?

Ethical Issue:

Is it a violation of the AICP Code of Ethics to take credit for the work of a colleague? Do you have a duty to report willfully misleading conduct that results in the misappropriation of what you believe to be your intellectual property?

Action Alternatives:

1.   Do nothing. The code is silent on the specific topic of plagiarism.
2.   Contact the awards jury chair and offer to send a copy of the original document and ask that a co-award be made and announced in the chapter's newsletter.
3.   Ask Ewing to contact the state chapter officers, apologize for her oversight and offer to return her award.
4.   Ask Ewing to write a personal letter of apology to you acknowledging the nature of the joint effort. Promise her you will publish it if she ever pulls a similar stunt.
5.   Other.

Code Citations:

A.3   A planner must strive to provide full, clear, and accurate information on planning issues to citizens and governmental decision-makers.
C.1   A planner must protect and enhance the integrity of the profession and must be responsible in criticism of the profession.
C.4   A planner must share the results of experience and research which contribute to the body of planning knowledge.
D.4   A planner must accurately represent professional qualifications, education, and affiliations.

Advisory Ruling:

5.   A planner who knows of unethical conduct must report it. (See appendix for full text.)

Discussion:

There is a distinction between sharing the results of experience and research and having your creative and original thinking incorporated into work products of others. How does this distinction play out in this scenario?

When a product is completed for a public agency, it resides in the public domain, but that doesn't mean the individuals who created the work do not deserve credit and professional recognition for their efforts. When Ewing recycles the results of a team project and creates a title page on which she lists herself as the only author, she fails in her responsibility to provide full, clear, and accurate information. The error would be compounded if her resume were revised to reflect her designation as a master planner. At that point, she may be failing to accurately represent her qualifications.

This scenario asks what Bell should do. Alternatives 2, 3, and 4 are ethical. Only alternative 1, turning the other cheek, is both ethical and inappropriate given Ewing's lack of remorse. Advisory Ruling No. 5, which requires reporting of unethical conduct when one has certain knowledge, obligates Bell to do something. If Bell is reluctant to publicly state his objections, the chapter professional development officer could be enlisted to prepare an article for the chapter newsletter on the subject.

It also should be noted that because the practice of sharing work is usual and customary, it is unlikely that the AICP Ethics Committee would uphold even a well-documented accusation of unethical conduct related to plagiarism. The process of notifying Ewing of the accusation, however, would have a sobering effect on conduct and could trigger the well-deserved apology to Bell.

GROCERY STORE MARKET ANALYSIS

You are a planning consultant and you respond to a fairly typical request for proposals and scope of services for a market analysis. You are hired by the city's planning director to analyze the potential market for a new grocery store in a low-income community. Currently, the only grocery store is a small liquor/convenience store. A federal grant is in sight to construct a shopping center that will include a supermarket. In discussing the work, you are instructed to push the definition of "potential market" to its limits. You are to make a strong case that the community would be a highly successful location for a new store. What should you do?

Ethical Issues:

From the consultant's point of view: How do you fulfill your responsibility to act independently and provide complete information when being directed to make a specific finding?

From the city planning director's point of view: How do you fulfill your responsibility to expand choice and opportunity for all persons, recognizing a special responsibility to plan for the needs of disadvantaged groups and persons, and urge the alteration of policies, institutions, and decisions that oppose such needs.

Action Alternatives for the Consultant:

1. Conduct the analysis called for in the scope of services and let the chips fall where they may. Essentially, you ignore the planning director.

2. Run the numbers for several scenarios that demonstrate how the neighborhood might support a grocery. Lay out your projections based on varying assumptions, including those of the planning director, and make it clear just how optimistic some of the assumptions are.

3. Concur with the planning director's objective of getting a grocery store in the area and assist in securing the grant. Adjust the numbers accordingly.

4. Decide not to do the work for the city based on the terms specified by the planning director.

5. Other.

Code Citations:

A.3 A planner must strive to provide full, clear, and accurate information on planning issues to citizens and governmental decision-makers.

A.5 A planner must strive to expand choice and opportunity for all persons, recognizing a special responsibility to plan for the needs of disadvantaged groups and persons, and must urge the alteration of policies, institutions, and decisions that oppose such needs.

B.1 A planner must exercise independent professional judgment on behalf of clients and employers.

B.2 A planner must accept the decisions of a client or employer concerning the objectives and nature of the professional services to be performed unless the course of action to be pursued involves conduct that is illegal or inconsistent with the planner's primary obligation to the public interest.

Advisory Ruling:

4. "Honest in the Use of Information," (see appendix for full text). Many daily pressures do battle against honesty. We are pressed to be effective advocates for a community, a private client…. It is part of professional conduct to communicate ethical standards to clients, employers and the public…. There should be no need to explain what the code requires is full, clear, and accurate information. Half-truth, deceptions, and undocumented assertions don't pass. A half-truth is a whole lie. Don't cook the numbers.

Discussion:

There are two factors at play in this scenario: (1) respecting the decisions of the employer and serving the client, and (2) telling the truth even when pressured to do otherwise. You cannot ignore your responsibility to tell the truth even if an employer should urge you to shade the facts. Planners must always be committed to making sure the numbers they use are the best that can be provided.

The AICP code demands a commitment and a determination to police your own behavior. Your responsibility to provide clear and accurate information overrides loyalty to an employer and, therefore, only alternative 3, adjusting your numbers, is unacceptable. Some of the alternatives might appear to imply that as a consultant you have a flexible definition of the truth. To avoid such accusations, you will need to be thorough in drafting your assumptions and explaining their varying degree of reasonableness.

The planning director who advocates that everything in the study be arranged in a way to ensure receipt of the federal grant is operating from a premise that the end justifies the means. You may even share her commitment to community revitalization. Low-income residents often experience a double burden in that few grocery store choices make food shopping more expensive. And you may be able to assist her in achieving the goal through different methods, such as identifying other sources of funding or interested, socially-responsible investors.

Either alternative 1 (doing the job consistent with your understanding of responsible financial analysis) or 2 (describing alternative assumptions under which the conclusions might vary) would be acceptable, as would alternative 4 (bailing out). However, the latter would be an extreme choice.

WHO DETERMINES THE REAL NUMBERS?

You are a young consulting planner working for a national planning and economic development firm in a northern California branch office. You recently have been given your first opportunity to manage a client engagement. The client is a major developer with subdivisions scattered throughout several counties. You are in a meeting with the developer's staff. Before your selection as project principal, your supervisor did a preliminary calculation of the likely profit on a new subdivision. At that time, your supervisor was acting as the project principal. Based on that initial calculation, the developer decided to proceed with land acquisition.

You have spent a lot of time looking at the project and running the numbers. Unfortunately, you think the project will generate somewhat less money. You report the lower figure to the client's staff. The attorneys and accountants employed by the developer immediately object. You are asked to leave the room. When you return, you are asked to adjust your figures. They argue that reasonable people can differ and that so much time and money has already been invested in making the deal work that it is too late to go back to square one. You consider whether they may be right.

Ethical Issues:

How do you fulfill your responsibility to act independently and provide complete information when your employer seems to be directing you to make a different set of conclusions?

Action Alternatives:

1.   Restate your conclusions and elaborate on your rationale so that those present can identify any errors in your assumptions which would affect the calculations.

2.   Offer to run the numbers again placing greater weight on other discretionary factors that might lead to a higher figure. But make no guarantees.

3.   Punt this one to your supervisor making it clear that while your numbers aren't likely to change, the firm's conclusions may vary.

4.   Other.

Code Citations:

A.3   A planner must strive to provide full, clear, and accurate information on planning issues to citizens and governmental decision-makers.

B.1   A planner must exercise independent professional judgment on behalf of clients and employers.

B.2   A planner must accept the decisions of a client or employer concerning the objectives and nature of the professional services to be performed unless the course of action to be pursued involves conduct that is illegal or inconsistent with the planner's primary obligation to the public interest.

Advisory Ruling:

4. "Honesty in the Use of Information" (see appendix for full text). Many daily pressures do battle against honesty. We are pressed to be effective advocates for a community, a private client.... It is part of professional conduct to communicate ethical standards to clients, employers and the public.... There should be no need to explain what the code requires is full, clear, and accurate information. Half-truth, deceptions, and undocumented assertions don't pass. A half-truth is a whole lie. Don't cook the numbers.

Discussion:

There are two factors at play in this scenario: (1) respecting the decisions of the employer and serving the client, and (2) telling the truth even when pressured to do otherwise. You cannot ignore your responsibility to tell the truth even if an employer should urge you to shade the facts. Planners must always be committed to making sure the numbers they use are the best that can be provided. (It is more likely that as the new project principal, you would have reviewed concerns with the supervisor before coming to the meeting so that you could come to a common understanding before the new numbers are presented. But the scenario is silent on this point. It leaves you to make the decision about what is the most appropriate thing to do without the comfort of checking with the boss.)

The AICP code demands a commitment and a determination to police your own behavior. Your responsibility to provide clear and accurate information overrides loyalty to an employer and, therefore, alternative 1, restating your conclusions with elaboration, is preferred. Alternatives 2 and 3 imply that you have a flexible definition of the truth. Therefore, they are less desirable choices.

PRICING THE COMPREHENSIVE PLAN

In the State of Nirvana, state purchasing law specifically lists only a few categories of professional services that are excluded from price consideration. Although architecture is excluded, planning is not. Therefore, when purchasing planning services, local governments must consider cost, although it is not the single determining factor. A city in Nirvana has proposed a detailed request for proposals (RFP) for a comprehensive plan. It does not include any information about how much money is available, although consultants are requested to submit a cost proposal. You are a consultant interested in the project. By checking the city's adopted budget, you are able to determine how much money the planning department has available for consultant studies this fiscal year. You believe the budget to be inadequate. In a public session with all of the potential consultants, you explicitly ask if your assumptions regarding the budget are correct. You are told that your conclusions about the amount of funding available are correct. You are thinking about responding to the RFP and submitting a cost proposal in line with the available budget. You assume that, if you are successful, you can always whittle down the number of deliverables required in order to maintain the firm's financial solvency.

Ethical Issues:

From the consultant's point of view: There is no ethical issue. The people who write the RFPs have no idea what they really need or how much things cost. I will give them a good product (I define good.) for a reasonable amount of money. Whether it exactly comports with what was in the original RFP is not the issue, because what was in the original RFP was probably just a grab bag of issues and ideas. There's not enough money; but, then, there never is.

From the city planning director's point of view: How do you establish a professional working relationship with a consultant team that responds to the RFP, as written, but which has no intention of doing the work detailed in the RFP? The RFP was reviewed extensively within your community by both private and public-sector planners, was endorsed by the planning commission, and responds in form and content to the major recommendations of the American Society of Consulting Planners' publications on working with consultants. If the job can't be done for the amount of money in the budget, why don't the consultants tell the truth and not respond or only respond in part? That way I might be able to get the city to increase the budget. What we have now is just a useless cycle. Besides, if they can't do the job as written, they have no business responding at all.

Action Alternatives for the Consultant:

1.   Business as usual. Respond to the RFP as written. Assume you can negotiate away aspects of the project that would unreasonably eliminate your ability to earn a profit.

2.   Respond to the RFP and make clear those aspects of the project that would fall outside the scope of work and the proposed budget.

3.   Respond to the RFP with a cost proposal in line with the work to be accomplished. You worry that this may exclude you from any further consideration, but at least it is realistic.

4.   Decide not to respond to the RFP.

5.   Contact the elected officials who will be making the final decision about whom to hire based on the staff recommendation. Share your observation that the funding may not be adequate to perform all of the activities listed in the RFP. Suggest they increase the budget.

6.   Other.

Code Citations:

B.2   A planner must accept the decisions of a client or employer concerning the objectives and nature of the professional services to be performed unless the course of action to be pursued involves conduct that is illegal or inconsistent with the planner's primary obligation to the public interest.

B.8.   A planner must not accept or continue to perform work beyond the planner's professional competence or accept work which cannot be performed with the promptness required by the prospective client or employer, or which is required by the circumstances of the assignment.

Discussion:

The scenario is silent on the point of how the budget for the consultant study was established. To have a worthwhile debate about the issues, it is necessary to assume that the public-sector planner carefully consulted colleagues as well as publications made available through the American Planning Association on working effectively with consultants. The scenario was written so as to preclude the use of a request-for-qualifications process, although in real life that's a good choice. Instead, the scenario tried to focus on the sometimes amiable, but altogether awkward, relationship that can exist between public planning agencies and the consultants working for them. This "dance" requires the consultant to insist that the budget always is inadequate. And the public planner is often vague about the job requirements, hoping to derive guidance from the consultant RFP. Aggravating the relationship is the knowledge that in some states similar professionals, such as engineers and architects, are exempt from haggling because state legislation precludes selecting architects and engineers based solely on price. Often, planners are classified differently and so must compete based on price as well as other considerations. The vagaries of the public purchasing system leave consultants playing games regarding true costs and price.

Language in the code regarding accepting the decisions of the employer precludes simply ignoring the requirements of the RFP and viewing it as a jumping off point.

Alternative 1, attempt to negotiate your troubles away, is the least desirable because it does nothing to improve the situation. Alternatives 2 and 3 both are appropriate. They differ only in how you handle what you believe to be inadequate funding. Not responding at all, alternative 4, is a personal decision. Alternative 5 is lobbying and it distorts the intent of the consultant selection process.

WHAT'S THE DIFFERENCE BETWEEN EXACTIONS AND EXTORTION?

You are the long-time planning director of a community in a southern coastal state where a large new development has been proposed. The mixture of land uses contemplated for the project requires that the developer secure approval as a conditional use. The city council will make the final decision after receiving comments from the planning commission.

Considering your staff analysis, it is obvious that the proposed project is too large for the site, but not entirely inconsistent with the adopted plan. The applicant is politically well connected, and you believe there is better than a fifty-fifty chance of approval by the city council. You also know that the planning commission is **not** likely to approve the project. In anticipation of this course of events, the commission will phrase its report carefully. The commission probably will suggest that the council, if it approves the project, attach a number of conditions. As the director, you believe that the developer is likely to accept the conditions to secure project approval. You ask your staff members to come up with a "wish list" of exactions (the term for conditions in your municipal code) that might be imposed as part of the conditional use approval. A staff planner objects to the assignment and says it looks like a case of kidnapping and ransom. "Just because he will agree to a lot of conditions doesn't mean that we should ask for them," says the planner. "I'm not going to be a part of any of this!" What should you do as the planning director?

Ethical Issues:

There are two issues of ethical concern in this scenario: (1) How do you manage dissent and disagreement within the office? (2) Is it ethical to attempt to "make lemonade from lemons" by securing the maximum public benefits to help mitigate an otherwise undesirable project. If you determine that the answer to the second question is "no," then you are guilty of asking your staff to behave unethically. There are two sets of action alternatives proposed below. The first set focuses on how to ethically respond to disagreement from staff members regarding the nature of work to be carried out. The second set of alternatives deals with whether the staff activity is ethical. To resolve the dilemma, responses will be needed to both issues.

Action Alternatives for Dissent and Disagreement:

1.   Meet privately with the staff planner. Explore the planner's concerns. Ask the planner to describe her actions in light of the code requirements. Express no opinion about whether you found her conduct to be acceptable.

2.   Orally counsel the employee. Emphasize your role as the supervisor who makes work assignments. Stress that you are ultimately accountable for the final staff report and that it will be you who defends it in public.

3.   Prepare a written warning for the employee and place a copy in the personnel file. The warning should address the employee's responsibility to carry out assigned work in a timely manner.

4.   Let the planner opt out of participation in the general activity as long as you get good ideas from other people. You value cordial working relations above administrative efficiency. It is not worth a battle.

5.   Other.

ACTION ALTERNATIVES FOR DEFINING THE EXACTIONS LEADING TO APPROVAL:

1.   These ideas should be based on a review of all plans and ordinances that might relate to the property. The public benefit can be more fully developed through a list of conditions that may bring the project into greater plan conformance.

2.   Unless the proposal is largely consistent with the adopted plan, the staff should recommend against the project and not in any way imply

that it can be made acceptable through a series of concessions. Writing a list of conditions implies that a plan can "purchase" consistency.

   3.   Other.

Code Citations:

   A.   A planner's primary obligation is to serve the public interest. While the definition of the public interest is constantly evolving, a planner owes allegiance to a conscientiously attained concept of the public interest, which requires special obligations.

   A.1   A planner must have special concern for the long-range consequences of present actions.

   B.   A planner owes diligent, creative, independent and competent performance of work in pursuit of the client's or employer's interest. Such performance should be consistent with the planner's faithful service to the public interest.

   B.1   A planner must exercise independent professional judgment on behalf of clients and employers.

   B.2   A planner must accept the decisions of a client or employer concerning the objectives and nature of the professional services to be performed unless the course of action to be pursued involves conduct that is illegal or inconsistent with the planner's primary obligation to the public interest.

   C.   A planner should contribute to the development of the profession by improving knowledge and techniques, making work relevant to solutions of community problems, and increasing public understanding of planning activities. A planner should treat fairly the professional views of qualified colleagues and members of other professions.

   C.3   A planner who reviews the work of other professionals must do so in a fair, considerate, professional, and equitable manner.

Discussion:

There are two different issues at play in this scenario. The first has to do with dissent among planning staff members. The second attempts to distinguish between two competing visions of the planner's role when reviewing development proposals. With respect to the second issue, planning law experts steadfastly maintain that contract zoning is illegal. Nonetheless, many of these same legal experts also have helped craft ordinances by which a marginally acceptable project can increase its likelihood of being approved if accompanied by a number of public benefits.

The first issue, dissent and disagreement in the planning office, calls to mind different elements of the code. Section B.2 states that a planner must accept the decisions of the employer concerning the objectives and nature of the professional services. The next section of the code also requires that a planner who reviews the work of others do so in a fair, considerate, professional, and equitable manner.

While each supervisor needs to create a process for accommodating dissent within the office, the supervisor also needs to make sure that the ongoing work of the office is not sidetracked. Therefore, in this scenario, the director should receive full information from the staff about what alternatives might exist. Generating those ideas does not imply an automatic commitment to use them as possible trade-offs with the developer. Even a proposal that is only somewhat consistent with the requirements of the plan may work to the benefit of a community.

Alternative 1, under dissent and disagreement, probably best meets the intent of the code. With alternative 1 you discuss the situation and the ethics with your employee. In such a setting you hear the employee's arguments, treating her views fairly. Keep in mind that both the director and the employee can find citations in the code to support their different perspectives. Ultimately, however, the code of ethics supports your right to request staff input by requiring employees to accept decisions by their employer.

Alternative 1 under defining exactions, is the most realistic. The exactions associated with such an approval should be in accordance with plans and ordinances. Certainly those specifically noted in an ordinance are most defensible. Usually, some legal guidance (or case law) can establish boundaries for the negotiations. Also, you know that the developer himself has opened the door to these negotiations suggesting that he would like to hear your ideas. You are not holding the project hostage by identifying other potential forms of public benefit. Ethically, one's primary duty is to serve the public interest.

Alternative 2, under exactions, is not unethical. But choosing this course of action allows you little impact on a development that is likely to occur anyway.

WHEN THE RULES OF THE GAME SEEM TO CHANGE

You are a professional consulting planner working for a small firm located in a large Pacific Northwest state. You have no particular expertise in transportation matters, but you are a well-versed generalist. The mayor appointed you to serve as a citizen representative to a Special Commission on Rail Selection (SCRS). The SCRS is evaluating competing bids to build a new light rail transportation system. Most of the appointees to the SCRS are well known because of their long-term involvement with both civic affairs and the political career of the mayor.

Three months have passed. The SCRS has met numerous times using the already-published bid document as a basis for its work. The SCRS prepared a detailed ranking scheme with more than forty-five factors for evaluating the bids. Based on the form, Firm A, a USA-based company, scored highest on two of the three most significant criteria: domestic content and local content. Firm B, a Japanese company, had the highest score on the third of the most significant criteria: technical competence.

When the SCRS met last week, the representative from the mayor's office (a voting member of the SCRS) proposed that greater weight be placed on technical competence. He explained that because the project will cost more than $1 billion, technical competence should be the most critical factor. Although there was discussion of the new proposal, no action was taken.

During the meeting you were in a quandary. The assertion seemed reasonable, but you were uncomfortable with changing the evaluation scheme after-the-fact. You also wondered about the influence of one of the mayor's close friends who is the former governor and the top lobbyist for the Japanese firm.

Today is the final meeting of the SCRS. The mayor's representative offers a more dramatic change to the scheme. The costs, he suggests, are to be compared not in terms of the total price, but on the dollars per point. This makes the more expensive Japanese bid seem like the lowest bid because it scored more points overall, though not on the most significant criteria. A lively debate ensues. Proponents of "Buy America" stress the need to secure more jobs for Americans through the purchase of equipment, rail cars, etc. produced in the United States. Others argue that subsidizing Americans while they learn the business of building rail cars is likely to be too expensive in the long run. "If you are spending the taxpayer's money, you need to make sure that the job is done right the first time," says another member of the SCRS. While you can understand the merits of the arguments on both sides, you consider this to be the wrong time in the process to be establishing new ranking criteria and you make this comment to the group. You are outvoted 7 to 6.

Ethical Issues:

When a process has been established for making a planning decision, and that process was developed in a public manner and published as the decision-making process, can it be changed with the effect of altering the outcome of the decision and still be ethical?

Action Alternatives:

1.   Contact the mayor and urge that another meeting be called to reconsider the matter. Explain that you believe the changes to the evaluation criteria will result in a final decision that lacks credibility.

2.   Do nothing. You recognize that in a democracy you sometimes come out on the losing side. You forcefully stated your arguments at the time the decision was made. No more can be expected.

3.   Telephone the editor of the major newspaper and suggest that a story be written about the details of the evaluation process. Offer to provide copies of documents and notes from meetings.

4.   Decide to contact a planner with greater expertise in the evaluation of bids for constructing rail systems and see if an objective outsider finds the mayor's scheme to be defensible, even if you personally dislike it.

5.   Resign from the SCRS. Do so in a public setting stating your reasons. You do this with the understanding that you will have few friends in the mayor's office, but you believe that you will have retained your integrity.

6.   Talk to the mayor's opposition on the city council. Encourage them to fight the SCRS's recommendation. Try to use your position to influence them to support the original public process in the interest of good government.

7.   Other.

Code Citations:

A.   A planner's primary obligation is to serve the public interest. While the definition of the public interest is formulated through continuous debate, a planner owes allegiance to a conscientiously attained concept of the public interest, which requires special obligations.

A.1   A planner must have special concern for the long-range consequences of present actions.

A.3   A planner must strive to provide full, clear, and accurate information on planning issues to citizens and governmental decision-makers.

B.2 A planner must accept the decisions of a client or employer concerning the objectives and nature of the professional services to be performed unless the course of action to be pursued involves conduct that is illegal or inconsistent with the planner's primary obligation to the public interest.

D. A planner should strive for high standards of professional integrity, proficiency, and knowledge.

D.5 A planner must systematically and critically analyze ethical issues in the practice of planning.

Advisory Ruling:

4. "Honesty in the Use of Information" (see appendix for full text). As professional givers of advice — advice that may affect the well being of communities and individuals for many years — we have a special obligation to cherish honesty in the use of information that supports our advice…. Yet many daily pressures do battled against honesty. We are pressed to be effective advocates for… an elected administration or a cause…. It is part of professional conduct to communicate our ethical standards to clients, employers, and the public.

Discussion:

Contacting the mayor, alternative 1, is not likely to solve the ethical dilemma. It is, however, a reasonable step to take in trying to address the questionable decision made by the SCRS. In this arena, you can fulfill your ethical responsibility to advise others on the standards of the profession. Will the mayor be persuaded? Maybe not, but it is a good first (but not final) effort because it tacks with the requirement of the code that your conduct reflect high standards of integrity.

This scenario goes beyond what happens when you lose an argument. It clearly suggests that the planner suspects that ethically inappropriate influence was used. Therefore, the planner should investigate and give further serious consideration to his or her responsibilities. Examine the work accomplished to date with a fresh perspective. If you find that the process is good overall, the results are likely to be good. Maybe the infraction was minor — merely an adjustment to the process. If these are your conclusions, then alternative 2 would be appropriate. It should be noted that the scenario was crafted to strongly suggest that it would be difficult to come to this conclusion; nonetheless it is valid to go through the exercise before settling upon another course of action.

Alternative 3, contacting the media, can be useful when different people have different opinions. Further investigation by others, like the media, could be helpful. One step on the checklist for ethical decision-making is to consider the test of publicity. Perhaps, the additional public scrutiny will help illuminate the existence of problems. Alternative 3 could have merit provided that the information you reveal is already a matter of public record. You also should be aware that the mayor and your fellow SCRS members will not like seeing another commissioner undermine the process by going to the media. Be certain you are ready to live with the consequences.

Alternative 4, which poses little risk, would be an appropriate intermediate step for any planner who wants to test whether issues do represent an ethical problem. However, once the transportation planner provides an opinion, you are left with the question, "Do I do anything further?"

Alternative 5, the public resignation, would be most appropriate after other actions have been taken and you remain convinced that the process has been tainted by improper political influence.

Alternative 6, lobbying other members of the city council, is troublesome in that you are seeking out people already known to oppose the mayor personally, instead of providing information to all of the members of the council. This alternative fails the test of providing full, clear and accurate information. It would not be acceptable.

Background:

Many planners who favor the professional role of technical advisor would agree that without further negative evidence, the material presented in this scenario does not represent a major ethical dilemma. The planner tried to act ethically and was thwarted. Only planners who see their role in a more holistic manner — as helping to define the agenda and the process of decision-making, and then testing the results of the decision against goals of social justice and equity — might take action consistent with alternatives 3 or 5.

USING THE PLANNING PROCESS TO STOP AN UNPOPULAR LAND USE

You are the planning director in a rural county. Your citizens are outraged over a proposed locally unwanted land use. A large national corporation wants to expand an existing landfill, which serves your county and several others. The landfill is a permissible use under the current plan and zoning regulations. You are ordered by the county manager to stop the project, at least for the next six months, until the next election is over. What should you do?

Ethical Issue:

How should you respond to requests to use the planning process to delay a politically controversial or unacceptable land use to advance the political interests of the elected officials whom you serve?

Action Alternatives:

1.   Review with extraordinary care those applications that the waste company must secure. You know that if you look long and hard at any application, you can always find some reason to recommend a delay or denial of the necessary permits.

2.   Draft appropriate ordinances to restrict the uses. Work with the county manager to implement an immediate emergency moratorium allowing for adequate time to discuss and adopt planning and zoning changes that would preclude substantial expansion of the landfill at that site.

3.   Recognize that this is purely a political matter and not a planning issue. Send the waste management company officials to the county manager's office. The manager can discuss and describe the current situation and the local concerns in whatever manner both meets his needs and those of the elected officials. You won't risk the credibility of the planning process in all of this.

4.   Research state laws and requirements. Carefully identify how parties can intervene to delay approval by the county and the state permitting authority.

5.   Other.

Code Citations:

A.3   A planner must strive to provide full, clear, and accurate information on planning issues to citizens and governmental decision-makers.

B.   A planner owes diligent, creative, independent and competent performance of work in pursuit of the client's or employer's interest. Such performance should be consistent with the planner's faithful service to the public interest.

B.1   A planner must exercise independent professional judgment on behalf of clients and employers.

B.2   A planner must accept the decisions of a client or employer concerning the objectives and nature of the professional services to be performed unless the course of action to be pursued involves conduct that is illegal or inconsistent with the planner's primary obligation to the public interest.

C.1   A planner must protect and enhance the integrity of the profession.... .

Discussion:

Your county manager has directed you to solve this problem. The manager assumes that you can be a creative team member and figure out how to stop these land uses. For a results-oriented manager, the ends could easily justify a variety of means. While a planner also would want to be helpful and responsive, the requirements of the laws and the canons of the code place some constraints on what can be accomplished. For the record, it doesn't sound as if the manager has a very good sense of the purpose of planning or respect for the process. He just wants the problem to temporarily disappear. At the same time, you have a responsibility to enhance the integrity of the profession.

Alternatives 1, finding administrative cover, and 2, issuing a moratorium, are unacceptable if the application already has been filed. It would be illegal, and you could end up being sued as well as jeopardizing the integrity of the planning process. Alternative 3, referring the applicant to the county manager, is appealing and might work depending on the temperament of the county manager. Keep in mind, however, that you may have been given this assignment specifically because the manager wanted it off his desk. Also, this is not a long-range solution. It does little more than buy you some time.

Despite what the county manager may wish, or may direct you to do, you have few options in terms of what you can do. If you find the facility is permissible and consistent with environmental constraints, you have a responsibility to so advise the manager and to sign any permits/approvals required by your office. This would not preclude your implementing alternative 4, which is consistent with your obligation to provide complete information. You can do the research and identify for the county manager what the options are for the community at this point.

Bernie Dworski, APA Legal Counsel, provided assistance in drafting this scenario.

IS SOMETHING SERIOUS REALLY GOING ON?

You and an old friend are having dinner. Your friend is currently the director of environmental management in Kelso County, Florida. He supervised the completion of a multi-million dollar comprehensive watershed master plan. The study recommended stringent impervious cover limitations for each watershed. One effect of the plan was to make land in the watersheds with a 50 percent impervious cover limitation valuable. Land with a lower impervious cover standard became virtually unbuildable. In the meantime, the county has embarked on the construction of a variety of storm water detention facilities to further address water quality concerns in developed areas. The study rejected all non-structural techniques such as berms, levees, and swales, in favor of concrete tunnels and streams. A citywide drainage fee that appears on residential utility bills has financed construction.

Over a second bottle of wine, your friend mutters about how the consultant selection process is dominated by political contributions. You nod sympathetically. You have seen, on more than one occasion, how the number four or five ranked firm mysteriously rises to the top.

Only later, after you return to your office, do you give your colleague's remarks further consideration. You had assumed that he was referring to the contracting process. But what if he was alluding to something even more sinister? What if the science in the watershed master plans had been skewed by political concerns? Massive amounts of money are being made and lost by land speculators and developers as a result of the study's recommendations. You are profoundly troubled and wonder if you have a duty to report? Report what? To whom? Do you first have a responsibility to contact your colleague and confirm your understanding? If he is corrupt, your giving notice will only make it easier for him to continue to cover his tracks. If he isn't, then he and his organization can surely withstand a little scrutiny.

Ethical Issues:

If you believe that there may have been corrupt activity by a planner, should you follow-up? Is it possible to follow up without appearing overly inquisitive and failing to respect the confidence of a friend? If you believe the science or the planning has been subverted for illegal purposes, to whom would you make such an accusation? Would such an accusation have any impact if the system is corrupt?

Action Alternatives:

1. Do nothing. The report was completed several years ago. Surely if something were amiss, someone else would have raised the issues by now.

2. Give a copy of the report to a friend who is an environmental engineer. Without describing your concerns, ask the engineer to review the scientific integrity of the assumptions, the analysis, and the conclusions.

3. Call your friend and explain in general terms the questions raised over your last meal together and seek clarification.

4. Other.

Code Citations:

A.3 A planner must strive to provide full, clear, and accurate information on planning issues to citizens and governmental decision-makers.

A.6 A planner must strive to protect the integrity of the natural environment.

C.1 A planner must protect and enhance the integrity of the profession and must be responsible in criticism of the profession.

D.1 A planner must not commit a deliberately wrongful act which reflects adversely on the planner's professional fitness.

D.4 A planner must accurately represent professional qualifications, education, and affiliations.

Advisory Rulings:

4. "Honesty in the Use of Information," (see appendix for full text). As professional givers of advice — advice that may affect the well-being of communities and individuals for many years — we have a special obligation to cherish honesty in the use of information that supports our advice. Yet many daily pressures do battled against honesty. We are pressed to be effective advocates for... an elected administration or a cause. It is part of professional conduct to communicate our ethical standards to clients, employers, and the public.

5. A planner who knows of unethical conduct must report it. (See appendix for full text.)

6. "Illegal conduct should be reported, even if it means revealing confidential information." (See appendix for full text.)

Discussion:

This is a distressing circumstance and a true test of character. Do you do the right thing even when no one is watching?

As a seasoned professional, you have learned to rely on your instincts. You should not ignore them here. You sense that something wrong may have occurred. Your alternatives certainly are not very challenging. Alternative 1, do nothing, is the least appropriate. First, it implies that ethical obligations fade over time. Secondly, it suggests that responsibilities can be avoided by assuming someone else will take care of the issue.

Alternatives 2 and 3, pursuing additional information, are reasonable and in no way threaten your friend. Rulings 5 and 6 preclude ignoring the circumstances.

The scenario does not deal with the more challenging issue of how you would proceed if your informal inquiries indicated evidence of corruption.

PLANNER SPIES ENDANGERED SPECIES

You are a former fire fighter. Several years ago you returned to graduate school, earned a degree in planning and, since then, have been working as a land-planning consultant. An individual seeking to build a single-family home on a five-acre lot with steep slopes and a pond has retained your services. The local planning board was concerned as to whether the access proposed by the applicant would provide adequate fire-fighting capability. After studying the site plan and a field inspection, you determined that it would.

While on the property, however, you noted what you believe to be a blue heron rising from the applicant's pond. In your state, the heron is a threatened species. The state law requires a 150-foot setback from any pond used as a feeding or nesting area for a threatened species. The current site plan only calls for a 50-foot setback. Because of your familiarity with the site constraints, you believe that if the applicant were to provide a 150-foot setback, he would not be able to build on the lot at all. You discuss your bird sighting with a colleague who points out that you are not an ornithologist; it might have been another species. Also, you did not actually see the bird take off. You assumed that it was in the pond because it was flying so low. It might just have been passing through. You realize that you would not be a very credible witness if you were called to testify in a court of law. But that is not the point. Using a test of reasonableness, you are pretty sure that it was a blue heron and that it probably did take off from the pond. You worry that, at the least, you will be regarded as a troublemaker and that your firm might lose this client. You also wonder if perhaps the property owner already knew of the bird's presence and was just hoping that no one else would find out. What is the most ethical course of action?

Ethical Issues:

Should you report on information inadvertently gathered? What do you do when the effect of reporting the information may be to preclude a landowner from using his property in the way he wants?

Action Alternatives:

1.   Advise the property owner of your findings and indicate that, after further investigation, the site plan will probably have to be revised.

2.   Discuss this matter with your supervisor and seek advice. Find out if the firm has an established policy on what you should do.

3.   A single sighting of a single bird does not really establish the presence of a species. You were hired for your expertise in fire suppression, not bird sighting. You are required to do nothing.

4.   Contact the local planning officials and advise them of your conclusions. Allow them to use (or not use) the information as they see fit.

5.   Other.

Code Citations:

A.   A planner's primary obligation is to serve the public interest. While the definition of the public interest is constantly evolving, a planner owes allegiance to a conscientiously attained concept of the public interest, which requires special obligations.

A.1   A planner must have special concern for the long-range consequences of present actions.

A.3   A planner must strive to provide full, clear, and accurate information on planning issues to citizens and governmental decision-makers.

A.6   A planner must strive to protect the integrity of the natural environment.

Advisory Ruling:

4.   "Honesty in the Use of Information" (see appendix for full text). As professional givers of advice — advice that may affect the well being of communities and individuals for many years — we have a special obligation to cherish honesty in the use of information that supports our

advice.... Yet many daily pressures do battle against honesty. We are pressed to be effective advocates for... an elected administration or a cause.... It is part of professional conduct to communicate our ethical standards to clients, employers, and the public.

Discussion:

In considering what the planner might do in this scenario, discussions might start with "What is the planner legally required to do?" If the law requires one to report a sighting, then there is no question about the appropriate next steps. In this case the law calls for the protection of the species and the habitat. The scenario deals with the matter not in terms of the minimum we are legally required to do but, rather, what would constitute ethical behavior?

Alternative 1 would be the most desirable alternative, both legally and ethically. You were on the property at the owner's request and you are obliged to tell him what you found. If possible, you could offer to redesign the site at little or no charge. By allowing the property to be developed without the necessary setback, you are ignoring your responsibility to uphold the public interest as defined in legislation protecting endangered species. In a sense, you become an accomplice.

While seeking advice from a supervisor is an acceptable first step, it would not constitute a sufficient course of action in and of itself. What if the supervisor was to suggest that the relevant data be suppressed? Further, failing to advise the client properly could backfire if the data were subsequently revealed through another source. The client would be justified in feeling that he had not been well represented by the firm.

To do nothing fails both the legal and ethical tests. It also jeopardizes the reputation of the firm by not providing complete information that is relevant to the client's needs.

Advising the planning department on the side, alternative 4, is equivalent to blind-siding the client. The property owner is paying the consulting firm to bring him accurate information so that he can develop his property legally.

In using this scenario in training sessions, other creative alternatives have been mentioned including:

1.   The planner could seek out a knowledgeable individual from the Audubon Society who might be able to establish a more reliable database about the presence of herons in the area.

2.   The property owner could volunteer to have a reputable biologist study the bird population in the area and establish the suitability of the pond as habitat.

Neither of these alternatives, however, are superior to alternative 1, telling the landowner what you have found.

ARE WETLANDS AN ETHICAL ISSUE?

You are the chairperson of the APA Environmental Division. A member of AICP appears before the division at its annual business meeting and asks the division to support proposed federal changes to the definition of wetlands. The revised definition would, among other things, reduce the amount of land classified as wetlands. The planner argues that protecting wetlands to the exclusion of all other factors does not meet the ethical requirements to pay special attention to the inter-relatedness of decisions. The planner provides examples of proposals to develop low-income housing that have been rejected because of their impact on wetlands. He asks that you take this action in advance of the upcoming APA Delegates Assembly on Wetlands Preservation hoping that your action will influence all of the chapter delegates. What should you do?

Ethical Issue:

Should the need to protect the environment take precedence over other ethical obligations of the AICP code?

Action Alternatives:

1.   You explain to the planner that the procedure for formulating national APA policy on wetlands does not rest with solely with the division. You encourage the individual to press her/his case through the Chapter Delegate Assembly.

2.   You agree that the legislation would, at least occasionally, help support low-income housing and you consider low-income housing more important than the "marginal" wetlands that might be lost. You encourage the division to support the legislation.

3.   You take seriously the request and attempt to derive specific guidance from the ethics statement. A full reading of the language supports balancing competing interests. Therefore you cannot personally conclude that low-income housing is always preferable to wetlands preservation.

4.   You think that the question is an interesting one. You support a motion to place this item on the agenda for action by the division officers at their next meeting.

5.   Other.

Code Citations:

A.2   A planner must pay special attention to the inter-relatedness of decisions.

A.5   A planner must strive to expand choice and opportunity for all persons, recognizing a special responsibility to plan for the needs of disadvantaged groups and persons, and must urge the alteration of policies, institutions, and decisions that oppose such needs.

A.6   A planner must strive to protect the integrity of the natural environment.

Discussion:

There are competing viewpoints that need to be resolved using an appropriate planning process. There is substantive competition between environmental goals and low-income housing goals. Should they be resolved at the national level or at the local level? Should APA take a position that would influence the national direction? Does the code favor one side over the other? Does it suggest one decision-making level as more appropriate than another?

The presence of the pertinent language addressing the protection of the environment and the needs of the disadvantaged encourages one to conclude that both issues are important. Where the code implies equal importance to competing objectives, the resolution to the conflict should come in the context of the planning process at the local level.

Because the specific proposal in the scenario is to comment on the federal legislation, you must have a basis for the analysis. This could be developed by assessing the impact of the legislation on the ability of the local planning process to address and resolve the issues. The legislation, as proposed, seems to suggest that a revised definition of wetlands would permit local governments to use a planning process to determine a future land use for area currently restricted from development consideration by definition. In theory, the local government would not be precluded from identifying these areas as environmentally sensitive anyway. For this reason, the division could make a case for supporting the change to the legislation as most consistent with the content of the code. While one cannot guarantee that additional low-income housing would result, it might.

Alternative 1 is an accurate statement, but does not fully respond to the request. Alternative 2, supporting the potential for low-income housing at the cost of wetlands, is not precluded. Alternative 3 merely gets you started; it does not lead you to a final decision.

It should be noted, however, that the basis of this scenario is a "real life" situation that was not resolved in the manner suggested above. At an APA Chapter Delegates Assembly, planners overwhelmingly voted to support stringent federal definitions of wetlands. Many commented that local elected officials were not likely to withstand the political pressure to develop these areas if the definition were to change. Few planners thought the development would result in low-income housing. Planners have consistently supported stronger, tougher federal laws to the exclusion of local autonomy or the local planning process. If the environment were seen as the beneficiary, the determination by planners to oppose the change in legislation would not be unethical. It would merely emphasize the federal decision-making process over the local one for this issue.

Alternative 4 is merely a way of avoiding the issue. However, it is not unethical.

In conclusion, the code encourages planners to look more deeply into many issues like this and it requires them to weigh the potential impact of alternative solutions carefully to select the most ethical.

DOES HISTORIC PRESERVATION OVERRULE RELIGIOUS RIGHTS?

As a planner in a large, Eastern seaboard city, you provide staff support to the historic preservation board. The city has a local ordinance and landmark designation program for significant prehistoric and historic sites. St. Meade's Church will be nominated as a landmark site at the historic preservation board meeting in two months. The church recently was researched and evaluated as part of an inventory of downtown historic architecture. While the church was notified according to the ordinance and state enabling legislation, the church's approval of the designation is not required.

Yesterday, a church official met with you to discuss problems resulting from the church's previous designation as "a significant heritage resource" under the ordinance. She explains that the church cannot afford to remove, restore, and replace the aging stained glass windows. Heating bills are expensive because of the cracked windows so the church wants to replace the stained glass with more energy-efficient and modern windows. To accomplish this, the church would like to be exempted from the ordinance's requirements to maintain the historic appearance of the church. If the exemption is not granted, she says, "The city will be forcing the church to abandon its inner-city ministry to the poor and homeless in order to fund building maintenance. The church believes it is called to serve. Buildings are only a means to that end." She gives you copies of past church budgets and a five-year financial plan. These documents provide clear evidence of financial strain and substantiate a significant resource commitment to the ministry of service. What should you do?

Ethical Issues:

If a planning program is being carried out as it was intended, yet causing hardship to a church that believes that government ought not to mandate how religious institutions spend money, is it ethical to bend the rules of the planning program? Should the needs of the disadvantaged take precedence over a desire to maintain a uniform community appearance?

Action Alternatives:

1.   You think that St. Meade's might qualify for the hardship exemption in the ordinance. The exemption hasn't been granted often, but it would seem to pertain here. You personally are moved by the church official's plea and agree to assist the official in reviewing city files so that an effective case can be built.

2.   Although you express great personal sympathy for the inquirer, the law should not, in your opinion, be waived just because a property owner is reluctant or even unable to spend the money necessary to comply. You tell the applicant that you believe the problem is not the ordinance, but the church's failure to have properly maintained the windows over time. You point out the repaired windows will generate energy savings which, over time, can help pay, for the cost of the repairs.

3.   It occurs to you that with some diligent research, you can make the case that St. Meade's is not as significant as the architectural survey stated. You believe that it may be possible to squash the designation. Due to the presence of other churches in the area, you believe that the windows are not particularly unique. You start your research immediately.

4.   You promise to request a delay in the designation so that the city can consider other options and programs that address the situation. You know that in some communities churches have been able to transfer

development rights to finance improvements. You suggest that the church work with you and the historic preservation board to pursue this option. In the meantime, the church must not change the windows and should plan to at least stabilize them so that there is no further deterioration.

    5.   Other.

Code Citations:

    A.1   A planner must have special concern for the long-range consequences of present actions.

    A.2   A planner must pay special attention to the inter-relatedness of decisions.

    A.3   A planner must strive to provide full, clear, and accurate information on planning issues to citizens and governmental decision-makers.

    A.7   A planner must strive for excellence of environmental design and endeavor to conserve the heritage of the built environment.

    B.1   A planner must exercise independent professional judgment on behalf of clients and employers.

    B.2   A planner must accept the decisions of a client or employer concerning the objectives and nature of the professional services to be performed unless the course of action to be pursued involves conduct that is illegal or inconsistent with the planner's primary obligation to the public interest.

Discussion:

The courts have addressed this issue and past rulings have favored the enforcement of historic preservation ordinances. Therefore, the designation of St. Meade's Church as a preservation landmark is not considered a violation of religious rights, even though it places a significant financial burden on the congregation. This is not a pleasant circumstance as planners are charged with the responsibility of considering the inter-relatedness of their decisions. If historic preservation programs were more comprehensive, perhaps the scenario would never arise. A planner in Florida offered a similar comment.

Many of our historic preservation programs are narrowly focused and fail to deal adequately with critical legal and economic issues... Very often it is easier for most communities to enact a law than devise a financial incentive program to accomplish preservation goals that conform with operative forces of land economics.... Ethical concerns for... planners should go beyond the fundamental issues of morality and also incorporate how well we do our job when devising policies and regulations to govern development of our client communities.

> Benjamin Withers, AICP
> Tampa, Florida

Alternative 1 would allow for the designation to proceed but ultimately sabotages the purpose of the designation, which is to maintain the historic and architectural character of the building. You cannot participate in programs that serve the public interest while simultaneously working to undermine them. However, if the hardship exemption exists, it is worthwhile understanding why it was created and its relevance to the current circumstances.

A planner is not precluded from assisting an applicant in seeking a waiver from the ordinance if such an option is part of the planning process. However, some agencies may view such assistance as undermining the intent of the ordinance, which is, after all, to secure compliance. In such an instance, the code's call for clear and complete information should override claims of loyalty to the intent of an ordinance, even if that means remaining silent about provisions of the ordinance.

> Just as planners should advocate for the "needs of disadvantaged groups and persons," it should not be discouraged for planners to promote the interests of these "disadvantaged" historic, non-renewable resources. The strength of citizen historic preservation and design review boards is the ability to brainstorm and draw from the various professional and law members' experience and expertise to arrive at innovative solutions.

> The guidance of a motivated, knowledgeable, professional planner advocating for the interests of the cultural resource while upholding the current policies of the local government is an invaluable component of the planning process, and one which should be utilized to its fullest extent.

> Robert J. Joiner, AICP
> Carson City, Nevada

If one is inclined to follow alternative 2, perhaps it can be made more palatable by offering assistance in finding appropriate contractors and favorable financing. Time spent in providing such help to the church or others is consistent with the code. However, in some agency settings, this type of activity may not be viewed with favor. The individual planner should check on these matters. If it is not the policy of the agency to provide such assistance, it would be appropriate for the planner to suggest such a change in the agency's process.

Alternative 3 is the only unacceptable course of action. Your responsibility as the designated staff person supporting the work of the historic preservation board, makes it unethical for you to actively seek to undercut the architectural survey, which underpins the implementation of the ordinance.

Alternative 4 has appeal for planners, and may work in some communities. Ethically speaking, however, one should be careful not to develop false or unrealistic hopes that some new technique used elsewhere can solve a problem. The planner should mention this alternative only if she believes there to be some realistic opportunity to implement it. Time may be better spent on other alternatives.

Note: The landscape is changing with new state and federal laws prescribing freedom to practice religion. New case law will emerge.

DISCLOSING YOUR EMPLOYER

You are a consulting planner engaged by an attorney. The attorney explains that although the client is K-Mart, you are under strict instructions not to divulge this information. Your assignment is to ensure that every aspect of the City of Gillette's development review process is conducted thoroughly, and that all potentially relevant facts are unearthed and carefully considered before city officials vote on a site plan for a new Target. The intention of your K-Mart employer is to delay final action on the Target application. The Target store is, coincidentally, proposed for a site near the K-Mart. You agree to the conditions and accept the assignment.

In pouring over the requirements of the local development regulations as well as state law, you are able to identify numerous opportunities to recommend, in public hearings, that actions to approve the development plan be deferred. One time you suggest the item be referred to the city's Environmental Board to consider whether the applicant must include a rainwater harvesting system on the roof. Another time you recommend that information be sought from the State Historic Commission regarding the presence of earlier settlements on the site. The previous existence of such settlements would trigger a requirement for an archeological examination, etc. Finally, at some point during a third public hearing, you suggest, on behalf of gardeners everywhere, that staff request another delay to examine the likelihood that the plants proposed in the landscaping plan would survive a winter frost. Frosts have occurred at least once every ten years and would leave the site completely denuded if one were to occur within the first two years, before the plantings are firmly established. After your comments, a planning commissioner demands to know what is motivating you. You decline to answer the question citing your right to participate as a member of the public.

The next day, you receive a phone call from the Gillette planning director who quotes the old saw, "Where you stand depends on where you sit." He thinks you ought to be more forthcoming. He asks you to write a letter to the chair of the planning commission providing the information requested. The director makes it clear to you that he understands you are working for a Target competitor and he doesn't appreciate having the planning process turned into a business delaying tactic. However, he doesn't intend to discuss his conclusion in public because there is a chance he may be wrong

Ethical Issues:

Is it ethical to refuse to divulge whom you represent when asked to do so in a public hearing? Is it ethical to accept a consulting engagement that is designed to delay or undermine the normal deliberative process?

Action Alternatives:

1.   Do nothing. You may choose to treat all matters that pass between you and a client as privileged communication.

2.   Answer fully and completely if you are asked again, in a public venue, whom you represent.

3.   Send a letter to the planning director, with a copy to the chair of the planning commission, informing him of the nature of your interest in the development plan.

4.   Form an association of concerned property owners in the community and declare yourself to be the representative of CORT — Citizens Organized to Remove Target. No one need know that only residents of

Gillette who also happen to be managers at K-Mart will be allowed to join.

5.　　Withdraw immediately from the engagement.

6.　　Other.

Code Citations:

A.　　A planner's primary obligation is to serve the public interest.

A.3　　A planner must strive to provide full, clear, and accurate information on planning issues to citizens and governmental decision-makers.

B.　　A planner owes diligent, creative, independent and competent performance of work in pursuit of the client's or employer's interest. Such performance should be consistent with the planner's faithful service to the public interest.

B.2　　A planner must accept the decisions of a client or employer concerning the objectives and nature of the professional services to be performed unless the course of action to be pursued involves conduct that is illegal or inconsistent with the planner's primary obligation to the public interest.

B.3　　A planner shall not perform work if there is an actual, apparent, or reasonably foreseeable conflict of interest, direct or indirect, or an appearance of impropriety, without full written disclosure concerning work for current or past clients and subsequent written consent by the current client or employer. A planner shall remove himself or herself from a project if there is any direct personal or financial gain including gains to family members. A planner shall not disclose information gained in the course of public activity for a private benefit unless the information would be offered impartially to any person.

B.9　　A planner must not reveal information gained in a professional relationship which the client or employer has requested be held inviolate. Exceptions to this requirement of non-disclosure may be made only when (a) required by process of law; (b) required to prevent a clear violation of law; or (c) required to prevent a substantial injury to the public. Disclosure pursuant to (b) and (c) must not be made until after the planner has verified the facts and issues involved and, when practicable, has exhausted efforts to obtain reconsideration of the matter and has sought separate opinions on the issue from the other qualified professionals employed by the client or employer.

C.1　　A planner must protect and enhance the integrity of the profession and must be responsible in criticism of the profession.

Discussion:

Public opposition to a variety of development interests is sometimes funded by corporations that may be motivated by business or other interests. Is it a problem? Neighborhood and environmental groups, generally under-funded, are grateful for the money and feel that the source of the funds is irrelevant. Sometimes the funding organization may itself be a non-profit group. For example, Mothers Against Drunk Drivers (MADD) has funded neighborhood organizations opposing liquor licenses for concert venues. When the funding connection is made public, MADD says it feels comfortable with an approach that tries to eliminate the number of places where teenagers are likely to drink too much and then drive. While not volunteering information about the source of funding, both the neighborhood groups and MADD have disclosed it upon request.

In this scenario, the competitor is seeking to increase the cost of entering a new marketplace. The strategy you are using is one of administrative intimidation — running down rabbit holes. While the administrative rabbit holes exist, they were established as components of a system that is supposed to serve the public interest. Undertaking such an engagement requires a legalistic point of view, not a planning perspective. You may have violated provision B.2 by accepting the engagement with the proviso that the client not be identified. You may have violated the code a second time if you further believed that, even with an identified client, the nature of the services were nevertheless not in the public interest. B.2 provides that work must be both legal and serve the public interest. Because ethical lapses already have occurred, the best course of action for you is to immediately withdraw from the engagement, alternative 5, and take any associated financial lumps.

You also failed a critical test when you declined to answer a direct question. This aspect of the planner's conduct is clearly inconsistent with the responsibility to provide accurate information and disclosure of personal interest. Because disclosing the confidential information does not work to your benefit, the prohibition against disclosure in the code does not pertain. The prohibition against revealing information gained in a professional relationship does not apply because the name of your employer hardly seems to be covered by the phrase "information gained" (although that point is probably debatable).

It is hard to see how you are serving the public interest. Clearly, a private interest is being served. An argument, although futile, could be made that the process is served by a thorough testing. But such testing is indirect, at best. You are close to distorting information to achieve a desired outcome. At the very least, you are subverting the process. Such an approach harms the public interest by instructing others that the process will not produce equitable outcomes but, instead, will operate like a court of law in which the outcome is often determined by who can afford the best attorney.

Doing nothing, alternative 1, fails to meet the standards of ethical conduct. Alternative 4 is unacceptable in terms of dissembling and abusing the process by creating a fake organization. Alternative 2, answering truthfully in the future, is fine and alternative 3, taking the initiative to disclose, is also acceptable. However, both 2 and 3 may subject you to a suit by the client for nonperformance. Therefore, alternative 5 is preferred.

Note: This issue of disclosure recently was addressed in a Notice of Censure published in the Winter/Spring 2000 issue of *Planners' Casebook*. In this instance, the notice stated:

> A planner is censured for her conduct in misrepresenting to the public the true client she was representing in presenting commentary relating to certain development projects. This is a case of first impression which deals with a planner's responsibility under the Code to balance the need to provide full public information with the need to respect a client's confidence. The planner violated the Code when the planner, as a planner in a private consulting firm, provided commentary on behalf of an assumed client to conceal the true identity of an actual client who asked to remain anonymous. The actual client had directed the planner to use the assumed identity.

> Notwithstanding the planner's adherence to Code Section B.9 which requires planners to hold their client's confidences inviolate, the Ethics Committee has nevertheless concluded that the above conduct violated Sections B., B.2, C.1, and D.1 of the AICP Code of Ethics and Professional Conduct. A planner's primary obligation is to serve the public interest. Misrepresentation of a planner's true client in a public forum violates that obligation and thereby violations Section A. of the Code. A planner must decline a proposed assignment from a client who wants the planner to deceive the public as to its true identity. The acceptance of such an assignment is a violation of Section B., and B.2 of the Code. Additionally, Section C.1 of the Code requires a planner to protect and enhance the integrity of the profession; and misrepresentation to the public as to the identity of one's client violates that mandate. Finally, Section D.1 of the Code, which requires a planner to refrain from deliberately wrongful conduct, is also violated when a planner engages in public misrepresentation concerning the identity of a client.

DAMSON PRESERVES

You are the principal of a small planning firm with offices in the town of Glitch, the last city before an Interstate exit to a national park. Your planning firm consults throughout the region and you have never done work for the town.

Near the interstate exit for Glitch, there are several large billboards advertising your good buddy's Burger King fast food restaurant. Joe Doyal's fast food emporium is located at the exit itself. This Burger King is Glitch's only fast food restaurant and also the last fast food stop before the national park. The Burger King is, by your estimation, a veritable cash cow for your friend Doyal. With no other vacant land served by local utilities, competition is non-existent. Doyal has shared this good fortune with the people of Glitch and has consistently supported every worthy cause, especially those involving young people.

Doyal had been one happy guy until an auto repair shop closed when the owner/operator died and his wife sold the property to a corporation that operates McDonald's franchises throughout the state. The newspaper story reporting the sale noted that the initial reaction of the local politicians and the public was that another fast food restaurant was highly desirable. Notwithstanding the need for a change in the base zoning, the location seems perfect.

When you read the newspaper over your morning coffee, your reaction is the same as others: a chance to grab a burger with a shorter wait. Not long after, the phone rings and Doyal asks if he can come by and commiserate with you. You then realize that at least one person is not happy with the news.

When Doyal arrives, he says he's been aware for some time that the vacant repair shop was a potential problem, but he had been outbid for it by a corporate entity that owned eight franchises elsewhere. As a trusted friend, Doyal now seeks your counsel. He's working on the details of a plan that will make it as difficult as possible for the new owners to secure the rezoning. He's made a list of all the professionals — engineers, attorneys, economists — who have what he deems to be the best political credentials. He asks for your political assessment.

Then, brightening, he reports that one line of thinking from the environmental engineer sounds very promising. The nature of materials and chemicals used in an automotive repair business are known to cause environmental problems, including serious soil contamination. It would be unsafe to allow children to play and eat in such circumstances.

He looks to you for confirmation and then describes his other strategy. This one he's already reviewed with one of your planners, Michelle Quinlan. Quinlan is ready to undertake the assignment, but not until you sign-off on the project. Your curiosity is obviously at a peak and you ask Doyal to explain what he has in mind. "Quinlan," he excitedly explains, "lives in Cluster Oaks. That subdivision is near the old auto repair site. You know how great she is at rabble rousing. She did a lot of community organizing before she went to work for you. Here's my brilliant plan. I'll hire your firm for general strategizing, but what I really want is Quinlan to organize massive opposition to the McDonald's. For this thing to work, though, no one can know that Quinlan, or your firm, is on my payroll. Quinlan says she can live with the arrangement if you can."

Doyal then passes you a packet of information from another Burger King franchisee who took a heavy hit when a corporate McDonald's came to his town. The photographs show McDonald's trash all over the neighborhood. There are even copies of police reports stating that the McDonald's, by extending hours of operation until 2:00 a.m., had become the hangout of choice for underage drinking and rowdy behavior, including fist fights. With this information, Doyal is convinced that Quinlan won't have any trouble scaring people into opposing the McDonald's.

Doyal even has a name for the opposition. Reminding you that his family just returned from a vacation at Knott's Berry Farm, he smiles as he says "Don't Allow McDonalds, Save Our Neighborhood, a.k.a., Damson Preserves." You smile uneasily and observe that the name is just a little too cute to garner credibility. Doyal acquiesces. "You and Michelle can call it whatever you like. But I've brought a check for you for $20,000 hoping that's enough of a retainer to get this show on the road." You wave off the check "for now" and say you need a day or two to think about the request. Doyal seems alarmed by your hesitation, and says: "Hey, pal, we're buddies. I can't believe you're going to let me down." You give Doyal a pat on the back as you walk him toward the door.

Ethical Issues:

Can you conceal your employer? Can you use arguments that will cause unreasonable fear to affect public opinion? How far can you go to help a friend who needs your expertise as a planner without compromising your ethics?

Action Alternatives:

1.   Tell Doyal that you'll be happy to advise him, although the fee seems excessive. Reduce the amount to $5,000 and set up a meeting with Quinlan to get things going.

2.   Explain that, as a friend, you can discuss strategy and, provided your firm doesn't need to be involved in any technical analysis, there won't be any charge. But there is a caveat. You'll be making your suggestions based on sound planning rationale. For example, the environmental arguments make no sense but concerns about increased traffic on residential streets might. Political advice is something you'll be happy to share.

3.   You agree to the assignment as proposed by Doyal with one caveat. Quinlan is able to keep things going without volunteering who is funding the effort, but if asked a direct question, she'll have to answer it truthfully.

4.   Other.

Code Citations:

A.   A planner's primary obligation is to serve the public interest.

A.3   A planner must strive to provide full, clear, and accurate information on planning issues to citizens and governmental decision-makers.

B.   A planner owes diligent, creative, independent and competent performance of work in pursuit of the client's or employer's interest. Such performance should be consistent with the planner's faithful service to the public interest.

B.2   A planner must accept the decisions of a client or employer concerning the objectives and nature of the professional services to be performed unless the course of action to be pursued involves conduct that is illegal or inconsistent with the planner's primary obligation to the public interest.

B.3   A planner shall not perform work if there is an actual, apparent, or reasonably foreseeable conflict of interest, direct or indirect, or an appearance of impropriety, without full written disclosure concerning work for current or past clients and subsequent written consent by the current client or employer. A planner shall remove himself or herself from a project if there is any direct personal or financial gain including gains to family members. A planner shall not disclose information gained in the course of public activity for a private benefit unless the information would be offered impartially to any person.

B.9   A planner must not reveal information gained in a professional relationship which the client or employer has requested be held inviolate. Exceptions to this requirement of non-disclosure may be made only when (a) required by process of law, or (b) required to prevent a clear violation of law; or (c) required to prevent a substantial injury to the public. Disclosure pursuant to (b) and (c) must not be made until after the planner has verified the facts and issues involved and, when practicable, has exhausted efforts to obtain reconsideration of the matter and has sought separate opinions on the issue from the other qualified professionals employed by the client or employer.

C.1   A planner must protect and enhance the integrity of the profession and must be responsible in criticism of the profession.

Discussion:

The initial question you must answer is one of balancing your friendship, which would urge you to assist you friend in any way a comrade thinks helpful, against your professional judgment, which may not support your friend's desires. Your instincts on this matter are sound. An on the spot decision to decline a check gives you time to evaluate alternatives and their likely consequences before accepting a new client.

To begin your ethical analysis, you quickly conclude that you are under no moral obligation to undertake an activity simply because it is urged upon you by a friend. It is called peer pressure and you decided at the age of 12 not to allow yourself to be coerced into a buddy's scheme.

Doyal is not your only friend in Glitch and, as a planning consultant, you have pondered the city's future on many occasions. It is both your personal and professional belief that Doyal's expectations regarding the desirable and likely outcome are unrealistic. Finally, you are uncomfortable with the concept of any form of subterfuge for two reasons: it's a small enough community that secrets don't remain so for very long, and it is inconsistent with the planner's responsibility to enhance the integrity of the profession.

Other relevant AICP code considerations include providing full, clear and accurate information. A planner should avoid even the appearance of impropriety. Your knowledge that a professional planner was censured for keeping a similar matter confidential is also of relevance. In that case, the planner's censure was reported in *Planners' Casebook*. The following information was also provided:

A planner is censured for her conduct in misrepresenting to the public the true client she was representing in presenting commentary relating to certain development projects. This is a case of first impression which deals with a planner's responsibility under the Code to balance the need to provide full public information with the need to respect a client's confidence. The planner violated the Code when the planner, as a planner in a private consulting firm, provided commentary on behalf of an assumed client to conceal the true identity of an actual client who asked to remain anonymous. The actual client had directed the planner to use the assumed identity.

Having established this ethical framework, you evaluate the alternative courses of action and reject alternatives 1 and 3. Alternative 2, advising Doyal informally and not as a consultant strikes you as the best choice. You decide that you'll call your friend this afternoon, explain you'll be happy to talk with him on a personal basis, and warn him that he may not like everything you have to say. You also decide to have a meeting with Quinlan and your other staff members to review your expectations for ethical conduct.

Bernie Dworski, Legal Counsel for APA and AICP, provided assistance in developing this scenario

WHEN YOUR PERSONAL VALUES CLASH WITH A PLANNING ASSIGNMENT

You work as a senior planner in a consulting firm. You are based in the southwest office. The firm has been engaged to advise a team of attorneys working on what you think is a First Amendment case. When you get to the first meeting, you are informed that the client wants to attack a community's ability to regulate the establishment of adult entertainment businesses. The Kitty Kat Lounge, the client, offers totally nude dancing as entertainment. The dancers are attacking the public decency law requiring dancers to wear pasties and G-strings. The dancers are claiming that the public decency law violates the First Amendment guarantee of free speech based on the premise that nude dancing performed for entertainment is a form of expressive conduct protected by the U.S. Constitution. The lounge owner wishes to open a new branch in a commercial corridor where zoning might allow a bar to operate with special conditions, but would preclude sexually oriented businesses because of proximity to a neighborhood school and churches.

Your job as the planning consultant will be to show that there are no negative externalities associated with sexually oriented businesses (SOBs) and, therefore, no need for special controls or regulations under an ordinance.

You are both professionally and personally offended. Professionally, you believe that the public welfare is served by regulating aspects of SOBs. Limitations on how close such businesses can be to public schools are an example of what you believe to be appropriate. Personally, you find it difficult to conceive of nude dancing as a form of speech. You also are concerned about your firm's reputation, which could suffer whether or not you perform the work. What should you do next?

Ethical Issues:

Should you be forced to carry out a planning assignment of dubious merit if it will advance a cause you find to be repugnant?

Action Alternatives:

1.   Be pleasantly non-committal. Then excuse yourself from the meeting and call your office to collect some facts. You want to know if the firm understood the assignment in detail.

2.   Indicate to the lawyers that a professional planner can't make the argument they are requesting. Do not mention your values and discomfort with their request.

3.   Simply say that you are not the right person for the assignment and that you will discuss the matter with your employer who will assign another planner to the task.

4.   Set aside personal views and do the job requested. Develop the arguments supporting your client's case as best you can. Work with the attorneys to provide the information that will help bolster the client's position.

5.   Other.

Code Citations:

B.   A planner owes diligent, creative, independent and competent performance of work in pursuit of the client's or employer's interest. Such performance should be consistent with the planner's faithful service to the public interest.

B.2   A planner must accept the decisions of a client or employer concerning the objectives and nature of the professional services to be performed unless the course of action to be pursued involves conduct that is illegal or inconsistent with the planner's primary obligation to the public interest.

C.1 A planner must protect and enhance the integrity of the profession and must be responsible in criticism of the profession.

C.5 A planner must examine the applicability of planning theories, methods, and standards to the facts and analysis of each particular situation and must not accept the applicability of a customary solution without first establishing its appropriateness to the situation.

Discussion:

Becoming a professional planner does not require you to abandon your personal feelings and values. In fact, it is personal values like a commitment to social change and progress that prompt many people to enter the profession. At the same time, you have a responsibility to your employer.

Alternative 1, checking back with the office, gives you some time to collect your thoughts. The real question you have to answer is whether this truly is an issue to be resolved under the code or whether it is a personal moral stance. That is not to diminish the importance of your feelings, but simply to acknowledge that not all of the conflicts we experience on the job are related to the AICP code. You may believe that the job should be declined because it violates sound planning principles. If the client's concerns are defensible from your perspective as a planner, then you cannot defend a personal moral stance by exclusively relying on the code. You should remember, however, that planners do not subscribe to the same principles as attorneys who believe everyone is entitled to the best possible defense money can buy.

Alternative 2, pointing out that information does not support their case, is an acceptable course of action, provided you believe it to be true. While you could soften this argument by offering to do some additional research into precedents for this case, you need to reserve the right to withdraw should you be unable to locate sound planning rationale. Data provided by local police officials generally indicate a crime incidence of five to six times the norm at bars that permit nude dancing. Police also have documented the correlation between drugs and other illegal activity and nude dancing establishments. Further, you must take into account the effect of increased criminal activity on the surrounding neighborhood.

Alternative 3, bailing out, is an appropriate course of action given your moral values, but it is not mandated by the code. Without additional information regarding the type of employer you work for, it would be difficult to say whether taking this stance would harm your position with the firm, or enhance your standing because you stood up for principles you consider important. Consider the possibility that your employer did not know the details of the assignment at the time it was handed to you. (And ignore the issue of whether the firm should have accepted the engagement and assigned staff without a clear understanding of the nature of the services being provided.) Perhaps the firm itself would not wish to be associated with this undertaking. Or, in the worst case, the firm may agree to release you from this engagement, and reassign it to a colleague. There also is the matter of whether your consulting firm could make a good legal case even if it wanted to.

Alternative 4, assisting the client, should only be pursued if you believe that you can provide a legitimate planning service to the client. Given your values, it is probably the least desirable course of action.

CHAPTER

3
Discussion Scenarios

WHEN A UNIVERSITY FLEXES ITS MUSCLE

You are the long-time economic and community development director of Glenview. Glenview is a suburb in a metropolitan community. The planning department is one of several under your jurisdiction. The local university, while not dominating the community's economy, is a major economic force. Currently, the planning commission is conducting public hearings on area amendments to the existing comprehensive plan.

As part of the current area plan amendment process, the city manager appointed a citizens' committee consisting of major property owners, neighborhood representatives, developers who have expressed interest in the area, and community organizations with citywide civic interests. The citizens' committee has been at work for several months and staff has made a number of changes to the proposed plan amendment to incorporate committee recommendations.

Recently one of Glenview's most respected staff planners advised you that he has serious reservations regarding the recommendations that the citizen's committee will soon present to the planning commission. The issues of concern are related to the potential negative impacts of proposed development. The problem affects two key members of the committee: the university that controls more than 30 percent of the land in the study area, and a private property owner who controls another 25 percent. Among the issues raised by the planner is the fact that all of the traffic generated by the potential development will have to travel on collector and arterial roads within the corporate limits of the nearby City of Reed Junction. No provision has been made for identifying improvements needed to the transportation system within Reed Junction. Committee members are not unaware of this circumstance, but believe that it is not their problem. Representatives of the adjacent city have expressed concern, but have found neither the time nor the money to fully address the anticipated difficulties. You expect these issues to be aired at the upcoming public hearing.

163

On the day scheduled for the final public hearing and adoption by the planning commission, you discover that the city manager has bypassed you and advised the planning staff to make no recommendation to the planning commission on the area plan amendment. The findings of the citizens' committee are to be reported as "The Administration's Recommendations," which the commission will be encouraged to quickly adopt. To your knowledge, this is the first time that such direction has been given to your department.

You discuss this matter with your planning staff. At first you are satisfied by the planning staff's intention to finesse the direction from the city manager by presenting the committee's recommendations and a couple of alternative proposals. The alternatives are based on new information that was not available at the time the committee completed its work.

During the hearing, representatives of Reed Junction are present and they prefer the staff alternatives. As the meeting progresses, you conclude that there is no easy compromise. The flaws of the committee's proposal seem real. Yet a university faculty member who serves on the planning commission is dominating the discussion, pushing "The Administration's Recommendations" toward adoption. What should you do? You decide to apply ethical decision-making rules.

Define the Problem

You have multiple concerns including inappropriate behavior by both the city manager and the university's representative. The city manager bypassed you. The university's representative is advocating something that will have a direct economic benefit to his employer. You are most concerned that the planning commission is about to make a decision without considering the impact of that decision on adjacent communities.

The list of stakeholders in this scenario is lengthy, as often is the case with real-world, complex, planning problems. Parties involved include you, the commission, the city manager, your planning staff, and representatives from Reed Junction, the university, and the citizens' committee.

Clarify Your Primary Goal

You conclude that your fundamental and immediate objective is to assure that the commission doesn't make an inappropriate decision that may negatively impact adjacent communities. Concern for the inter-relatedness of decisions is an aspect of planning covered in the AICP code. Although you know that some of your colleagues view the professional planner as merely a technician who leaves the process and content of decision-making to others, you find such an approach inconsistent with your understanding of how one serves the public interest. Simply letting events take their course would not be acceptable to you. This definition of your objective also means not dealing with how you have been treated by the city manager. That is probably an issue of administrative style.

Examine the Facts In Light of this Primary Goal and Your Problem Statement

Before you can identify possible courses of action, you need to sort out some of the details of the situation to see if it can be understood in discrete components.

1.   The city manager appointed what some might see as a biased committee. Her action regarding the staff's recommendation and the commissioner's actions (the one who is a faculty member) suggest that there may be a serious problem.

2.   The planning commissioner who works at the university seems to have abandoned the responsibility to be objective and to hear all of the facts before making a decision. You suspect that he has been given marching orders by the university and is moving accordingly.

3.   From questions raised by the planning commission, it appears certain that the citizens' committee did not fully consider all of the relevant facts. Some of the facts became known after its work was done.

4.   Your supervisor, the city manager, has limited the role you can play. Making a strong stand may strain your relationship with her and negatively impact other planning activities.

5.   You feel confident that the traffic problems will be severe, but there has been no formal technical analysis. You realize that this is a serious omission and admitting it will be embarrassing.

6.   There is real support from the university and city hall for the committee's proposals. But you don't know how widespread that support may be among the planning commission.

7.   Because there is no technical analysis of transportation, you know other entities that should have been consulted have not been involved. Is there a regional planning organization and what role, if any, can it play in this situation?

8.   You also should know if there are usual and customary delaying/stalling tactics (such as tabling an issue for lack of a motion) that the commission may use while you attempt to work with the planners in

Reed Junction to determine whether there is an actual transportation problem.

Brainstorm Alternative Courses of Action that You Might Pursue

1. Publicly discuss the influence of the university and the commissioner from the university. Suggest that the planning commissioner remove himself from the discussion.
2. Reveal the actions of the city manager. Suggest that the process has been manipulated.
3. Encourage the commission to reject the proposed area plan.
4. Be quiet and let the commission resolve the matter itself. There may be opportunities to work directly with the city council to improve the plan before final action.
5. Encourage postponement, allowing time for further study of the potential transportation issues. Coordinate the study with the planners in Reed Junction and other relevant planning entities at the regional or state level.

Evaluate the Alternatives and the Consequences That May Result from Your Course of Action

1. Exposing the university may appear ethical and appealing. But how will this achieve the goal of protecting the interests of Reed Junction? It will undoubtedly strain relations with the planning commission. In the future, you might want to have a workshop for the planning commission on defining and responding to conflicts of interest.
2. The city manager may have acted inappropriately. Exposing the conflict will not improve your working relations. Once again, how will public exposure address the transportation problem? Worse yet, this course of action has the potential for jeopardizing the public confidence in the planning process. You are bound by the decisions of your employer, according to the code of ethics. In this situation, you at least owe your supervisor the courtesy of a conversation to better understand the manager's motives and rationale.
3. Without being excessively judgmental of the ethics of the participants, you could well achieve your objective, for the time being, by encouraging the commission to reject the proposed area plan. However, this alternative does not deal with the long-range consequence, and the traffic problems would remain real and unquantified.

4.   Tempting this may be, but left to its own leadership, the commission appears ready to approve the plan. As the director, you need to exercise responsibility and take action. Your primary obligation is to serve the public interest.

5.   Postponement appears to be a good alternative. You get time to investigate the transportation problem. However, there may not be adequate staff or money to fully pursue the matter. You think that you might also use the time to pursue other suspicions you have about the process and to work with the planning commission about the concept of a conflict of interest.

Compare these Alternatives to the Code of Ethics

You mentally run through the AICP code of ethics to bring up points you might have missed. You think:

A.   A planner's primary obligation is to serve the public interest. This code requirement does not allow you the luxury of ignoring what is going on with the plan.

A.1   A planner must have special concern for the long-range consequences of present actions. Your best alternative will be one that works to address the long-term issues.

A.2   A planner must pay special attention to the inter-relatedness of decisions. This, in your mind, requires you to take action to provide all important and helpful information to the commission.

B.2   A planner must accept the decisions of a client or employer concerning the objectives and nature of the professional services to be performed unless that course of action to be pursued involves conduct that is illegal or inconsistent with the planner's primary obligation to the public interest. Given that the public hearing is in progress, you were probably right when you narrowly defined your goal for the day.

Select the Preferred Course of Action and Give It the Tests of Publicity and Whether It Feels Right

Alternative 5, postponement, is the best alternative. It protects the public interest of Reed Junction. It also is consistent with the code's emphasis on the need to look at the long-range consequences and inter-relatedness of decisions. An area plan amendment is not to be undertaken lightly nor with a degree of urgency that would preclude further analysis.

Try Your Plan of Action

You make your pitch to the planning commission. Your language focuses on the need to find the best solution for everyone involved. If necessary, you assign responsibility to you and your staff for the need to delay: you should have caught this problem earlier and been more prepared for the meeting.

Robert Joice, AICP, helped to develop this scenario and commentary.

AN EXERCISE IN DAMAGE CONTROL

You currently are a member of the executive committee of your APA chapter. Your chapter has a program called SCAT — Small Communities Assistance Teams. Cities can make application to the chapter for advice on planning matters. A team of planners visits for several days and submits recommendations. Communities are charged only the direct expenses incurred by the planners who volunteer their time.

Three years ago you and former members of the executive committee sent a SCAT to a small community called McLain. McLain had a population of less than 10,000 and had been identified as the site for a large new manufacturing facility. This designation had prompted the request for help. The town had never had a full-time planner before, although you know that it occasionally engaged a consultant. The planning commission lacked professional staff and was advised on planning matters by the city attorney who also sat as a member of the commission. In this capacity the city attorney provided legal counsel and also prepared staff recommendations. This overlap of duties concerned you. In your previous report you had recommended, among other things, that the community hire an AICP planner and that the role of the city attorney be revised. The second recommendation was partially acted upon.

Based on articles later published in the newspaper, you believe that some of that advice was followed directly, while most of it was at least carefully considered. The community's building inspector has called and invited you to lunch. He tells you that there have been some problems in town lately and he wants some help sorting them out. He is seeking advice from you, a professional planner who is independent of the circumstances in which he now finds himself.

Over lunch, the building inspector tells you that the manufacturing plant was built. Lots of spin-off development occurred. A planning director with AICP credentials was hired. It was decided that building inspection functions should remain outside of the planning department to accommodate the interests of other long-time city employees. The city attorney stepped down as a voting member from the planning commission, but retained his role as legal counsel. He now performs the same function for the board of adjustment and for the city council. The attorney also continues to maintain a small private practice. The new planning director makes recommendations to the planning commission. The building inspector makes recommendations to the board of adjustment. The commission makes recommendations to the city council. The attorney makes legal recommendations to all three.

The building inspector then describes his current difficulties. Several months ago a realtor visited the planning director to determine the zoning of a piece of property on the edge of the downtown commercial district. The property also is at the edge of a historic neighborhood. The zoning maps did not seem clear. They are old and the tick marks don't properly register. The director thinks that some of the property lines on the base map are inaccurate. He scaled the maps and decided that a zoning boundary line either bisected the property in question or included the property in its entirety. The planning director made a judgment call based on available information and informed the realtor that the parcel was within the downtown commercial area.

At the same time, the planning director was hard at work on a draft comprehensive plan. It was under review with the assistance of many citizen committees. The draft plan maps were regularly displayed and the above-referenced property always was shown as being within the commercial district. The citizens' committees and the planning commission approved the final plan maps accordingly. The narrative accompanying the plan map states that the commercial boundary in this area is to remain stable. The boundary in another area is identified for possible expansion, and in another for potential contraction as the result of more detailed sub-area planning.

The realtor again visited the planning director and sought to reconfirm the earlier understanding. The director confirmed his earlier statement, and even mentioned the topic at a meeting of the planning commission's steering committee. The steering committee includes the current and past commission chairs and the city attorney. The planning director's interpretation was affirmed in this informal setting.

Subsequently, the realtor purchased the property and spent an additional sum of money to renovate the building for her own office use. Residents adjacent to the property are aghast at what they see to be an intrusion of commercial activity into their residential enclave. They reported their dissatisfaction to the building inspector. The inspector decreed that, based on his long-term knowledge of the area, the planning director erred in the original interpretation of the boundary line and that the property is zoned residential. He made this comment based on his best judgment and not out of any personal rancor. As a result of what the building inspector said, the adjacent property owners insisted that the board of adjustment pursue the matter as a land use in violation of the city's adopted zoning map. The board of adjustment conducted a hearing. The city attorney advised the board to take a position consistent with the map included in the plan adopted by the city commission. The board, however, determined that the position of the building inspector is correct.

While waiting for the proper notice and hearing for the meeting of the board of adjustment, the comprehensive plan had been adopted by the city council with the map showing the property in the downtown commercial area. It was then suggested to the realtor that she seek a rezoning of the property consistent with the intent of the newly adopted comprehensive plan. The owner agreed and proceeded to request the rezoning. At the public hearing on the proposed zoning change, the planning director was candid in reviewing the history of the parcel. Based upon the many reviews of the maps of the plan, and the fact that the new property owner spent money in good faith, the planning director recommended that the property be rezoned. During the commission's discussion of the item, the following actions were taken:

• The city attorney was asked by the planning commission chair to remove himself from discussion of this item because he has represented the realtor's husband in other legal matters.

• The city attorney rejected the request of the commission chair. He claimed that the personal representations he undertakes do not affect his judgment concerning properties and zoning.

• The commission chair suggested that a fellow commissioner who resides in the historic area excuse herself from the debate because feelings are running so strongly in the neighborhood. The commissioner complied and left the chamber during the subsequent debate and vote.

• The planning commission, by a narrow margin, voted to approve the zone change using conformance with the newly adopted comprehensive plan as its primary reason.

After the commission meeting, the planning director learned that the city attorney was directly involved in the realtor's purchase of the property and had done the title search. The neighborhood association in the historic area insisted that the city attorney disqualify himself from participating on this matter when it comes before the city council. This time, the attorney agreed.

The planning commissioner who disqualified herself from the voting is disgruntled by the results. She suggested that perhaps the mayor, who knows the realtor well, had used special influence to persuade the planning director to support the rezoning request. The commissioner has gone so far as to suggest that the director intentionally misled the citizen committees and the commission and just "slipped this one by everyone's nose." The planning director is warned that the commissioner will seek to testify to this effect at the hearing before the city council.

The planning director, who was thinking about resigning for reasons unrelated to this zoning case, decides to do so. A resignation letter is submitted with an effective date of one week before the city council hearing on the rezoning.

The former consulting planner to the city still lives nearby. Miffed at not being offered the job of planning director, she has rejoiced in the downfall of her colleague. She also disagrees with elements of the newly adopted plan. She is expected to testify at the zoning hearing and use that opportunity to attack the former planning director and the credibility of the adopted document.

The building inspector will be appointed acting planning director and seeks your advice. He asks you what you think he should try to accomplish between today and the public hearing in two weeks.

Ethical Issues:

How can planners best perform in an environment where personal relationships and long-standing practices undermine best planning practices?

Action Alternatives:

1.   Make sure that an attorney is present at the hearing. Talk with the attorney, the mayor, and others to encourage the hearing to focus on the facts, not the individuals involved. Do not attempt to control who speaks as one never knows which participant will bring forward important information.

2.   See how the council intends to vote and develop materials to support the likely decision. Get this whole matter over with as fast as possi-

ble. Ask the former planning director, the attorney, the planning consultant, and the planning commissioner to stay away from the hearing,
reminding them that they all have personal conflicts.

3.   Check the political waters and then figure out who should take
the fall. The resigning planning director is an easy target. Blame everything on him. At all costs, protect the attorney; he probably controls the
building inspector's job.

4.   Other.

This scenario illustrates a complex yet common situation. Seemingly little mistakes mount up to major ethical difficulties. Well-intentioned people loose their perspective, but fortunately, as in this scenario, they may
come to you and ask for advice. At this point you should proceed with the
analytical steps suggested early in this text.

1.   Make sure your talk with the building inspector doesn't end
before you have a clear definition of the problem.

2.   You need to clarify your objectives. Presumably you want to help
him determine what his best course of action is. As you add your perspective, do you want to emphasize what is best for him, best for planning, best for the local community, or best for you as you might want to
apply for the newly vacated planning director's position? Certainly that
which is in the best interest of the local community should be paramount.

In pursuit of this objective, it would help to encourage the building
inspector to clarify what he hopes to accomplish. He may have a few conflicts or goals that he hasn't mentioned. One would hope that he would
share your interest in the good of the community and the integrity of the
planning process.

3.   Continue to review the facts in light of these goals. It may be necessary to read between the lines, to judge where honest mistakes occurred
or if anything truly devious was ever intended. History may well be an
indicator of what to expect at the upcoming meeting.

4.   Brainstorm alternatives beyond those suggested at the end of the
scenario. If you are going to advise the building inspector and attempt to
influence his actions, you certainly want to hear his ideas. Even after
lengthy discussion with you, he is likely to rely on a variation of one of
his own ideas as the first choice. He also knows more than you have dis-
covered so far during lunch, so keep listening.

5.   Evaluate your alternatives together. Such discussion may afford
you the greatest opportunity to influence his decision. When he first

asked for you to come and discuss the matter, he indicated he wanted your help. If the three alternatives listed are the only ones that come up, you must then use the ethical guidelines to evaluate them. The first alternative starts well, especially with the call for a new attorney to assist the council in the upcoming meeting. The alternative emphasizes one of the guidelines — that of providing full information to the decision-makers. While it is hard to guess the outcome of the meeting, it appears that provision of good information is necessary and should help the process.

6. The second alternative starts pragmatically, but not ethically. Staff should review the facts and attempt to make a clear, complete presentation. The presentation should be logical and cover the facts that support the staff recommendation, but not second-guess the council decision. Several key players in the scenario have personal conflicts that should be considered. The attorney should have bowed out long ago. The planning consultant needs to bury the hatchet, or stay out. The commissioner apparently recognizes that there is a conflict. At this point, the resigning planning director's reputation has become an issue and legal action could follow. The potential for personal conflict is evident. One must, however, weigh the impact of these people not being available against the degree of personal conflict. Furthermore, the scenario focuses upon what the building inspector, as acting planning director, should do. The building inspector should make sure that people are aware of the conflicts, but should not attempt to muzzle participants as they may bring pertinent facts to the attention of the decision-makers. Even the resigning planning director, abiding by the AICP code of ethics, could participate under these conditions. He should acknowledge the personal conflict, decline to make a recommendation, and be available for questioning. Given the complexity of the situation, his knowledge of specific facts may be invaluable to the council.

7. The third alternative is in no way consistent with serving the public interest, but it may be nearest and dearest to the heart of the building inspector.

8. Help the building inspector select an alternative, preferably the first. Ask him and yourself if this would stand the test of publicity. If he were inclined toward the second or third alternatives, and were asked what the public might think if they knew exactly what had gone on, it could help eliminate these alternatives from consideration.

9. Praise the building inspector for coming to you for advice and encourage him to call back as he proceeds. You may be able to help him refine his approach.

Commendations to you as well. It is important for planners to help one another deal with ethical dilemmas. You should also be concerned, however, about the welfare of the planning director and you should consider taking the initiative to discuss the current situation in terms of providing help in securing a new job!

WHISTLE BLOWING OR BLOWING IN THE WIND

You are a young urban planner looking for work. Prior to attending graduate school, you were employed by a regional council of governments (COG). The COG was the officially-designated metropolitan planning organization (MPO) doing long-range regional transportation planning. Three years ago (when you were working for the COG), the COG endorsed a $3 billion rail transit system for the region. The system was supported by the mayor of the largest city in the region, and was strongly endorsed by the local chambers of commerce, realtors' associations, and the transit authority. Many academics, some congressional representatives, and city council members from outlying areas were opposed to the proposed rail system.

You felt at the time, after careful study and analysis, that the only reasons for supporting the proposal were political. You think your employer acted foolishly in preparing reports that concluded the rail system would be a good public investment. You believe that forecasting models were designed to favor the rail system, and that unrealistic assumptions were used to make the proposal seem attractive.

Your boss was the head of the COG's transportation planning department when the decision was made to support the rail system. At the time, you told him that, in your opinion, the rail system was a poor public investment. He said he understood your point of view and that he agreed with you. But, he explained, it was the job of all COG employees to support the agency's positions. Not satisfied with that response, you sought out the director of the COG. You laid out your point of view carefully to her. You cited data and gave examples of inappropriate methods and assumptions being used by the organization. The COG director, like the head of transportation planning, expressed personal warmth toward you and did not try to talk you out of your position. Instead, the director noted that planning agencies often must support programs of questionable technical merit if the political head of the organization, in this case the board of directors, approves the proposal. You do not agree. You argued that concern for the public interest requires planners to tell the truth, even if they must take some heat from their political directors. You parted from your meeting with the director on friendly terms.

You then prepared a scathing editorial for the op-ed page of the largest newspaper in the region. You carefully documented the unreasonable assumptions that were used in the COG's formal analysis. You argued that the rail investment was a pork-barrel project of little technical merit. Your letter showed how similar projects in other cities failed to live up to projected patronage, and exceeded costs. Without mentioning your employment status in the article or the Council of Governments by name, you explicitly attacked the COG's position and its technical analysis. The newspaper accepted the editorial for publication, and did not inform the COG prior to publishing it. The paper identified you in the "credits" box under the editorial as "a transportation planner with the local Council of Governments."

The day that the article was published, you were called into the office of the COG director. The head of the transportation planning department was present. They told you that employees may not publish anything without their approval. You responded that you knew they would not have approved publication had you submitted the editorial to them in advance. You claimed that everything you wrote is the truth, and that you saw it as your obligation to the public interest to write the editorial. They did not attempt to change your mind about the rail system, but they did tell you that you must be loyal, in public, to the agency's adopted positions. You argued that you have never been shown a rule that forbids employees to publish without approval of a superior, and claimed that they have no right to limit your freedom to express yourself as a citizen.

The director of transportation planning asks you about one particular statement in the editorial and inquired where you found out about a statistic because it had not yet been published in any of the agency's technical reports. You, in all candor, admitted that you saw an internal memo lying on the director's desk one day after five o'clock, and you borrowed it for a few minutes to read it over. You then made a photocopy of a few paragraphs that were related to your interest in the regional rail system. The two directors asked you to leave the room so they could confer with one another. Not long after, you were invited to return. You were told that you would never be promoted while employed by the COG and that you had better look for another job. You asked whether you were being fired. You were told, "No, but you will be given no opportunity to advance, no favorable recommendation, nor any increased responsibility."

Upon reflection, you left the COG to attend graduate school out of state. Later you returned to the metropolitan area. You applied for jobs with the regional transit authority, the county planning commission, and eight consulting firms. All tell you that you are "unqualified," or that they have no current openings. In the case of each position, however, jobs were either advertised or individuals with similar qualifications were recently hired.

You have asked your roommate, a planner and a member of AICP, his opinion. Were you unfairly treated for being a whistle blower, or did your action constitute something other than whistle blowing because nobody in the organization had violated any law by supporting the transit proposal?

Your roommate tells you that:

1. He believes the two directors acted unfairly in telling you to leave the COG instead of firing you.

2. He believes that you violated the ethical canons of the AICP by using data from a report that was not in the public domain.

3. He thinks you should try to get the AICP to take up your cause. It seems as if the word has been put out on the street.

4. Other.

Code Citations:

A.3 A planner must strive to provide full, clear, and accurate information on planning issues to citizens and governmental decision-makers.

B. A planner owes diligent, creative, independent and competent performance of work in pursuit of the client's or employer's interest. Such performance should be consistent with the planner's faithful service to the public interest.

B.2 A planner must accept the decisions of a client or employer concerning the objectives and nature of the professional services to be performed unless the course of action to be pursued involves conduct that is illegal or inconsistent with the planner's primary obligation to the public interest.

B.9 A planner must not reveal information gained in a professional relationship which the client or employer has requested be held inviolate. Exceptions to this requirement of non-disclosure may be made only when (a) required by process of law, or (b) required to prevent a clear violation of law; or (c) required to prevent a substantial injury to the public. Disclosure, pursuant to (b) and (c), must not be made until after the planner has verified the facts and issues involved and, when practicable, has exhausted efforts to obtain reconsideration of the matter, and has sought separate opinions on the issue from the other qualified professionals employed by the client or employer.

D. A planner should strive for high standards of professional integrity, proficiency, and knowledge.

D.1 A planner must not commit a deliberately wrongful act that reflects adversely on the planner's professional fitness.

Discussion:

At the outset, it is worthwhile noting that in the United States there is little status or respect accorded to the whistle blower. Conversely, studies in Great Britain show that whistle blowers go on to more important positions. Here, they are likely to remain unemployed for a prolonged period of time because our culture places such great weight upon loyalty to one's employer, even to the exclusion of other important values. Other deterrents to whistle blowing include fear of personal retaliation and fear of prosecution, since whistle blowing can require one to do something illegal such as copying confidential records. Finally, institutions themselves often prohibit whistle blowing by emphasizing in their written policies different aspects of obedience, loyalty, and confidentiality.

Despite such constraints, whistle blowing will continue to take place because institutions will continue to make mistakes and the public is increasingly willing to accept allegations of wrongdoing. Also, bonds of loyalty to one's employer are weakening. Still, whistle blowing is not likely to increase significantly because one can reasonably expect to lose one's job as a result. In the State of Texas, a whistle blower who revealed safety violations in the construction of a nuclear power facility was fired. The employee sued, and was awarded a substantial judgment. The State has refused to pay the judgment leaving the whistle blower a hollow victory.

The code is silent on whistle blowing. However, a thorough reading of the document would imply a set of responsibilities for whistle blowers.

1. They must be able to clearly define what they are objecting to.
2. They must know what laws are being broken or specific harm is being done.
3. They must have adequate and accurate information about the wrongdoing.
4. They must know whether they need additional information and how to get it.
5. They must try to report the wrongdoing to someone within the organization.

6. They must have a clear sense that failure to report the matter is a violation of the law or shirking of one's duty.

7. They should know to whom they would report outside of the organization and whether to do the reporting by name or anonymously.

8. They should know what is likely to be the response of those they inform both inside and outside of the organization.

9. They should know what they hope to achieve by revealing their concerns both inside and outside of the organization.

10. They should know whether they can live with the consequences of not speaking out.

In this case, you followed the rules by notifying your colleagues and superiors of your concerns and made an effort to secure a reconsideration of the matter. You tried to make sure you had the facts; although it appears you acquired some of those facts from confidential sources.

Democratic societies recognize the importance of the free discussion of ideas, Where the potential public impact is great, organizations should not seek to prohibit disclosure. The overall cost to society of restricting the marketplace of ideas is too great. However, when the disclosure involves the release of unauthorized information, another set of factors comes into play. This is because the negative consequences of releasing otherwise confidential information can outweigh the benefits obtained as a result of exposure. Your value to society as a whistle blower must be recognized. Whistle blowing won't eliminate all wrongdoing. It can be an important factor in maintaining democratic freedom and, as such, is to be valued by your employer. The scenario implies that the organization accepted internal dissent and might have tolerated external dissent. The problem lies with the manner in which you acquired some of the data to build this case. Using a "means justify the ends" philosophy, you were comfortable with what you did. Others, who operate from an approach that certain behaviors cannot be justified regardless of the provocation, would not be willing to accept such actions on your part.

Alternative 1 may show great loyalty from your roommate, but limited skills in ethical analysis. In fact, the supervisor was kind in allowing you to display a resignation rather than a firing on your resume. This alternative, in which emotion would overrule common sense, would be the response of a friend who had abandoned all objective standards.

Alternative 2 is the most logical response from your roommate. However, if he is your friend as well as your roommate, this response could seem cold-hearted.

Alternative 3 is the weakest of the proposals. To be candid, there are few instances of either AICP or APA coming to the aid of planners who are whistle blowers. Planners are most likely to be counseled to resign when circumstances dictate an unacceptable course of action.

Source: Martin Wachs, AICP, University of California for scenario. Carolyn Torma provided assistance in developing the commentary.

PRIORITIZING NON-WORK THAT OCCURS AT THE OFFICE

As the planning director of a public agency, how would you prioritize the acceptability of the following "thefts" of public property or misuse of public resources? Place each of the following activities into one of the four categories listed below:

1.   Activities you might encourage as appropriate when suggested by staff or by an outside source. (Mark these E.)

2.   Activities you might quietly allow to occur unless there is a negative impact upon other pressing work requirements. (Mark these A.)

3.   Activities you generally would discourage if you were consulted in advance. (Mark these D.)

4.   Activities you would prohibit in written office policies. (Mark these P.)

_____ Taking home office supplies for after-hours work

_____ Use of typewriter or computer after hours for personal items

_____ Secretarial assistance with personal typing

_____ Photocopying personal items

_____ Providing maps to others without the normal charge

_____ Use of office computer after hours for an otherwise acceptable moonlighting project

Planner's office time spent on the following:

_____ General APA activities

_____ Preparation for teaching a class

_____ Preparation for teaching a class when the planner will be well compensated beyond covering expenses

_____ Reading the newspaper

_____ Preparing medical insurance reimbursement paperwork

_____ Paying bills

_____ Writing a book or article about planning

_____ Extended lunch hours to exercise at a health club

_____ Leaving early for Friday afternoon fun as a group

_____ Writing the newsletter for a neighborhood association

_____ Vacation planning

_____ Job hunting

Planner's office time spent on providing planning assistance as a volunteer to:

_____ Religious institution

_____ Private school

_____ Scouts

_____ Child Abuse Center

_____ Sexual Crisis Center Advisory Board

_____ Minority business owner

_____ Another governmental jurisdiction

_____ Homeless shelter

Code Citations:

A.4   A planner must strive to give citizens the opportunity to have a meaningful impact on the development of plans and programs. Participation should be broad enough to include people who lack formal organization or influence.

A.5   A planner must strive to expand choice and opportunity for all persons, recognizing a special responsibility to plan for the needs of disadvantaged groups and persons, and must urge the alteration of policies, institutions, and decisions that oppose such needs.

B.   A planner owes diligent, creative, independent and competent performance of work in pursuit of the client's or employer's interest. Such performance should be consistent with the planner's faithful service to the public interest.

C. A planner should contribute to the development of the profession by improving knowledge and techniques, making work relevant to solutions of community problems, and increasing public understanding of planning activities. A planner should treat fairly the professional views of qualified colleagues and members of other professions.

C.4 A planner must share the results of experience and research that contribute to the body of planning knowledge.

C.6 A planner must contribute time and information to the professional development of students, interns, beginning professionals, and other colleagues.

D. A planner should strive for high standards of professional integrity, proficiency, and knowledge.

D.3 A planner must strive to continue professional education.

D.6 A planner must strive to contribute time and effort to groups lacking in adequate planning resources and to voluntary professional activities.

Discussion:

Approval of the kinds of non-work that can go on in an office varies by custom. For example, some private planning firms enforce a policy that requires all time spent at work to be billable. Others view time spent on some non-work as a form of marketing and are supportive. In many public sector agencies, a practice has evolved of allowing planning staffers considerable leeway as to what they can do during regular work hours in recognition of the many uncompensated hours spent at night meetings. Sometimes the informal practices that govern behavior of key staff become the norm of an entire agency, thereby reducing the level of productivity. As a planning director, you need to determine whether the pattern of behavior among your employees is appropriate. A good operational rule is to anticipate ethical behavior; but to be prepared to set out your expectations for what constitutes ethical conduct. As an employee, you need to be scrupulous in making sure that your employer (whether public or private) receives a full day's work for a full day's pay.

Additional information is needed in this scenario to help with the evaluation of the alternatives. Several issues deserve serious consideration prior to establishing formal policy. The appropriateness of the activities listed above depends, in part, upon whether:

1.   employees are expected to work overtime without compensation;
2.   the jurisdiction has a policy regarding compensation for overtime or the noted activities;
3.   the rules are different for the professional versus the clerical staff;
4.   there are some issues that are firm departmental policies and others that vary according to circumstance.

Overall, the goal must be to create a workplace in which there is a high degree of logic and consistency in the application of both the written and the unwritten rules. Therefore, personal values must not interfere. For example, a planning director who opposes gun control should not single out the National Rifle Association as the only organization that is precluded from the office environment. Establishing detailed procedures can be counter productive and create a perception that your public planners are employed in a police state.

As the director, you have a primary responsibility to make sure the work of the department is progressing. Is there is a proliferation of non-work in your office? What example are you setting? Do you efficiently organize work so that staffers always have something to keep them occupied? Do people know what they are supposed to be doing?

The aspirational standards of the code, although not particularly explicit in terms of what can and cannot be done, do provide guidance for responding to this scenario. The activities listed above could be ranked based upon whether they contribute to the development of the profession or colleagues, and as to whether they help to improve planning knowledge and techniques. Contributing to the public understanding of planning activities also would be an appropriate weighting criterion. Finally, the test of public exposure should be applied. Would you be willing to defend spending your time on this, or defend a member of your staff doing this, in public? If you cannot honestly answer in the affirmative, then the activity ought not to be condoned. For example, a planner charged with developing low-income housing strategies might legitimately work on a grant application for a church group that is seeking to build subsidized apartments. Assisting a community group with planning resources might generally be approved; leaving work early to avoid the rush hour should not.

ARNOLD OIL COMPANY CONDITIONAL USE APPLICATION

This is a role-playing scenario. It works well in larger groups if they are divided into smaller units of no more than ten. Individuals without assigned roles should be designated as planning commissioners.

Make name tags for the assigned roles and distribute them, along with a specific role description, to the eight individuals with parts to play. For example, Darwin McKeen would get a name tag reading, "Darwin McKeen, Planning Commissioner." He also would get a piece of paper with the brief description of his personal orientation, listed in "The Participants" section below.

Each participant should receive the statement of facts as well as the assignment. The group should select the recorder. The recorder will need the notes section to record the results of the activity.

For interest, authorize one person in the group to behave unethically, but caution that individual not to reveal this until after the role-playing is completed.

Allow ten minutes to read the facts and study the participant role, then take twenty minutes to allow each group to conduct its public meeting. A final five minutes per group should be reserved for reporting back.

The Facts:

The City of Allendale, in 1931, approved a zoning map that designated parts of the city by their ethnic population. Many of the Hispanic neighborhoods, in the eastern portion of Allendale, had parcels zoned for industrial use. Since then, numerous homes have been built on land zoned for industrial purposes. (Allendale used a cumulative form of zoning.) Allendale residents who live in the eastern part of the city are angry about issues of incompatibility. They want to eliminate all industrial uses in areas adjacent to homes, even if properties are properly zoned for industrial use. The topic of environmental racism frequently surfaces in public shouting matches.

In response to the concerns of the East Allendale area, the planning commission recommended, and the city council adopted, an overlay ordinance. The ordinance makes the establishment or expansion of an industrial use or industrial-type use in East Allendale a conditional use requiring a public hearing and an affirmative vote by the planning commission.

Arnold Oil has applied for approval of a site plan to expand its business in East Allendale. The business has occupied its current site for twenty-one years and has seventy-five employees, a third of whom live in the immediate neighborhood. When the issues of the conditional overlay were first being discussed in the neighborhood, Arnold Oil came to the city and applied for a downzoning of its property from industrial to commercial. At that time, company officials explained their plans to the neighborhood for the eventual expansion of their business. The officials felt that seeking the downzoning voluntarily demonstrated their desire to be a good neighbor.

The new warehouse would be equipped with a sprinkler system, and would be complemented by trees and a wrought iron fence. It would replace a lumber shed made of gray weathered wood, which is a tinderbox in the 100-degree days of Allendale. The lumber yard itself is strewn with debris. To make the project more acceptable to the neighborhood, Arnold Oil proposes less impervious cover than is permitted by the code; hoods on all night lights; no use of reflective materials on the exterior of the building; no operations at night; and no structure higher than thirty feet, which is the residential use height restriction.

Further, Arnold Oil is mostly an auto parts business. Company officials say they need additional storage room and the new 28,000 square-foot warehouse would roughly double the available space.

This case will be the first test of the new East Allendale zoning overlay, which was enacted by the city council in response to years of complaints by residents about the industrial facilities in their midst. Industries are blamed for health problems as well as degrading the overall quality of life.

The Participants:

Steve Cutler, manager of Arnold Oil Co., can't understand why some East Allendale residents object to his company's plan to replace the crumbling, rat-infested lumber shed next door with a gleaming new auto parts warehouse. Cutler notes that about twenty-five of the company's seventy-five employees live in East Allendale and that the surrounding area of East Sixth Street is a commercial corridor with few homes. He also notes that several nearby business owners have endorsed Arnold Oil's plans. Cutler will have to respond to questions as to why Arnold Oil, which purchased the lumberyard in 1995, has yet to clean up the site.

Cathy Rodriguez represents residents who oppose the expansion of Arnold Oil. Arnold may have been a good neighbor, but a new warehouse is exactly the sort of thing the law was created to prevent. Rodriguez owns property adjacent to the lumber yard and there is some dispute about whether her driveway encroaches on Arnold Oil property. Rodriguez also is the publisher of *La Prensa,* a bilingual newspaper, whose office is located on the property adjacent to the lumber yard. Rodriguez would be a neighbor of the new warehouse. *La Prensa* has campaigned thoughtfully and vigorously against the expansion of Arnold Oil. "The bottom line is that there was a promise made to citizens of East Allendale when the overlay was enacted. That promise was that this would be the beginning of revitalization and increasing property values. We feel that this is an obvious expansion of the kinds of uses we do not want anymore. He's going to increase his holding capacity so he can have more oil and more parts. That's going to mean more trips," Rodriguez wrote. "There is going to be an increase in traffic because there's going to be an increase in his business."

The zoning law enacted last summer is designed to limit industry in East Allendale. So why, Rodriguez asks, would the council approve expanding one of those businesses? "Is the city serious about turning East Allendale around, or is it just rhetoric?" she wonders. "We don't want to have something that's just a paper tiger." Rodriguez also is a former planning commissioner.

Art Navarone is a planning commissioner who is seeking to balance the interests of East Allendale residents, who want tranquil neighborhoods, and the rights of business owners who followed city zoning rules when they set up shop. He, himself, is a business owner with major aspirations to run for citywide elective office. He chairs the planning commission.

Dudly Dunderdonk, the traffic consultant, contends that the expansion will reduce traffic in the neighborhood. Currently, 18-wheel trucks block traffic when they back into Arnold Oil's site to load or unload parts. The new facility will have a circular driveway where the trucks can park.

Ernesto Garcia, another business owner in the area, is ready to testify before the planning commission that, "They're good neighbors; we get along." Garcia owns a tortilla factory nearby. "As long as it's an improvement, and it's not overlapping or harming anybody else, I don't know why there would be resistance to it."

Alice Glass, the planning director, wants the process to be fair and respectful to all parties involved. Her staff drafted the conditional overlay ordinance and this is its first test.

Jean Rather is a planning commissioner. Intense and devoted, Rather wants to do the right thing. She has lived in Allendale for many years and sympathizes with the concerns of the minority community.

Darwin McKeen, a planning commissioner, is concerned about the impact of planning proposals on the African-American community. A businessman, he seeks to make sure that every point of view is represented. He asks for both information and opinion from those appearing before the planning commission.

Your assignment:

The conditional use overlay covers basic industry, warehouses, recycling centers, light manufacturing, kennels, vehicle storage, construction sales and certain other businesses that are near homes, schools, parks, houses of worship, or day-care centers. It requires a public hearing and planning commission approval before existing businesses expand significantly or new businesses move in. The law doesn't apply to a new property owner who uses the land in the same way, as long as activity does not cease for more than 90 days. The law does not change the underlying zoning.

Conduct a short planning commission meeting on the conditional use application to expand Arnold Oil. You should ask the applicant and staff for presentations. Those in support and those in opposition to the conditional use should have an opportunity to speak.

Take a vote at the end of your commission meeting. You may recommend denial of the application to expand or approve the application with conditions.

Assign one of the participants the role of recorder and ask that individual to report back to the larger group regarding the following:

Recorder's Notes:

What decision did the planning commission make?

What process was followed for conducting the commission meeting?

What facts were brought out?

What were the strongly held positions and why?

Did everyone behave ethically? Why or why not?

Appendix

SCENARIOS ORGANIZED BY APPLICABLE CODE ELEMENTS

A. Serve the public interest

When the Planning Director Wants Affordable Housing
Window Dressing Minority Contracting
Planner Spies Endangered Species
Moving the Airport
Planner Suspects Developer Influence on Planning Commission
Annexation Analysis Blues
Street Vendors vs. Corporate America
What's the Difference between Exactions and Extortion?
When the Rules of the Game Seem to Change
Balancing Compassion and Enforcing the Sign Ordinance
Disclosing Your Employer
When a University Flexes Its Muscles

A.1. Have special concern for long range consequences

Planner Spies Endangered Species
Planner Suspects Developer Influence on Planning Commission
A Simple Office Conversion
Annexation Analysis Blues
Street Vendors vs. Corporate America
Does Historic Preservation Overrule Religious Rights?
Making Time for Planning on the Planning Commission Agenda
What's the Difference between Exactions and Extortion?
When the Rules of the Game Seem to Change
Balancing Compassion and Enforcing the Sign Ordinance
Where Have All the Affordable Rental Houses Gone?
When a University Flexes Its Muscles
Whistle Blowing or Blowing in the Wind

A.2. Pay special attention to inter-relatedness of decisions

When a University Flexes Its Muscles
Moving the Airport
Planner Suspects Developer Influence on the Planning Commission
Annexation Analysis Blues
Street Vendor vs. Corporate America
Are Wetlands an Ethical Issue?
Does Historic Preservation Overrule Religious Rights?

Where Have All the Affordable Rental Houses Gone?
When a University Flexes Its Muscles

A.3.   Provide full, clear accurate information

What Are You Willing to Do to Keep Your Job?
When the Planning Director Wants Affordable Housing
Temporary Toilets
Public Decision-Making without Public Input
Planner Wonders if Community Understands Development's Impact
Planner Spies Endangered Species
Moving the Airport
Planner Suspects Developer Influence on Planning Commission
Annual Birthday Dinner
Being Offered Confidential Information
Annexation Analysis Blues
Street Vendors vs. Corporate America
Does Historic Preservation Overrule Religious Rights?
When the Rules of the Game Seem to Change
Using the Planning Process to Stop an Unpopular Land Use
Senior Planner Questions Competence of Director
Who Determines What Are the Real Numbers
Preserving Indian Artifacts
Grocery Store Market Analysis
Where Have All the Affordable Rental Houses Gone?
Disclosing Your Employer
Whistle Blowing or Blowing in the Wind

A.4.   Give opportunities for meaningful citizen participation

When the Planning Director Wants Affordable Housing
Public Decision-Making without Public Input
Planner Wonders If Community Understands Development Impact
Moving the Airport
Being Offered Confidential Information
Annexation Analysis Blues
Street Vendors vs. Corporate America
Being Responsive to Hispanic Community Values
Where Have All the Affordable Rental Houses Gone?
Prioritizing Non-Work That Goes On at the Office

A.5.   Expand choice and opportunity

When the Planning Director Wants Affordable Housing
Temporary Toilets
Public Decision-Making without Public Input

Moving the Airport
Annexation Analysis Blues
No Home for Group Homes
Street Vendors vs. Corporate America
Are Wetlands an Ethical Issue?
Being Responsive to Hispanic Community Values
Using the Zoning Ordinance to Eliminate Feeding Programs
Balancing Compassion and Enforcing the Sign Ordinance
Grocery Store Market Analysis
Where Have All the Affordable Rental Houses Gone?
Prioritizing Non-Work That Goes On at the Office

A.6. Protect integrity of the natural environment

Planner Spies Endangered Species
Are Wetlands Ethical Issues?
Preserving Indian Artifacts

A.7. Strive for excellence of design and conserve heritage of the built environment

A Simple Office Conversion
Street Vendors vs. Corporate America
Does Historic Preservation Overrule Religious Rights?
Preserving Indian Artifacts
Where Have All the Affordable Rental Houses Gone?

B. Planner owes competent, independent performance of work

When the Planning Director Wants Affordable Housing
Temporary Toilets
Public Decision-Making without Public Input
A Simple Office Conversion
When an Appointed Official Seeks Permit Approval
Making Time for Planning on the Planning Commission Agenda
What's the Difference between Exactions and Extortion?
Being Responsive to Hispanic Community Values
Using the Planning Process to Stop Unpopular Land Uses
When Your Personal Values Clash with a Planning Assignment
Where Have All the Affordable Rental Houses Gone?
What Happens when A Consultant Takes On Too Much Work
Disclosing Your Employer

Whistle Blowing or Blowing in the Wind
Prioritizing Non-Work that Goes On at the Office

B.1. Exercise independent professional judgment

When the Planning Director Wants Affordable Housing
Temporary Toilets
Public Decision-Making without Public Input
Planner Suspects Developer Influence on Planning Commission
A Simple Office Conversion
When an Appointed Official Seeks Permit Approval
Does Historic Preservation Overrule Religious Rights?
Making Time on the Planning Commission Agenda
What's the Difference between Exactions and Extortion?
Being Responsive to Hispanic Community Values
Using the Planning Process to Stop Unpopular Land Uses
Balancing Compassion and Enforcing the Sign Ordinance
Who Determines the Real Numbers?
Grocery Store Market Analysis

B.2. Accept decisions of employer or client

What Are You Willing to Do to Keep Your Job?
Temporary Toilets
Planning Director Browbeats Consultant
Public Decision-Making without Public Input
Planner Suspects Developer Influence on the Planning Commission
No Home for Group Homes
Does Historic Preservation Overrule Religious Rights?
What's the Difference between Exactions and Extortion?
When the Rules of the Game Seem to Change
Being Responsive to Hispanic Community Values
Using the Planning Process to Stop Unpopular Land Uses
When Your Personal Values Clash with a Planning Assignment
Senior Planner Questions Competence of Director
Who Determines the Real Numbers?
Pricing the Comprehensive Plan
Grocery Store Market Analysis
Do You Have a Duty to Report and Publicize Suspicious Conduct?
Disclosing Your Employer
When a University Flexes Its Muscles
Whistle Blowing or Blowing in the Wind

B.3. **Not perform work when there is a conflict of interest**

Can You Be a Consultant to the Public Agency for Which You Once
  Worked?
Off-the-Job Social Relationships Affecting On-the-Job Performance
Private Enterprise Seeks a Public Official
Planner Works Part-time in Real Estate Sales
Annual Birthday Dinner
Developer Offers Summer Employment to Planner's Children
Do You Have a Duty to Report Suspicious Conduct?
Disclosing Your Employer

B.4. **Not represent a client for a year after leaving public
employment on matter previously influenced**

Can You Be a Consultant to the Public Agency for Which You Once
  Worked?
Private Enterprise Seeks a Public Official

B.5. **Not solicit clients or employment through false claims**

The Consultant's Brochure

B.6. **Not sell services by implying ability to influence through
improper means**

The Consultant's Brochure
Private Enterprise Seeks a Public Official

B.7. **Not improperly use power of office to seek a special
advantage**

Can You Be a Consultant to the Public Agency for Which You Once
  Worked?
Private Enterprise Seeks a Public Official
Annual Birthday Dinner
Developer Offers Summer Employment to Planner's Children

B.8. **Not accept work unable to perform**

Doing Outside Professional Work on Office Time
Being Responsive to Hispanic Community Values
Senior Planner Questions Competence of Director
Consultant's New Staff

Pricing the Comprehensive Plan
What Happens when the Consultant Takes On Too Much Work?

B.9.   Not reveal information

Private Enterprise Seeks a Public Official
Whistle Blowing or Blowing in the Wind
Disclosing Your Employer

C.   Contribute to development of profession

Planning Director Browbeats Consultant
Window Dressing Minority Contracting
Public Decision-Making without Public Input
Making Time on the Planning Commission Agenda
What's the Difference between Exactions and Extortion?
Balancing Compassion and Enforcing the Sign Ordinance
Senior Planner Questions Competence of Director
Prioritizing Non-Work That Occurs at the Office

C.1.   Protect and enhance integrity of profession

Planning Director Browbeats Consultant
Negative Comments about Consultant Work
The Consultant's Brochure
Using the Planning Process to Stop Unpopular Land Uses
When Your Personal Values Clash with a Planning Assignment
Using the Zoning Ordinance to Eliminate Feeding Programs for the
    Homeless
Senior Planner Questions Competence of Director
The Consultant's New Staff
Do You Have a Duty to Report Suspicious Conduct?
Whistle Blowing or Blowing in the Wind

C.2.   Accurately represent views of colleagues

Negative Comments about Consultant Work
Consultant's New Staff

C.3.   Review work in professional manner

Planning Director Browbeat Consultants
Window Dressing Minority Contracting
Negative Comments about Consultant Work
Off-the-Job Social Relationships Affecting On-the-Job Performance

What's the Difference between Exactions and Extortion?
Using the Zoning Ordinance to Eliminate Feeding Programs for the
    Homeless
Senior Planner Questions Competence of Director
Consultant's New Staff
Preserving Indian Artifacts
Do You Have a Duty to Report Suspicious Conduct?

C.4. Share results of experience and research

Doing Outside Professional Work on Office Time
Prioritizing Non-Work That Occurs at the Office

C.5. Establish appropriateness of solutions

When the Planning Director Wants Affordable Housing
Temporary Toilets
Annexation Analysis Blues
Street Vendors vs. Corporate America
Senior Planner Questions Competence of Director
When Your Personal and Professional Values Seem to Clash
Balancing Compassion and Enforcing the Sign Ordinance
Preserving the Indian Artifacts

C.6. Contribute time and information to development of others

Doing Outside Professional Work on Office Time
Prioritizing Non-work That Goes On at the Office

C.7. Strive to increase opportunities for women and minorities

Window Dressing Minority Contractor
Dealing with Allegations of Sexual Harassment

C.8. Not commit an act of sexual harassment

Dealing with Allegations of Sexual Harassment

D. Strive for high standards of integrity, proficiency, and knowledge

Planning Director Browbeats Consultant
Off-the-Job Social Relationships Affecting On-the-Job Performance

When the Rules of the Game Seem to Change
Senior Planner Questions Competence of Director
Whistle Blowing or Blowing in the Wind
Prioritizing Non-Work that Goes On at the Office

D.1.   Not commit a deliberately wrongful act

What Are You Willing to Do to Keep Your Job?
Dealing with Allegations of Sexual Harassment
No Home for Group Homes
Balancing Compassion and Enforcing the Sign Ordinance
Whistle Blowing or Blowing in the Wind

D.2.   Respect rights of others

Planning Director Browbeats Consultants
Dealing with Allegations of Sexual Harassment
Street Vendors vs. Corporate America

D.3.   Strive to continue education

Senior Planner Questions Competence of Director
Prioritizing Non-Work That Goes On at the Office

D.4.   Accurately represent qualifications

Consultant's Brochure
Consultant's New Staff

D.5.   Analyze ethical issues

What Are You Willing to Do to Keep Your Job?
Can You Be a Consultant to the Public Agency for Which You Once
    Worked?
Doing Outside Professional Work on Office Time
Private Enterprise Seeks a Public Official
Annual Birthday Dinner
When an Appointed Official Seeks Permit Approval
Street Vendors vs. Corporate America
When the Rules of the Game Seem to Change
Using the Zoning Ordinance to Eliminate Feeding Programs.
An Exercise in Damage Control
Whistle Blowing or Blowing in the Wind

D.6. Contribute time to groups lacking planning resources

When the Planning Director Wants Affordable Housing
Planner Wonders If Community Understands Development's Potential
    Impact
Doing Outside Professional Work on Office Time
Moving the Airport
Street Vendors vs. Corporate America
Prioritizing Non-Work that Goes On at the Office

RULINGS

1. Sexual harassment

Dealing with Allegations of Sexual Harassment

2. When a public planner has a stake in private development

A Planner Works Part-Time in Real Estate Sales

3. Outside employment or moonlighting

Doing Outside Professional Work on Office Time
Planner Works Part-time in Real Estate Sales

4. Honesty in the use of information

Temporary Toilets
Planner Spies Endangered Species
When the Rules of the Game Seem to Change
Who Determines the Real Numbers
Preserving the Indian Artifacts
Grocery Store Market Analysis

5. Planners who know of unethical conduct must report it

What Are You Willing to Do to Keep Your Job?
Planning Director Browbeats Consultants
Annexation Analysis Blues
The Consultant's Brochure
Using the Zoning Ordinance to Eliminate Feeding Programs for the
    Homeless
Do You Have a Duty to Report Suspicious Conduct?

6. **Disclosure of confidential information when there may be a violation of law**

Being Offered Confidential Information

AICP/APA ETHICAL PRINCIPLES IN PLANNING
(AS ADOPTED MAY 1992)

This statement is a guide to ethical conduct for all who participate in the process of planning as advisors, advocates, and decision-makers. It presents a set of principles to be held in common by certified planners, other practicing planners, appointed and elected officials, and others who participate in the process of planning.

The planning process exists to serve the public interest. While the public interest is a question of continuous debate, both in its general principles and in its case-by-case applications, it requires a conscientiously held view of the policies and actions that best serve the entire community. Section A presents what we hold to be necessary elements in such a view.

Planning issues commonly involve a conflict of values and, often, there are large private interests at stake. These accentuate the necessity for the highest standards of fairness and honesty among all participants. Section B presents specific standards.

Those who practice planning need to adhere to a special set of ethical requirements that must guide all who aspire to professionalism. These are presented in Section C.

Section D is the translation of the principles above into the AICP Code of Ethics and Professional Conduct. The Code is formally subscribed to by each certified planner. It includes an enforcement procedure that is administered by AICP. The Code, however, provides for more than the minimum threshold of enforceable acceptability. It also sets aspirational standards that require conscious striving to attain.

The ethical principles derive both from the general values of society and from the planner's special responsibility to serve the public interest. As the basic values of society are often in competition with each other, so do these principles sometimes compete. For example, the need to provide full public information may compete with the need to respect confidences. Plans and programs often result from a balancing among divergent interests. An ethical judgment often also requires a conscientious balancing, based on the facts and context of a particular situation and on the entire set of ethical principles.

This statement also aims to inform the public generally. It is also the basis for continuing systematic discussion of the application of its principles that is itself essential behavior to give them daily meaning.

A. The planning process must continuously pursue and faithfully serve the public interest.

Planning process participants should:
1. Recognize the rights of citizens to participate in planning decisions;
2. Strive to give citizens (including those who lack formal organization or influence) full, clear and accurate information on planning issues and the opportunity to have a meaningful role in the development of plans and programs;

3. Strive to expand choice and opportunity for all persons, recognizing a special responsibility to plan for the needs of disadvantaged groups and persons;
4. Assist in the clarification of community goals, objectives and policies in plan-making;
5. Ensure that reports, records and any other non-confidential information which is, or will be, available to decision makers is made available to the public in a convenient format and sufficiently in advance of any decision;
6. Strive to protect the integrity of the natural environment and the heritage of the built environment;
7. Pay special attention to the inter-relatedness of decisions and the long-range consequences of present actions.

B. Planning process participants continuously strive to achieve high standards of integrity and proficiency so that public respect for the planning process will be maintained.

Planning process participants should:
1. Exercise fair, honest and independent judgment in their roles as decision makers and advisors;
2. Make public disclosure of all "personal interests" they may have regarding any decision to be made in the planning process in which they serve, or are requested to serve, as advisor or decision maker (see also Advisory Ruling Number 2, "Conflicts of Interest When a Public Planner Has a Stake in Private Development" under Section D)
3. Define "personal interest" broadly to include any actual or potential benefits or advantages that they, a spouse, family member or person living in their household might directly or indirectly obtain from a planning decision;
4. Abstain completely from direct or indirect participation as an advisor or decision maker in any matter in which they have a personal interest, and leave any chamber in which such a matter is under deliberation, unless their personal interest has been made a matter of public record; their employer, if any, has given approval; and the public official, public agency or court with jurisdiction to rule on ethics matters has expressly authorized their participation;
5. Seek no gifts or favors, nor offer any, under circumstances in which it might reasonably be inferred that the gifts or favors were intended or expected to influence a participant's objectivity as an advisor or decision maker in the planning process;
6. Not participate as an advisor or decision maker on any plan or project in which they have previously participated as an advocate;
7. Serve as advocates only when the client's objectives are legal and consistent with the public interest.

8. Not participate as an advocate on any aspect of a plan or program on which they have previously served as advisor or decision maker unless their role as advocate is authorized by applicable law, agency regulation, or ruling of an ethics officer or agency; such participation as an advocate should be allowed only after prior disclosure to, and approval by, their affected client or employer; under no circumstance should such participation commerce earlier than one year following termination of the role as advisor or decision maker;

9. Not use confidential information acquired in the course of their duties to further a personal interest;

10. Not disclose confidential information acquired in the course of their duties except when required by law, to prevent a clear violation of law or to prevent substantial injury to third persons; provided that disclosure in the latter two situations may not be made until after verification of the facts and issues involved and consultation with other planning process participants to obtain their separate opinions;

11. Not misrepresent facts or distort information for the purpose of achieving a desired outcome (see also Advisory Ruling Number 4: "Honesty in the Use of Information" under Section D);

12. Not participate in any matter unless adequately prepared and sufficiently capacitated to render thorough and diligent service;

13. Respect the rights of all persons and not improperly discriminate against or harass others based on characteristics which are protected under civil rights laws and regulations (see also Advisory Ruling Number 1: "Sexual Harassment").

C. APA members who are practicing planners continuously pursue improvement in their planning competence as well as in the development of peers and aspiring planners. They recognize that enhancement of planning as a profession leads to greater public respect for the planning process and thus serves the public interest.

APA members who are practicing planners:
1. Strive to achieve high standards of professionalism, including certification, integrity, knowledge, and professional development consistent with the AICP Code of Ethics;

2. Do not commit a deliberately wrongful act which reflects adversely on planning as a profession or seek business by stating or implying that they are prepared, willing or able to influence decisions by improper means;

3. Participate in continuing professional education;

4. Contribute time and effort to groups lacking adequate planning resources and to voluntary professional activities;

5. Accurately represent their qualifications to practice planning as well as their education and affiliations;

6. Accurately represent the qualifications, views, and findings of colleagues;
7. Treat fairly and comment responsibly on the professional views of colleagues and members of other professions;
8. Share the results of experience and research which contribute to the body of planning knowledge;
9. Examine the applicability of planning theories, methods and standards to the facts and analysis of each particular situation and do not accept the applicability of a customary solution without first establishing its appropriateness to the situation;
10. Contribute time and information to the development of students, interns, beginning practitioners and other colleagues;
11. Strive to increase the opportunities for women and members of recognized minorities to become professional planners;
12. Systematically and critically analyze ethical issues in the practice of planning. (See also Advisory Ruling Number 3: "Outside Employment or Moonlighting").

Section D consists of the AICP Code of Ethics and Professional Conduct, Advisory Rulings, and Procedures.

AICP CODE OF ETHICS AND PROFESSIONAL CONDUCT (ADOPTED OCTOBER 1978, AMENDED OCTOBER 1991)

This Code is a guide to the ethical conduct required of members of the American Institute of Certified Planners. The Code also aims at informing the public of the principles to which professional planners are committed. Systematic discussion of the application of these principles, among planners and with the public, is itself essential behavior to bring the Code into daily use.

The Code's standards of behavior provide a basis for adjudicating any charge that a member has acted unethically. However, the Code also provides more than the minimum threshold of enforceable acceptability. It sets aspirational standards that require conscious striving to attain.

The principles of the Code derive both from the general values of society and from the planning profession's special responsibility to serve the public interest. As the basic values of society are often in competition with each other, so also do the principles of this Code sometimes compete. For example, the need to provide full public information may compete with the need to respect confidences. Plans and programs often result from a balancing among divergent interests. An ethical judgment often also requires a conscientious balancing, based on the facts and context of a particular situation and on the precepts of the entire Code. Formal procedures for filing of complaints, investigation and resolution of alleged violations and the issuance of advisory rulings are part of the Code.

The Planner's Responsibility to the Public

A. A planner's primary obligation is to serve the public interest. While the definition of the public interest is formulated through continuous debate, a planner owes allegiance to a conscientiously attained concept of the public interest, which requires these special obligations:
1. A planner must have special concern for the long-range consequences of present actions.
2. A planner must pay special attention to the inter-relatedness of decisions.
3. A planner must strive to provide full, clear and accurate information on planning issues to citizens and governmental decision-makers.
4. A planner must strive to give citizens the opportunity to have a meaningful impact on the development of plans and programs. Participation should be broad enough to include people who lack formal organization or influence.
5. A planner must strive to expand choice and opportunity for all persons, recognizing a special responsibility to plan for the needs of disadvantaged groups and persons, and must urge the alteration of policies, institutions and decisions which oppose such needs.
6. A planner must strive to protect the integrity of the natural environment.

7. A planner must strive for excellence of environmental design and endeavor to conserve the heritage of the built environment.

The Planner's Responsibility to Clients and Employers

B. A planner owes diligent, creative, independent and competent performance of work in pursuit of the client's or employer's interest. Such performance should be consistent with the planner's faithful service to the public interest.

1. A planner must exercise independent professional judgment on behalf of clients and employers.
2. A planner must accept the decisions of a client or employer concerning the objectives and nature of the professional services to be performed unless the course of action to be pursued involves conduct which is illegal or inconsistent with the planner's primary obligation to the public interest.
3. A planner shall not perform work if there is an actual, apparent, or reasonably foreseeable conflict of interest, direct or indirect, or an appearance of impropriety, without full written disclosure concerning work for current or past clients and subsequent written consent by the current client or employer. A planner shall remove himself or herself from a project if there is any direct personal or financial gain including gains to family members. A planner shall not disclose information gained in the course of public activity for a private benefit unless the information would be offered impartially to any person.
4. A planner who has previously worked for a public planning body should not represent a private client, for one year after the planner's last date of employment with the planning body, in connection with any matter before that body that the planner may have influenced before leaving public employment.
5. A planner must not solicit prospective clients or employment through use of false or misleading claims, harassment or duress.
6. A planner must not sell or offer to sell services by stating or implying an ability to influence decisions by improper means.
7. A planner must not use the power of any office to seek or obtain a special advantage that is not in the public interest nor any special advantage that is not a matter of public knowledge.
8. A planner must not accept or continue to perform work beyond the planner's professional competence or accept work which cannot be performed with the promptness required by the prospective client or employer, or which is required by the circumstances of the assignment.
9. A planner must not reveal information gained in a professional relationship which the client or employer has requested to be held inviolate. Exceptions to this requirement of non-disclosure may be made only when (a) required by process of law, or (b) required to prevent a clear violation of law, or (c) required to prevent a substantial injury to

the public. Disclosure pursuant to (b) and (c) must not be made until after the planner has verified the facts and issues involved and, when practicable, has exhausted efforts to obtain reconsideration of the matter and has sought separate opinions on the issue from other qualified professionals employed by the client or employer.

The Planner's Responsibility to the Profession and to Colleagues

1. A planner should contribute to the development of the profession by improving knowledge and techniques, making work relevant to solutions of community problems, and increasing public understanding of planning activities. A planner should treat fairly the professional views of qualified colleagues and members of other professions.
2. A planner must protect and enhance the integrity of the profession and must be responsible in criticism of the profession.
3. A planner must accurately represent the qualifications, views and findings of colleagues.
4. A planner who reviews the work of other professionals must do so in a fair, considerate, professional and equitable manner.
5. A planner must share the results of experience and research which contribute to the body of planning knowledge.
6. A planner must examine the applicability of planning theories, methods and standards to the facts and analysis of each particular situation and must not accept the applicability of a customary solution without first establishing its appropriateness to the situation.
7. A planner must contribute time and information to the professional development of students, interns, beginning professionals and other colleagues.
8. A planner must strive to increase the opportunities for women and members of recognized minorities to become professional planners.
9. A planner shall not commit an act of sexual harassment.

The Planner's Self-Responsibility

C. A planner should strive for high standards of professional integrity, proficiency and knowledge.
   1. A planner must not commit a deliberately wrongful act which reflects adversely on the planner's professional fitness.
   2. A planner must respect the rights of others and, in particular, must not improperly discriminate against persons.
   3. A planner must strive to continue professional education.
   4. A planner must accurately represent professional qualifications, education and affiliations.
   5. A planner must systematically and critically analyze ethical issues in the practice of planning.
   6. A planner must strive to contribute time and effort to groups lacking in adequate planning resources and to voluntary professional activities.

Procedures under the Code of Ethics and Professional Conduct (amended 2000)

1. Informal Advice and Formal Advisory Rulings: Any person may seek informal advice on ethics from the Executive Director of the AICP or from the Chair of a Chapter Professional Development Committee. Such advice shall not be binding upon the AICP.

    Any person may file a written request with the Executive Director of the AICP for a formal advisory ruling on the propriety of any professional planner conduct. The request should contain sufficient facts, real or hypothetical, to permit a definitive opinion. If appropriate, the Executive Director shall then prepare and furnish a written formal advisory ruling to the inquiring party. This ruling may be published if endorsed by the AICP Ethics Committee as commentary on the Code and a guide to its application. Published rulings, however, shall not include any actual names and places without the written consent of all persons to be named. A ruling may be relied upon by the person who requested it whether or not published.

2. Charges Alleging Misconduct by an AICP Member: Any person may file in writing with the Executive Director of the AICP a charge of misconduct against an AICP member. The charge shall state the facts upon which it is based. A person may file a charge anonymously. Anonymous filers shall have the option of designating a em-mil or post office address in the event they need to be contacted by the Executive Director. Persons who file charges anonymously shall not be sent notification as to the disposition of the charge, shall have no right to appeal if the charge is dismissed, and shall not be sent findings of fact, determinations, and opinions of the AICP Ethics Committee. The Executive Director shall furnish a copy of the charge to the respondent member.

The Executive Director shall determine whether the charge warrants an investigation.

The Executive Director with or without an investigation may dismiss the charge or issue a complaint against the respondent. In either event, notice shall be sent to the charging party and to the respondent advising of the determination and of the charging party's right to appeal the dismissal of the charge.

The Executive Director's decision to dismiss a charge may be appealed by the charging party within thirty days of receipt of written notification. The Executive Director shall promptly forward copies of the appeal to the members of the AICP Ethics Committee. The Ethics Committee may remand the charge to the Executive Director for further investigation and/or reconsideration, or the Committee may reverse the Executive Director's decision if it is contrary to the provisions of the Code or to prior Committee opinions.

If the Executive Director issues a complaint against a member, the latter shall have thirty days from receipt of the complaint to respond. In the absence of extraordinary circumstances which, in the opinion of the Ethics Committee, warrant a special exception, the failure of a respondent to deny any fact alleged in the complaint within the thirty day period will be deemed an admission of such fact.

If the response to the complaint reveals any disputed material fact, the respondent shall be granted a hearing before the Ethics Committee of the AICP or before any member or members of the Ethics Committee designated by the Committee's Chair to conduct the hearing. The hearing shall proceed without application of formal rules of evidence; however, the substantive rights of the respondents shall at all times be protected.

If a hearing is held, those conducting it shall promptly issue findings of fact which shall be transmitted to the full Committee, the respondent and the charging party. If no material fact was in dispute and no hearing held, the Ethics Committee need not issue findings of fact.

On the basis of the findings of fact and admissions, the Ethics Committee shall determine whether the Code has been violated and issue an opinion. A copy of the opinion shall be transmitted to the respondent, the charging party and the Commission. The Ethics Committee may concurrently submit a recommendation to the Commission that the respondent be expelled, suspended, publicly censured, or privately reprimanded. The respondent shall be given no less than thirty days' notice to respond, in person and/or in writing before it is voted on by the Commission, which vote shall be within one year of the issuance of the complaint. Disciplinary action against a member and the official publication of an expulsion, suspension or public censure shall require the affirmative vote of two-thirds of the Commission.

The Executive Director shall publish all written opinions endorsed by the Commission or by the Ethics Committee, but shall omit actual names and places unless authorized by an affirmative vote of two-thirds of the Commission or in writing by the respondent.

AICP ADVISORY RULINGS

Ethics Advisories. The AICP Code of Ethics and Professional Conduct provides for advice by the executive director on specific problems and questions concerning ethical behavior by members. The AICP Ethics Committee asked that such advice be codified as advisory rulings specified by the code.

Advisory Ruling No. 1: Sexual Harassment

Sexual harassment is unethical under the AICP Code of Ethics and Professional Conduct. Sexual harassment is also subject to penalty under law. The U.S. Equal Employment Opportunity Commission defines sexual harassment as: Unwelcome sexual advances, requests for sexual favors, and other verbal or physical conduct of a sexual nature constitute sexual harassment when: 1) Submission to such conduct is made either explicitly or implicitly a term or condition of an individual's employment; 2) Submission to or rejection of such conduct by an individual is used as the basis for employment decisions affecting such individual; or 3) Such conduct has the purpose or effect of unreasonably interfering with an individual's work performance or creating an intimidating, hostile, or offensive working environment.

Two of the general principles in the Code are applicable to specific instances of harassment: Principle D (1) of the Code says that a planner must not commit a deliberately wrongful act which reflects adversely on the planner's professional fitness; and Principle D (2) of the Code says that a planner must respect the rights of others and, in particular, must not improperly discriminate against persons. Unlawful sexual harassment as defined by the EEOC is a deliberately wrongful act.

Respecting the rights of others, under the Code, requires a standard of behavior higher than that defined as coercive or intimidating by EEOC. Conduct that may not have illegal effect may nevertheless be harassment. Joking or bantering about sexual subjects, comments suggesting sexual attractiveness, and comments disparaging women or men or their abilities generally may constitute petty harassment. If any such behavior is found offensive, offended persons should so say. The offensive behavior becomes harassment if continued after the offender is notified.

Negligence or omission on the part of an employer who is dismissive of a complaint of sexual harassment, and encourages the complainant to be tolerant of the offense is itself a form of harassment. So is a deliberately false accusation of sexual harassment.

Harassment is decidedly distinct from behavior occasioned when a genuinely mutual affection springs up between co-workers. (May 1988).

Advisory Ruling No. 2: Conflicts of Interest when a Public Planner has a Stake in Private Development

The Code of Ethics and Professional Conduct addresses conflicts of interest in Principal B (3): "A planner must not, without the consent of the client or employer, and only after full disclosure, accept or continue to perform work if there is an actual, apparent, or reasonably foreseeable conflict between the interests of the client or employer and the personal or financial interest of the planner or of another past or present client or employer of the planner."

Conflicts of interest are reasonably foreseeable when a planner attempts to serve a real estate development client while also serving a public agency that may have a role in reviewing or approving projects of that client.

Inquiries from planners who contemplate combining activity in real estate business with public planning work have fallen into a pattern as have the responses:

Real estate is a popular investment, and planners, knowing a lot about it, are attracted to it.

"I have an opportunity to invest in a small development, but the proposal will come before my agency for approval. What do you advise?" Don't do it. There are other investment opportunities.

"What if it's put in my wife's name?" Your wife's financial interest is your financial interest and yours is hers.

"But, when it comes before us, I will exclude myself from the decision, and only other staff members will recommend on the proposal. I won't take part at all." Your colleagues work with you, know that your interests are involved, and can't eliminate the influence of your relationship with them, even if unexpressed.

"My influence really can be a positive one on the developer. I know what would be good for the public and can work for a good design." That's when your agency is there for, and that's why it has the power to review and approve.

"But what if I disclose everything to the director, and he gives his consent...?" He shouldn't. I certainly would advise him not to.

"I will work for a broker in a neighboring jurisdiction across the state line. He doesn't have a license in that state." No, but some of his colleagues do. And some of the decisions affecting the broker's business are regional decisions involving both jurisdictions.

A code of ethics should not be a what-can-I-get-away-with code. It should not be tortured into loopholes and technicalities that would allow a person to be formally correct while ethically wrong. The AICP Code looks for "more than the minimum threshold of enforceable acceptability. It sets aspirational standards that require conscious striving to attain."

Developers can benefit from professional planning services and are just as entitled to fully conscientious advocacy of their interests as a public planning agency. A conflict of interest is inherent, however, in any assumption of both roles simultaneously.

There may also be a conflict when the roles overlap. A planner may move from employment by a public agency to employment by a private client. A conflict arises as soon as discussion is initiated for such a move. The public employer must, therefore, be notified promptly that such discussion has taken place whether or not it matures in a change of employment. This is decidedly earlier notice than is normal for a job change and it is notice of a change that may not take place. It is necessary, however, to guard against the substantial conflicts that would occur if a planner is in a position to influence the resolution of certain issues in public employ that will later affect the interests of a new, private employer.

Private planners and consultants who undertake work for a public agency, or change employment from private to public, must disclose any conflicts or potential conflicts to the public agency employer. (May 1988).

Advisory Ruling No. 3: Outside Employment or Moonlighting

A planner's responsibility to an employer places significant restraints on accepting work for employers outside of the full-time commitments to the primary employer. A full-time member of a planning agency staff owes loyalty, energy and powers of mind primarily to its service.

The Principles in the Code that concern conflict of interest B (3) and using an office to seek special advantage B (7) must especially be applied.

A planning staff member must take no employment outside of official duties unless such employment creates no conflict with those duties either in the interests to be served or in competition for time and energy. If the planner decides that there will be no such conflicts, then outside employment must, in addition, receive the explicit approval of the employer.

No outside employment must be undertaken if its performance will reduce the quality or dispatch with which the staff member executes primary responsibilities. The number of hours and the scheduled times devoted to outside employment must not interrupt or interfere with the time that the primary responsibilities demand.

Outside employment must never deal with any matter that may require an action or recommendation by the primary employing agency. Neither must employment be taken with any person or organization that does business with any agency of the primary employer.

Public property must not be used for any private purpose including work that is performed for other employers.

Principle B (8) says that "A planner must not accept ... work beyond the planner's professional competence or accept work which cannot be performed with the promptness required..." Since the schedules, deadlines, priorities and unanticipated time demands of the primary employer must always take precedence, the volume of outside work must necessarily be small and an outside employer must be informed that prompt execution will not necessarily be satisfied. Both the planner requesting, and the authority giving, approval for outside employment should consider the main justification for approval is a demand for whatever special professional knowledge and experience the planner has that is not otherwise readily available. Service as a teacher or instructor is outside employment that is most justifiable and an unspecialized, general consulting practice least justifiable. (May 1988).

Advisory Ruling No. 4: Honesty in the Use of Information

As professional givers of advice—advice that may affect the well being of communities and individuals for many years—we have a special obligation to cherish honesty in the information that supports our advice.

Yet, many daily pressures do battle against honesty. We are pressed to be effective advocates for a community, a private client, an elected administration or a cause. A political agenda is often formed before dispassionate study; those who have campaigned for it then look with passion for studies to support. Decision-makers may demand a greater degree of certainty, or impose more rigorous criteria for decision, than the capability of analysis or sufficiency of data can satisfy.

The Code of Ethics and Professional Conduct is filled with prescriptions for honesty:

A (3) "provide full, clear and accurate information on planning issues to citizens and governmental decision-makers."

B (3) "only after full disclosure" (on conflicts of interest)."

B (5) "must not ... through use of false or misleading claims."

B (8) "must not accept ... work beyond the planner's professional competence."

C (1) "must protect and enhance the integrity of the profession."

C (2) "must accurately represent the qualifications, views and findings of colleagues."

D (4) "must accurately represent (one's own) professional qualifications, education and affiliations."

In some situations, planners must not provide full information. Planners frequently have the role of negotiators whose effectiveness depends on not disclosing final positions that are acceptable. And, as the Code points out, "the need to provide full public information may compete with the need to respect confidences." Information that is disclosed in such circumstances must, however, be honest and accurate.

It is part of professional conduct to communicate our ethical standards to clients, employers and the public. Communicating them early, before they need to be applied to a specific controversy, may erase pressures to abuse them.

There should be no need to explain what the code requires as full, clear and accurate information. Half-truths, deceptions and undocumented assertions don't pass. A half-truth is a whole lie. Don't cook the numbers.

There is also a positive duty on behalf of ethical treatment of information. In reporting the results of studies, planners must follow the scholar's rule of making it possible for others to follow in our footsteps and check our work. Document the sources of data. Report the statistical procedures used, what was done to bring the raw data into the form that is reported. What assumptions were made at different stages in the study?

Public decision-makers must often leap beyond the cautions and reservations of a careful study to achieve political solutions. Planners must take pains that our studies and recommendations are not wrongly interpreted, and that a clear distinction is made between factual findings and policy decisions. (March 1991).

Advisory Ruling No. 5: Certain Duties of Planners to Ensure Effective Enforcement of the Code of Ethics and Professional Conduct

Principle C (1) of the Code of Ethics and Professional Conduct requires that a "planner must protect and enhance the integrity of the profession. The Code itself sets standards of behavior for planners and effective enforcement of Code provisions is essential to the integrity of the profession.

To achieve effective enforcement of the Code, the following behaviors are required by Principle C (1):

1. A planner who has certain knowledge of clearly unethical conduct on the part of the certified planner has a duty to file a charge of misconduct with the Executive Director. A corollary obligation is that a planner should never use the threat of filing an ethics charge relating to current or past misconduct in order to gain, or attempt to gain, an advantage in dealings with another planner.

2. A planner who desires to file a charge of misconduct has an obligation to do so pursuant to the Procedures under the Code of Ethics and Professional Conduct. The charge would be transmitted only to the Executive Director who will then send a copy to the respondent. A planner should not make public allegations of Code violations against another planner, but rather should trust the processes of the Institute to determine if a violation has occurred and, if so, the sanctions to be applied.

3. A planner against whom a charge of misconduct has been filed has a duty to cooperate fully with the Executive Director and the Ethics Committee to ensure that all information which may be relevant to the charge (or Complaint) is made available. This includes an obligation to encourage others with relevant information, whether favorable to unfavorable, to cooperate, as well. The Ethics Committee may determine that allegations not admitted by the planner are proven if it finds that the planner has failed to fully cooperate at any point in the process.

4. A planner against whom a charge of misconduct has been filed has a duty not to retaliate in any manner against a person who filed the charge or cooperated in the investigation and/or resolution thereof. (January 1998)

Formal Advisory Ruling No. 6: Concerning disclosure of information gained in a professional relationship when there may be a violation of law.

A planner is generally prohibited by Code B (9) from revealing "information gained in a professional relationship which the client or employer has requested to be held inviolate." However, one of the exceptions to the general rule permits disclosure "to prevent a clear violation of law... after the planner has verified the facts and issues involved and, when practicable, has exhausted efforts to obtain reconsideration of the matter and has sought separate opinions on the issue from other qualified professionals employed by the client or employer.

A planner who is expected by an employer not to make public disclosure of conduct that the planner, after verifying the facts and issues, views as clearly illegal is often faced with difficult personal choices. A planner who angers an employer by going public with such information is subject to retaliatory conduct, including direct or constructive termination, inferior pay and promotion treatment and other sanctions short of dismissal. In many situations, the planner's right to administratively or judicially appeal retaliatory conduct is limited or non-existent.

The planner facing such a dilemma should first consider whether it is practicable to try, as diplomatically as possible, to urge the employer to recognize that the conduct is illegal and should either be avoided or, if in the past, acknowledged and remedied. However, if the employer's past conduct indicates that such an effort will be unwelcome, the planner should avoid a confrontation with the employer and next consider whether it is practicable "to obtain separate opinions to verify the planner's conclusion from other qualified professionals employed by the same employer."

If the planner reasonably fears that the employer would retaliate upon learning of a possible challenge to its integrity, the planner may not deem it practicable to raise the matter with other professionals working for the same employer. This includes co-employed attorneys, who may feel a fiduciary duty to report immediately to the client employer upon learning of the planner's potential challenge to its conduct.

One option, not mentioned in the Code, is for the planner to consult with an unconflicted, personal attorney prior to concluding whether to go public with confidential information that could embarrass the employer. It would be desirable to seek the counsel of an attorney who has expertise in matters of public or private employment law and who is thus familiar with the rights and remedies available within the jurisdiction if the employer were to retaliate. And, even though attorneys, with narrow exceptions, are ethically barred from revealing client confidences, it may still be desirable to get advance assurance in writing from the attorney concerning non-disclosure. To hold down costs, the planner should prepare for the attorney a concise, confidential memorandum setting out the verified facts and issues so that the attorney can assist the planner more efficiently in determining the ethically required course of action.

In the final analysis, the planner may determine that the only ethical option is to go public with the information and face employer retaliation. It can only be hoped that in such situations available legal remedies furnish adequate protection and/or that a public outcry has a similar effect. (October 1999).

ANSWER SHEET FOR ETHICS WORKSHOP

Circle preferred alternatives and add your own comment.

A. Scenario:

1.   2.   3.   4.   5.

Other Comments: _____

_____

B. Scenario:

1.   2.   3.   4.   5.

Other Comments: _____

_____

C. Scenario:

1.   2.   3.   4.   5.

Other Comments: _____

_____

D. Scenario:

1.   2.   3.   4.   5.

Other Comments: _____

_____

E. Scenario:

1.   2.   3.   4.   5.

Other Comments: _____

_____

THE SOCIAL RESPONSIBILITY OF THE PLANNER

These Guidelines for the Social Responsibility of the Planner were adopted by the Board of Governors of the American Institute of Planners in 1972. These Guidelines were developed and reviewed by the membership of AIP in recognition that the planning profession is closely involved in public policies and decisions which affect the interests of minorities and other disadvantaged groups.

This booklet is published to help create better understanding among professional planners public officials, and the public at large as to the effects which public decisions have on all segments of the population served by Planning.

The American Institute of Planners for several years has had a state objective to foster social equality through the practice of applying. The AIP Code of Professional Responsibility contains a Canon which states that "A planner shall seek to expand choice and opportunity for all persons, recognizing a special responsibility to plan for the needs of disadvantaged groups and persons, and shall urge the alteration of policies, institutions, and decisions which mitigate against such objectives." These Guidelines on the Social Responsibility of the Planner help explain that Canon. This booklet contains General Guidelines and three specific short sections with Guidelines for planners in local areas, regional jurisdictions and state and federal programs.

The American Institute of Planners is the national professional society of urban and regional planners in the United States. Its members work primarily for local and state governments and other public agencies.

General Guidelines

1. The professional planners should recognize that a sound planning process requires familiarity with political and social realities, including the continuing need for, and real value in, working with directly with those affected by the planning process. Of special importance is the need to identify the human consequences of alternative public actions, including identification of positive social and cultural values to be preserved, as well as short-term and long-term social costs and benefits of alternative courses of action.

2. The professional planner owes faithful, creative, and efficient performance of work in pursuit of his client's interest, but also owes allegiance to a conscientiously attained concept of the public interest and a primary commitment to maximize opportunity and expand the extent of choice available to those restricted by social, economic, personal or other constraints. When a professional planner considers that planing policies, instruments, organizations or institutions are not in the interests of those intended to be served by the planning process, he must strive diligently to ensure that they are altered to reflect such interests.

3. The professional planner involved in controversial social issues related to planning activities should determine and recommend the soundest source of action based on his profession judgment, regardless of the controversy attendant upon such recommendation.

4. The professional planner should explain clearly to local, state, and national officials leaders the seriousness of existing, emerging, and anticipated social problems relating to community planning and development, so that solutions will be given proper priority in allocation of resources and other public actions. Similarly, the urgency of social needs and undesirable or inequitable human consequences resulting from public actions should be transmitted to those with power to influence those actions.

5. The professional planner should use all available forms of communication to make effective presentations on planning issues, planning alternatives, and their likely social effects, that they are more readily understandable by the public, particularly those affected.

6. The professional planner should seek to expand flexibility of governmental procedures and institutions to ensure greater constructive citizen participation and involvement in the planning process and to foster leadership in all groups, especially those neglected in public decision-making because of gaps in organization, leadership, or articulation of values and needs. The planner should be intimately concerned with the judgments, values, and needs of specific groups and subgroups.

7. The professional planners should recognize the wide human and intellectual diversity within a planning area, and devise appropriate institutions to accommodate and respect that diversity without unwarranted compromise resulting in mediocrity.

8. The professional planners should carefully examine planning standards and theory to determine their realism and their applicability to particular situations. This may call for new research of the systematic monitoring of progress or performance.

9. The professional planner should recommend the services of other professionals, whenever their specialized skills are needed in the constructive identification or measurement of social implications.

10. The professional planner should review achievements in collateral fields of social planning and reconcile such efforts with his own. The role of the advocate planner must be related to the many forms of planning activity and the advocate's functions acknowledged and supported.

11. The professional planner should seek opportunities to increase minority representation in the planing profession. This could be achieved by increasing minority representation in the Planning Department through adoption of a general minorities hiring policy, promoting planning education among minority groups, by providing scholarship support, summer internship programs, and directly involving minorities in professional and paraprofessional duties in areas of predominant minority group population.

12. The professional planners should seek very available opportunity to assist citizens in understanding the planning process. This should not be limited to advisory committees or other institutional forms of citizen participation in a project, but should be extended to voluntary participation by the planner himself in citizen organizations in which he may have an interest. This will thereby provide useful technical insights, intimate working relation-

ships with other members, assistance in understanding technical steps in the planning process and comprehensive of planning nomenclature. However, the professional planner must avoid conflicts of interests in such undertakings, especially the premature or unauthorized revelation of confidential information.

Guidelines for Planners in Local Areas

1. The process of preparing and updating the comprehensive plan and elements thereof deserves critical attention. This process has been considered by critics to have institutionalized economic and social bias, or to have ignored social injustice by focusing on policies which ignore economic and social consequences of physical planning proposals.

2. Participation in plan-making by professionals fully aware of the problems of minorities and the poor, and who can represent the viewpoints of such groups, would aid in ensuring that the comprehensive plan reflects their aspirations. If the requisite combination of skills, understanding and independence is not available in staff personnel, they must be sought elsewhere.

3. Problems affecting areas of minority and low income concentration with which planning should deal include: The quality, supply, availability and location of low and moderate-income housing; transportation accessibility to employment opportunities, shopping areas, medical services, recreation areas, day care centers, and educational facilities; location and adequacy of community and neighborhood facilities and services reasonably accessible to minorities, the poor, the young, the handicapped; the lower priority often given to environmental or physical development needs when compared to such immediate concerns as jobs, education, and housing; location near ghetto areas of employers who utilize labor-intensive operations which can draw on workers who are residents of the area; and opportunities for minority group members to establish their own businesses.

4. Where leadership in underrepresented areas is lacking or obscure, token representation, acknowledgment of self-appointed spokesmen or co-optation of groups in the planning process should be avoided in favor of an effort to develop adequate representation and real spokesmen.

5. The planning process should involve means by which residents of low income and minority neighborhoods with inadequate experience due to prior unfamiliarity, may identify effects of proposed plans on their neighborhood.

6. A key point in the plan-making process is determination of program content. Program components should assure adequate attention to social problems and needs of the community, as well as identification of positive cultural and social values to be preserved. In communities where there is a built-in reluctance to deal directly with controversial social questions, the planner must develop a strategy to ensure their inclusion in the work program.

7. Technical analysis may subordinate social sensitivity unless there is a conscious evaluation of standards and approach. Technical studies must be conducted broadly enough to determine social impacts.

8. Functional or element plans (e.g., for housing, transportation, health, natural resources, personal and public safety, education, etc.) should reflect underlying social concerns. Appropriate coordination among functional planning and programming efforts should assure that activity in one function does not cancel out the social effectiveness of actions in others. This concern for the social impact of planning is as important for natural and man-made physical environmental planning as it is for planning dealing with social and economic environments.

Guidelines for Professional Planners in Regional Jurisdictions (County, Metropolitan, and Regional)

1. At the regional scale, there is a significant opportunity to reduce inequities established and perpetuated at the local level. Planners in regional jurisdictions should be aware of the unequal effects of local taxation and service costs, residential and economic discrimination, and poor accessibility to employment, and should seek to reduce such inequities, including critical review of local plans.

2. Regional and metropolitan planners should foster communication among local planners who should meet regularly with counterparts in surrounding communities to improve mutual understanding of related or parallel problems.

3. Regional or metropolitan planners should provide information services for local planners, with more limited resources in evaluating social impacts of planning actions.

Guidelines for Professional Planners in State and Federal Programs

1. Distance from the neighborhood, where social issues are most apparent, demands from the state and federal planner caution in applying general panning standards or theories to a range of diverse situations. At these higher levels, where many decisions affecting the allocation of resources to local jurisdictions are made, social awareness is imperative.

2. State and federal planning should allow flexibility and choice within planning and a recognition that life styles and values vary significantly.

3. Planners working at state and federal levels should be especially careful that in drafting legislation and administrative guidelines, they reflect a concern for the individual's opportunity to develop his abilities and to move socially and economically within American society.

4. Program administration can often provide the most important opportunities to assure freedom of choice and foster economic and social mobility. For

instance, often state and federal programs are over-subscribed and choices must be made among the applicants; the planner should make every effort to give priority to proposals and projects which are socially significant.

5. State and federal planners must pursue changes in national priorities and resource allocation that contribute to alleviation of poverty and inequity, and should convey such concerns to those with the power and resources to change them. They should initiate needed legislative change relating to issues which have human consequences.

6. New forms of research and program monitoring should be pursued vigorously to maintain responsiveness and social awareness of ongoing state and federal programs.

ICMA CODE OF ETHICS WITH GUIDELINES

The ICMA Code of Ethics was adopted by the ICMA membership in 1924, and most recently amended by the membership in May 1998. The Guidelines for the Code were adopted by the ICMA Executive Board in 1972, and most recently revised in July 1998.

The purposes of ICMA are to enhance the quality of local government and to support and assist professional local administrators in the United States and other countries. To further these objectives, certain principles, as enforced by the Rules of Procedure, shall govern the conduct of every member of ICMA, who shall:

1. Be dedicated to the concepts of effective and democratic local government by responsible elected officials and believe that professional general management is essential to the achievement of this objective.
2. Affirm the dignity and worth of the services rendered by government and maintain a constructive, creative, and practical attitude toward local government affairs and a deep sense of social responsibility as a trusted public servant.

Guideline

Advice to Officials of Other Local Governments. When members advise and respond to inquiries from elected or appointed officials of other local governments, they should inform the administrators of those communities.

3. Be dedicated to the highest ideals of honor and integrity in all public and personal relationships in order that the member may merit the respect and confidence of the elected officials, of other officials and employees, and of the public.

Guidelines

Public Confidence. Members should conduct themselves so as to maintain public confidence in their profession, their local government, and in their performance of the public trust.

Impression of Influence. Members should conduct their official and personal affairs in such a manner as to give the clear impression that they cannot be improperly influenced in the performance of their official duties.

Appointment Commitment. Members who accept an appointment to a position should not fail to report for that position. This does not preclude the possibility of a member considering several offers or seeking several positions at the same time, but once a bona fide offer of a position has been accepted, that commitment should be honored. Oral acceptance of an employment offer is considered binding unless the employer makes fundamental changes in terms of employment.

Credentials. An application for employment should be complete and accurate as to all pertinent details of education, experience, and personal history. Members should recognize that both omissions and inaccuracies must be avoided.

Professional Respect. Members seeking a management position should show professional respect for persons formerly holding the position or for others who might be applying for the same position. Professional respect does not preclude honest differences of opinion; it does preclude attacking a person's motives or integrity in order to be appointed to a position.

Confidentiality. Members should not discuss or divulge information with anyone about pending or completed ethics cases, except as specifically authorized by the Rules of Procedure for Enforcement of the Code of Ethics.

Seeking Employment. Members should not seek employment for a position having an incumbent administrator who has not resigned or been officially informed that his or her services are to be terminated.

4. Recognize that the chief function of local government at all times is to serve the best interests of all of the people.

Guideline

Length of Service. A minimum of two years generally is considered necessary in order to render a professional service to the local government. A short tenure should be the exception rather than a recurring experience. However, under special circumstances, it may be in the best interests of the local government and the member to separate in a shorter time. Examples of such circumstances would include refusal of the appointing authority to honor commitments concerning conditions of employment, a vote of no confidence in the member, or severe personal problems. It is the responsibility of an applicant for a position to ascertain conditions of employment. Inadequately determining terms of employment prior to arrival does not justify premature termination.

5. Submit policy proposals to elected officials; provide them with facts and advice on matters of policy as a basis for making decisions and setting community goals; and uphold and implement local government policies adopted by elected officials.

Guideline

Conflicting Roles. Members who serve multiple roles—working as both city attorney and city manager for the same community, for example—should avoid participating in matters that create the appearance of a conflict of interest. They should disclose the potential conflict to the governing body so that other opinions may be solicited.

6. Recognize that elected representatives of the people are entitled to the credit for the establishment of local government policies; responsibility for policy execution rests with the members.

7. Refrain from all political activities which undermine public confidence in professional administrators. Refrain from participation in the election of the members of the employing legislative body.

Guidelines
Elections of the Governing Body. Members should maintain a reputation for serving equally and impartially all members of the governing body of the local government they serve, regardless of party. To this end, they should not engage in active participation in the election campaign on behalf of or in opposition to candidates for the governing body.

Elections of Elected Executives. Members should not engage in the election campaign of any candidate for mayor or elected county executive.

Elections. Members share with their fellow citizens the right and responsibility to exercise their franchise and voice their opinion on public issues. However, in order not to impair their effectiveness on behalf of the local governments they serve, they should not participate in any political activities (including but not limited to fundraising, endorsing candidates, and financial contributions) for representatives to city, county, special district, school, state, or federal offices.

Elections in the Council-Manager Plan. Members may assist in preparing and presenting materials that explain the council-manager form of government to the public prior to an election on the use of the plan. If assistance is required by another community, members may respond. All activities regarding ballot issues should be conducted within local regulations and in a professional manner.

Presentation of Issues. Members may assist the governing body in presenting issues involved in referenda such as bond issues, annexations, and similar matters.

8. Make it a duty continually to improve the member's professional ability and to develop the competence of associates in the use of management techniques.

Guidelines
Self-Assessment. Each member should assess his or her professional skills and abilities on a periodic basis.

Professional Development. Each member should commit at least 40 hours per year to professional development activities that are based on the practices identified by the members of ICMA.

9. Keep the community informed on local government affairs; encourage communication between the citizens and all local government officers; emphasize friendly and courteous service to the public; and seek to improve the quality and image of public service.

10. Resist any encroachment on professional responsibilities, believing the member should be free to carry out official policies without interference, and handle each problem without discrimination on the basis of principle and justice.

Guideline
Information Sharing. The member should openly share information with the governing body while diligently carrying out the member's responsibilities as set forth in the charter or enabling legislation.

11. Handle all matters of personnel on the basis of merit so that fairness and impartiality govern a member's decisions, pertaining to appointments, pay adjustments, promotions, and discipline.

Guideline
Equal Opportunity. Members should develop a positive program that will ensure meaningful employment opportunities for all segments of the community. All programs, practices, and operations should: (1) provide equality of opportunity in employment for all persons; (2) prohibit discrimination because of race, color, religion, sex, national origin, political affiliation, physical handicaps, age, or marital status; and (3) promote continuing programs of affirmative action at every level within the organization.

It should be the members' personal and professional responsibility to actively recruit and hire minorities and women to serve on professional staffs throughout their organizations.

12. Seek no favor; believe that personal aggrandizement or profit secured by confidential information or by misuse of public time is dishonest.

Guidelines
Gifts. Members should not directly or indirectly solicit any gift or accept or receive any gift—whether it be money, services, loan, travel, entertainment, hospitality, promise, or any other form—under the following circumstances: (1) it could be reasonably inferred or expected that the gift was intended to influence them in the performance of their official duties; or (2) the gift was intended to serve as a reward for any official action on their part.

It is important that the prohibition of unsolicited gifts be limited to circumstances related to improper influence. In de minimus situations, such as meal checks, some modest maximum dollar value should be determined by the member as a guideline. The guideline is not intended to isolate members from normal social practices where gifts among friends, associates, and relatives are appropriate for certain occasions.

Investments in Conflict with Official Duties. Member should not invest or hold any investment, directly or indirectly, in any financial business, commercial, or other private transaction that creates a conflict with their official duties.

In the case of real estate, the potential use of confidential information and knowledge to further a member's personal interest requires special consideration. This guideline recognizes that members' official actions and decisions can be influenced if there is a conflict with personal investments. Purchases and sales which might be interpreted as speculation for quick profit ought to be avoided (see the guideline on "Confidential Information").

Because personal investments may prejudice or may appear to influence official actions and decisions, members may, in concert with their governing body, provide for disclosure of such investments prior to accepting their position as local government administrator or prior to any official action by the governing body that may affect such investments.

Personal Relationships. Member should disclose any personal relationship to the governing body in any instance where there could be the appearance of a conflict of interest. For example, if the manager's spouse works for a developer doing business with the local government, that fact should be disclosed.

Confidential Information. Members should not disclose to others, or use to further their personal interest, confidential information acquired by them in the course of their official duties.

Private Employment. Members should not engage in, solicit, negotiate for, or promise to accept private employment, nor should they render services for private interests or conduct a private business when such employment, service, or business creates a conflict with or impairs the proper discharge of their official duties.

Teaching, lecturing, writing, or consulting are typical activities that may not involve conflict of interest, or impair the proper discharge of their official duties. Prior notification of the appointing authority is appropriate in all cases of outside employment.

Representation. Members should not represent any outside interest before any agency, whether public or private, except with the authorization of or at the direction of the appointing authority they serve.

Endorsements. Members should not endorse commercial products or services by agreeing to use their photograph, endorsement, or quotation in paid or other commercial advertisements, whether or not for compensation. Members may, however, agree to endorse the following, provided they do not receive any compensation: (1) books or other publications; (2) professional development or educational services provided by nonprofit membership organizations or recognized educational institutions; (3) products and/or services in which the local government has a direct economic interest.

Members" observations, opinions, and analyses of commercial products used or tested by their local governments are appropriate and useful to the profession when included as part of professional articles and reports.

ICMA DECLARATION OF IDEALS

The International City/County Management Association was founded with a commitment to the preservation of the values and integrity of representative local government and local democracy and a dedication to the promotion of efficient and effective management of public services. To fulfill the spirit of this commitment, the International City/County Management Association works to maintain and enhance public trust and confidence in local government, to achieve equity and social justice, to affirm human dignity, and to improve the quality of life for the individual and the community. Members of the International City/County Management Association dedicate themselves to the faithful stewardship of the public trust and embrace the following ideal of management excellence, seeking to:

1. Provide an environment that ensures the continued existence and effectiveness of representative local government and promotes the understanding that democracy confers privileges and responsibilities on each citizen.
2. Recognize the right of citizens to influence decisions that affect their well-being; advocate a forum for meaningful citizen participation and expression of the political process; and facilitate the clarification of community values and goals.
3. Respect the special character and individuality of each community while recognizing the interdependence of communities and promotion coordination and cooperation.
4. Seek balance in the policy formation process through the integration of the social, cultural, and physical characteristics of the community.
5. Promote a balance between the needs to use and to preserve human, economic, and natural resources.
6. Advocate equitable regulation and service delivery, recognizing that needs and expectations for public services may vary throughout the community.
7. Develop a responsive, dynamic local government organization that continuously assesses its purpose and seeks the most effective techniques and technologies for serving the community.
8. Affirm the intrinsic value of public service and create an environment that inspires excellence in management and fosters the professional and personal development of all employees.
9. Seek a balanced life through ongoing professional, intellectual, and emotional growth.
10. Demonstrate commitment to professional ethics and ideals and support colleagues in the maintenance of these standards.
11. Take actions to create diverse opportunities in housing, employment, and cultural activity in every community for all people.

Index

A

Acting on Ethics in City Planning (Howe), 28

Adult-oriented businesses
   clash of personal values and planning assignment involving, 159–162
   location of, 54–55

Affordable housing
   annexation analysis and, 51–53
   balancing need for, and rate of return on property, 49–51
   location of rental, 42–45
   planning director's desire for, 29–31
   potential impact of, 40–42

African American
   neighborhoods, 63
   planner, 40-41

African Americans, understanding of potential impact of development on, 40–42

AICP Code of Ethics and Professional Conduct, 7, 203–207
   advisory ruling on duties of planners in ensuring effective enforcement, 211–212
   procedures under, 206–207
   relationship of APA Statement of Ethical Principles to, 10
   summary of, 8–9
   tone of, 1

AICP Commission, action on misconduct charges by, 25

Airport location, 63–65

Alleged facts, 22–23

All other things being equal qualifier, 2

Alternative courses of actions
   comparing, to code of ethics, 167
   evaluating, 13, 166–167
   positive and negative effects of, 6
   possible outcomes and, 16

American City Management Association, 27

American Institute of Certified Planners (AICP)
   adoption of Guidelines for the Social Responsibility of the Planner by, 215–219
   Advisory Rulings
      on conflicts of interest, 208–209
      on disclosure of information, 140, 212–213
      on duties of planners in ensuring enforcement of Code of Ethics and Professional Conduct, 36, 52, 90, 91, 109, 115–116, 140, 211–212
      on honesty in use of information, 33–34, 118, 135, 140, 210–211
      on outside employment, 210
      on sexual harassment, 103, 207–208